| DATE | | | |
|---|---|---|---|
|  |  |  |  |
|  |  |  |  |
|  |  |  |  |
|  |  |  |  |
|  |  |  |  |
|  |  |  |  |
|  |  |  |  |
|  |  |  |  |
|  |  |  |  |
|  |  |  |  |
|  |  |  |  |
|  |  |  |  |
|  |  |  |  |

# EMOTIONS AND THE FAMILY
## For Better or for Worse

# EMOTIONS AND THE FAMILY

## For Better or for Worse

EDITED BY
**ELAINE A. BLECHMAN**
University of Colorado at Boulder

LEA  LAWRENCE ERLBAUM ASSOCIATES, PUBLISHERS
1990  Hillsdale, New Jersey          Hove and London

Lawrence Erlbaum Associates, Inc., Publishers
365 Broadway
Hillsdale, New Jersey 07642



**Library of Congress Cataloging-in-Publication Data**

Emotions and the family : for better or for worse / edited by Elaine
  A. Blechman.
      p.  cm.
  Includes bibliographical references and index.
  ISBN 0-8058-0136-7 (case)
  1. Emotions.  2. Family—Psychological aspects.  I. Blechman,
  Elaine A.
  BF511.E56  1990
  152.4—dc20                                         90-39732
                                                        CIP


Printed in the United States of America
10  9  8  7  6  5  4  3  2  1

To my mother, Sara Atkins Rosenfield,
and my daughter, Reva Michal Blechman.

# Contents

# Introduction

"Why is every critical moment in the fate of the adult or child so clearly colored by emotion?" (Vygotsky, 1987, p. 335). Emotion-free human behavior may be unimaginable (Buck, 1984; Leventhal & Tomarken, 1986), because emotion reveals the structure and the function of behavior. As a response to a demanding environment becomes more energetic, it becomes more emotional (Cowan, 1982; Dodge, 1989; Piaget, 1954/1981). Since all responses to a challenge vary from low to high on reactivity, behavior can never be unemotional. As the consequences of behavior becomes more hedonically relevant to the individual, the consequences gain in functional impact, and the behavior they consequate becomes more emotional (Darwin, 1896/1955; Skinner, this volume; Zajonc, 1989). Because consequences for individuals vary from low to high in functional impact and are controlled by these consequences, behavior can never be unemotional.

Never unemotional, behavior is at its emotional peak at home, where the heart is. Families, therefore, provide a natural laboratory for investigation of emotional experience and expression. This volume is unique for its thorough scientific coverage of emotions in the context of family life.

Although contributors differ about the structure of emotions, they are in accord about emotions' adaptive function. All contributors portray family members' competence as dependent on the way emotions are experienced and expressed within the group.

The book opens with a position paper by Skinner titled *Outlining a*

*Science of Feeling* (originally titled *The Place of Feelings in the Analysis of Behavior*). The other contributors reacted to Skinner's argument as they presented their perspectives and findings. Following Skinner, the first four chapters focus on basic psychological processes governing the expression of emotion in close relationships (Hatfield & Rapson, Plutchik & Plutchik, Saarni & Crowley, Wills) from social psychological (Hatfield & Rapson, Wills), developmental (Saarni & Crowley), and personality theory (Plutchik & Plutchik) vantage points. The next five chapters (Lindahl & Markman, Fruzzetti & Jacobson, Greenberg & Johnson, Dumas, Jouriles & O'Leary) consider how emotional experience and expression go wrong in dysfunctional families and how innovative family therapy methods can prevent conflict (Lindahl & Markman), restore intimacy (Fruzzetti & Jacobson; Greenberg & Johnson), and promote nurturance (Dumas; Jouriles & O'Leary). In the concluding chapter, I summarize and integrate the contributions to this volume and my research within the framework of a model of effective family communication.

## REFERENCES

Buck, R. (1984). *The communication of emotions.* New York: Guilford.

Cowan, P. (1982). The relationship between emotional and cognitive development. In D. Cicchetti & P. Hesse (Eds.), *Emotional development.* (Vol. 16, pp. 49–82). San Francisco: Jossey-Bass.

Darwin, C.R. (1955). *The expression of emotion in man and animals.* New York: Philosophical Library. (Original work published 1896)

Dodge, K.A. (1989). Coordinating response to aversive stimuli; Introduction to a special section on the development of emotion regulation. *Developmental Psychology, 25,* 339–342.

Leventhal, H., & Tomarken, A.J. (1986). Emotions: Today's problems. *Annual Review of Psychology, 37,* 565–610.

Piaget, J. (1981). Intelligence and affectivity; Their relationship during child development. Palo Alto, CA: Annual Reviews. (Original work published 1954)

Vygotsky, L.S. (1987). Lecture 4. Emotions and their development in childhood. In R.W. Riebar & A.S. Carton (Eds.), *The collected works of L.S. Vygotsky: Volume 1. Problems of general psychology* (pp. 325–338). New York: Plenum.

Zajonc, R.B. (1989). Feeling and facial efference: Implications of the vascular theory of emotions. *Psychological Review, 96,* 395–417.

# Acknowledgments

Credit for this volume must be shared with my colleagues in the NIMH Family Research Consortium, Bob Cole, Phil Cowan, John Gottman, Mavis Hetherington, Shep Kellam, Ross Parke, Gerald Patterson, Dave Reiss, Joy Schulterbrandt and Irv Sigel, who inspired me to account for the impact of emotions in a behavioral formulation of family communication. Gratitude for my emotional resilience as I worked on this book goes to my wise and loving colleagues, students, friends, and family: Ronna Abrams, Arthur Beck, Reva Blechman, Richard Carr, Steven Cohen, Chip Deming, Geri Doane, Kay and Jason Field, Norman Fleischer, Ann Helpern, Adele Kostellow, Phyllis Laufer, Gene Morrill, Allen Norin, Jane Seley, and Herb Scheinberg.

# CHAPTER 1

# Outlining a Science of Feeling*

## B.F. Skinner

A review of Gerald Zuriff's *Behaviorism: A conceptual reconstruction* in the *TLS* of July 19, 1985, begins with a story about two behaviourists. They make love, and then one of them says, "That was fine for you. How was it for me?" The reviewer, P. N. Johnson-Laird, insists that there is a "verisimilitude" with behaviourist theory. Behaviourists are not supposed to have feelings, or at least to admit that they have them. Of the many ways in which behaviourism has been misunderstood for so many years, that is perhaps the commonest.

A possibly excessive concern for "objectivity" may have caused the trouble. Methodological behaviourists, like logical positivists, argued that science must confine itself to events that can be observed by two or more people; truth must be truth by agreement. What one sees through introspection does not qualify. There is a private world of feelings and states of mind, but it is out of reach of a second person and hence of science. That was not a very satisfactory position, of course. How people feel is often as important as what they do.

Radical behaviourism has never taken that line. Feeling is a kind of sensory action, like seeing or hearing. We see a tweed jacket, for example, and we also feel it. That is not quite like feeling depressed, of course. We know something about the organs with which we feel

---

*Skinner, B. F. (1987, May 8). Outlining a science of feeling (Author's own title: The place of feeling in the analysis of behavior). *The Times Literary Supplement*.

the jacket but little, if anything, about those with which we feel depressed. We can also feel *of* the jacket by running our fingers over the cloth to increase the stimulation, but there does not seem to be any way to feel *of* depression. We have other ways of sensing the jacket, and we do various things with it. In other words, we have other ways of knowing what we are feeling. But what are we feeling when we feel depressed?

William James anticipated the behaviourist's answer: what we feel is a condition of our body. We do not cry because we are sad, said James, we are sad because we cry. That was fudging a little, of course, because we do much more than cry when we feel sad, and we can feel sad when we are not crying, but it was pointing in the right direction: what we feel is bodily conditions. Physiologists will eventually observe them in another way, as they observe any other part of the body. Walter B. Cannon's *Bodily Changes in Pain, Hunger, Fear, and Rage* (1929) was an early study of a few conditions often felt. Meanwhile, we ourselves can respond to them directly. We do so in two different ways. For example, we respond to stimuli from our joints and muscles in one way when we move about and in a different way when we say that we feel relaxed or lame. We respond to an empty stomach in one way when we eat and in a different way when we say that we are hungry.

The verbal responses in those examples are the products of special contingencies of reinforcement. They are arranged by listeners, and they are especially hard to arrange when what is being talked about is out of the listener's reach, as it usually is when it is within the speaker's skin. The very privacy which suggests that we ought to know our own bodies especially well is a severe handicap for those who must teach us to know them. We can teach a child to name an object, for example, by presenting or pointing to the object, pronouncing its name, and reinforcing a similar response by the child, but we cannot do that with a bodily state. We cannot present or point to a pain, for example. Instead, we infer the presence of the pain from some public accompaniment. We may see the child take a hard fall, for example, and say, "That must have hurt", or we see the child wince and ask, "Does something hurt?" We can respond only to the blow or the wince, but the child also feels a private stimulus and may say "hurt" when it occurs again without a public accompaniment. Since public and private events seldom coincide exactly, words for feelings have never been taught as successfully as words for objects. Perhaps that is why philosophers and psychologists so seldom agree when talking about feelings and states of mind, and why there is no acceptable science of feeling.

For centuries, of course, it has been said that we behave in given ways because of our feelings. We eat because we feel hungry, strike because we feel angry, and in general do what we feel like doing. If that were true, our faulty knowledge of feelings would be disastrous. No science of behaviour would be possible. But what is felt is not an initial or initiating cause. William James was quite wrong about his "becauses." We do not cry *because* we are sad or feel sad *because* we cry; we cry *and* feel sad because something has happened. (Perhaps someone we loved has died.) It is easy to mistake what we feel as a cause because we feel it while we are behaving (or even before we behave), but the events which are actually responsible for what we do (and hence what we feel) lie in the possibly distant past. The experimental analysis of behaviour advances our understanding of feelings by clarifying the roles of both past and present environments. Here are three examples.

LOVE. A critic has said that for a behaviorist "I love you" means "You reinforce me." God behaviorists would say "You reinforce my behavior" rather than "You reinforce me," because it is behavior, not the behaving person, that is being reinforced, in the sense of strengthened; but they would say much more. There is no doubt a reinforcing element in loving. Everything lovers do that brings them closer together or keeps them from being separated is reinforced by those consequences, and that is why they spend as much time together as they can. We describe the private effect of a reinforcer when we say that it "pleases us" or "makes us feel good," and in that sense "I love you" means "You please me or make me feel good." But the contingencies responsible for what is felt must be analyzed further.

The Greeks had three words for love, and they are still useful. Mentalistic psychologists may try to distinguish among them by looking at how love feels but much more can be learned from the relevant contingencies of selection, both natural selection and operant reinforcement. *Eros* is usually taken to mean sexual love, in part no doubt because the word erotic is derived from it. It is that part of making love that is due to natural selection; we share it with other species. (Many forms of parental love are also due to natural selection and are also examples of *eros*. To call mother love erotic is not to call it sexual.) Erotic lovemaking may also be modified by operant conditioning, but a genetic connection survives, because the susceptibility to reinforcement by sexual contact is an evolved trait. (Variations which have made individuals more susceptible have increased their sexual activity and hence their contribution to the future of the species.) In most other species the genetic tendency is the stronger. Courtship rituals and modes of copulation vary little from individual to individual and are usually related to optimal times of conception and seasons for the bearing of offspring. In *homo sapiens* sexual reinforcement predominates and yields a much greater frequency and variety of lovemaking.

*Philia* refers to a different kind of reinforcing consequences and, hence, a different state to be felt and called love. The root *phil* appears in words like philosophy (love of wisdom) and philately (love of postage stamps), but other things are loved in that way when the root word is not used. People say they "love Brahms" when they are inclined to listen to his works—perform them, perhaps, or go to concerts where they are performed, or play recordings. People who "love Renoir" tend to go to exhibitions of his paintings or buy them (alas, usually copies of them) to be looked at. People who "love Dickens" tend to acquire and read his books. We say the same thing about places ("I love Vienna"), subject-matters ("I love astronomy"), characters in fiction ("I love Daisy Miller"), kinds of people ("I love children"), and, of course, friends in whom we have no erotic interest. (It is sometimes hard to distinguish between *eros* and *philia*. Those who "love Brahms" may report that they play or listen to his works almost erotically, and courtship and lovemaking are sometimes practiced as forms of art.)

If we can say that *eros* is primarily a matter of natural selection and *philia* of operant conditioning, then *agape* represents a third process of selection—cultural evolution. Agape comes from a word meaning to welcome or, as a dictionary puts it, "to receive gladly." By showing that we are pleased when another person joins us, we reinforce joining. The direction of reinforcement is reversed. It is not our behaviour, but the behaviour of those we love that is reinforced. The principal effect is on the group. By showing that we are pleased by what other people do, we reinforce the doing and thus strengthen the group.

The direction of reinforcement is also reversed in *eros* if the manner in which we make love is affected by signs that our lover is pleased. It is also reversed in *philia* when our love for Brahms, for example, takes the form of founding or joining a society for the promotion of his works, or when we show our love for Venice by contributing to a fund to preserve the city. We also show a kind of *agape* when we honour heroes, leaders, scientists, and others from whose achievement we have profited. We are said to "worship" them in the etymological sense of proclaiming their worth. (When we say that we venerate them the *ven* is from the Latin *venus*, which meant any kind of pleasing thing.) Worship is the commoner word when speaking of the love of god, for which the New Testament used *agape*.

A reversed direction of reinforcement must be explained, especially when it calls for sacrifice. We may act to please a lover because our own pleasure is then increased, but why should we do so when it is not? We may promote the works of Brahms or help save Venice because we then have more opportunities to enjoy them, but why should we do so when that is not the case? The primary reinforcing consequences of *agape* are, in fact, artificial. They are contrived by our culture and contrived, moreover, just because the kind of thing we then do has helped the culture solve its problems and survive.

ANXIETY. Very different states of the body are generated by aversive stimuli, and they are felt in different ways. Many years ago W. K. Estes and I were rash enough to report an experiment in the *Journal of Experimental Psychology* (1941, *29*, pp 390–400) under the title, "Some quantitative properties of anxiety", although we were writing about rats. A hungry rat pressed a lever at a low, steady rate, under intermittent reinforcement with bits of food. Once or twice during an hour-long session, we sounded a tone for three minutes and then lightly shocked the rat through its feet. At first neither the tone nor the shock had any marked effect on the rate of responding, but the rat soon began to respond more slowly while the tone was sounding and eventually stopped altogether. Under rather similar circumstances a person might say, "I stopped what I was doing because I felt anxious".

In that experiment, the disrupted behaviour was produced by inter- mittent operant reinforcement, but the disruption would usually be attributed to respondent (classical or Pavlovian) conditioning. There is a problem, however. A change in probability of responding or rate of responding is not properly called a response. Moreover, since the shock itself did not suppress responding, there was no substitution of the stimuli. The reduced rate seems, paradoxically, to be the innate effect of a necessarily conditioned stimulus.

A paraphrased comment of Freud's begins as follows: "A person experiences anxiety in a situation of danger and helplessness." A "situation of danger" is a situation that resembles one in which painful things have happened. Our rat was in a situation of danger while the tone was sounding. It was "helpless" in the sense that it could do nothing to stop the tone or escape. The state of its body was presumably similar to the state a person would feel as anxiety, although the verbal contingencies needed for a response comparable to "I feel anxious" were lacking.

The paraphrase of Freud continues: "If the situation threatens to recur in later life, the person experiences anxiety as a signal of impend- ing danger." (It would be better to say "impending harm", because what threatens to recur is the aversive event—the shock for the rat and perhaps something like an automobile accident for the person, but what actually recurs is the condition that preceded that event— the tone, or say, riding with a reckless driver.) The quotation makes the point that the condition felt as anxiety begins to act as a second conditioned aversive stimulus. As soon as the tone began to generate a particular state of the rat's body, the state itself stood in the same relation to the shock as the tone, and it should have begun to have the same effect. Anxiety thus becomes self-perpetuating and even self-intensifying. A person might say, "I feel anxious, and something terrible always happens when I feel that way", but the contingencies yield a better analysis than any report of how self-perpetuated anxiety feels.

FEAR. A different result would have followed in our experiment if the shock had been contingent upon a response—in other words, if pressing had been punished. The rat would also have stopped pressing, but the bodily state would have been different. It would probably have been called fear. Anxiety is perhaps a kind of fear (we could say that the rat was "afraid another shock would follow"), but that is different from being "afraid to press the lever" because a shock will follow. A difference in the contingencies is unmistakable.

Young behaviourists sometimes contribute an example of fear, relevant here, when they find themselves saying that something pleases them or makes them angry and are embarrassed for having said it. The etymology of embarrassment as a kind of fear is significant. The root is *bar,* and young behaviourists find themselves barred from speaking freely about their feelings because those who have misunderstood behaviourism have ridiculed them when they have done so. An analysis of how embarrassment feels, made without alluding to antecedents or consequences, would be difficult if not impossible, but the contingencies are clear enough. In general, the more subtle the state felt, the greater the advantage in turning to the contingencies.

Such an analysis has an important bearing on two practical questions: how much can we ever know about what another person is feeling, and how can what is felt be changed? It is not enough to ask other people how or what they feel, because the words they will use in telling us were acquired as we have seen, from people who did not quite know what they were talking about. Something of the sort seems to have been true of the first use of words to describe private states. The first person who said, "I'm worried" borrowed a word meaning "choke" or "strangle". ("Anger", "anguish" and "anxiety" also come from another word that meant "choke".) But how much like the effect of choking was the bodily state the word was used to describe? All words for feelings seem to have begun as metaphors, and it is significant that the transfer has always been from public to private. No word seems to have originated as the name of a feeling.

We do not need to use the names of feelings if we can go directly to the public events. Instead of saying, "I was angry", we can say, "I could have struck him". What was felt was an inclination to strike rather than striking, but the private stimuli must have been much the same. Another way to report what we feel is to describe a setting that is likely to generate the condition felt. After reading Chapman's translation of Homer for the first time, Keats reported that he felt "like some watcher of the skies/When a new planet swims into his kin". It was easier for his readers to feel what an astronomer would feel upon discovering a new planet than what Keats felt upon reading the book.

It is sometimes said that we can make direct contact with what other people feel through sympathy or empathy. Sympathy seems to be reserved for painful feelings; we sympathize with a person who has lost a fortune but not with one who has made one. When we empathize, we are said to project our feelings into another person, but we cannot actually be moving feelings about, because we also project them into things—when, for example, we commit the pathetic fallacy. What we feel of Lear's rage is not quite what we feel in a raging storm. Sympathy and empathy seem to be effects of imitation. For genetic or personal reasons we tend to do what other people are doing and we may then have similar bodily states to feel. When we do what other *things* are doing, it is not likely that we are sharing feelings.

Sympathy and empathy cannot tell us exactly what a person feels, because part of what is felt depends upon the setting in which the behaviour occurs, and that is usually missing in imitation. When lysergic acid diethylamide first attracted attention, psychiatrists were urged to take it in order to see what it felt like to be psychotic, but acting like a psychotic because one has taken a drug may not create the condition felt by those who are psychotic for other reasons.

That we know what other people feel only when we behave as they behave is clear when we speak of knowing what members of other species feel. Presumably we are more likely to avoid hurting animals if what they would do resembles what we should do when hurt in the same way. That is why we are more likely to hurt the kinds of animals— fish, snakes and insects, for example—which do not behave very much as we do. It is a rare person, indeed, who would not hurt a fly.

To emphasize what is felt rather than the feeling is important when we want to change feelings. Drugs, of course, are often used for that purpose. Some of them (aspirin, for example) break the connection with what is felt. Others create states that appear to compete with or mask troublesome states. According to American television commercials, alcohol yields the good fellowship of *agape* and banishes care. But these are temporary measures, and their effects are necessarily imperfect simulations of what is naturally felt in daily life because the natural settings are lacking.

Feelings are most easily changed by changing the settings responsible for what is felt. We could have relieved the anxiety of our rat by turning off the tone. When a setting cannot be changed, a new history of reinforcement may change its effect. In his remarkable book *Émile,* Rousseau described what is not called desensitization. If a baby is frightened when plunged into cold water (presumably an innate response), begin with warm water and reduce the temperature a degree a day. The baby will not be frightened when the water is finally cold. Something of the sort could also be done, said Rousseau, with social reactions. If a child is frightened by a person wearing a threatening mask, begin with a friendly one and change it slightly day by day until it becomes threatening, when it will not be frightening.

Psychoanalysis is largely concerned with discovering and changing feelings. An analysis sometimes seems to work by extinguishing the effects of old punishments. When the patient discovers that obscene, blasphemous, or aggressive behavior is tolerated, the therapist emerges as a non-punitive audience. Behaviour "repressed" by former punishments then begins to appear. It "becomes conscious" simply in the sense that it begins to be felt. The once offending behaviour is not punished, but it is also not reinforced, and it eventually undergoes extinction, a less troublesome method of eradication than punishment.

Cognitive psychologists are among those who most often criticize behaviourism for neglecting feelings, but they themselves have done very little in the field. The computer is not a helpful model. Cognitive psychologists specialize in the behaviour of speakers and listeners. Instead of arranging contingencies of reinforcement, they often simply describe them. Instead of observing what their subjects do, they often simply ask them what they would probably do. But the kinds of behaviour most often associated with feelings are not easily brought under verbal control. "Cheer up" or "Have a good time" seldom works. Only operant behaviour can be executed in response to advice, but if it occurs only for that reason, it has the same shortcomings as imitative behaviour. Advice must be taken and reinforcing consequences must follow before the bodily condition that is the intended effect of the advice will be felt. If consequences do not immediately follow, the advice ceases to be taken or the behaviour remains nothing more than taking advice.

Fortunately, not everything we feel is troublesome. We enjoy many states of our bodies, and, because they are positively reinforcing, do what is needed to produce them. We read books and watch television and, to the extent that we then tend to behave as the characters behave, we feel and possibly enjoy relevant bodily states. Drugs are taken for positively reinforcing effects (but the reinforcement is negative when they are taken primarily to relieve withdrawal symptoms). Religious mystics cultivate special bodily states—by fasting, remaining still or silent, reciting mantras, and so on. Dedicated joggers often report a jogging high.

To confine an analysis of feelings to what is felt may seem to neglect an essential question: what is *feeling*, simply as such? We can ask a similar question about sensory process—for example, what is *seeing*? Philosophers and cognitive psychologists avoid that question by contending that to see something is to make some kind of copy—a "representation", to use the current word. But making a copy cannot be seeing, because the copy must in turn be seen. Nor is it enough, of course, to say simply that seeing is behaving; it is only part of behaving. It is "behaving up to the point of acting". Unfortunately, what happens up to that point is out of reach of the instruments and methods of the behaviour analyst and must be left to the physiologist. What remains for the analyst are the contingencies of reinforcement under which things come to be seen and the verbal contingencies under which they come to be described. In the case of feeling, both the conditions felt and what is done in feeling them must be left to the physiologist. What remain for the behaviour analyst are the genetic and personal histories responsible for the bodily conditions the physiologist will find.

There are many good reasons why people talk about their feelings. What they say is often a useful indication of what has happened to them or of what they may do. On the point of offering a friend a glass of water, we do not ask, "How long has it been since you last drank any water?" or "If I offer you a glass of water, what are the chances you will accept it?" We ask "Are you thirsty?" The answer tells us all we need to know. In an experimental analysis, however, we must have a better account of the conditions that affect hydration and a better measure of the probability that a subject will drink. A report of how thirsty the subject feels will not suffice.

For at least 3,000 years, however, philosophers, joined recently by psychologists, have looked within themselves for the causes of their behaviour. For reasons which are becoming clear, they have never agreed upon what they have found. Physiologists, and especially neurologists, look at the same body in a different and potentially successful way, but even when they have seen it more clearly, they will not have seen initiating causes of behaviour. What they will see must in turn be explained by ethologists, who look for explanations in the evolution of the species, or by behaviour analysts, who look at the histories of individuals. The inspection or introspection of one's own body is a kind of behaviour that needs to be analysed, but as the source of data for a science it is largely of historical interest only.

# CHAPTER 2

# Emotions: A Trinity

**Elaine Hatfield**
**Richard Rapson**
University of Hawaii

Recently, at the University of Iowa's summer program on social psycho-physiology, I watched a demonstration. An undergraduate who worked in John Cacioppo's laboratory was wired up with electrodes designed to measure facial EMG, heart rate, breathing rate, and skin conductance. He was instructed to think about anything he wished. Some trainees watched the student on a television monitor. All they saw was a blank, relaxed, impassive face. Others of us watched the pens on a 10-channel Grass poly-graph recorder. Now and then we would spot dramatic changes on the printout. For example, at one point, the electrodes connected to the corru-gator supercilli muscle showed a sudden jump. "What are you thinking about?" we asked. "An argument with my roommate." Later there was a powerful movement around the orbicular oris. It was so powerful that it was interfering with all the other readings. We looked at the television monitor to see what the student was doing, but we could detect no sign of movement. "What is going on?", we asked. "I've just thought of a great argument," he answered. "Well, quit," we said. "Just imagine you are lis-tening to what he has to say." He did, and the pens immediately quieted down. (Carlson & Hatfield, in press)

In chapter 1 of this book, B. F. Skinner argued that intimate conversa-tions will go best if people speak the same emotional language—the language of behavior. We disagree. We believe that, in the light of abundant and remarkable new research, Skinner's concept of the nature of emotion is too simple. In this chapter, we review what scientists now know about emotion. In the process, it becomes clear

**11**

that emotional experiences leave complex cognitive and physiological, as well as behavioral tracings. To understand emotion, one must be prepared to speak many languages. Let us begin our discussion by defining what we mean by emotion.

## DEFINING EMOTION

We, like many other theorists, view emotions as a *system* that activates cognitive, physiological, and behavioral components. For example, consider Izard and Buechler's (1986) definition:

> A fundamental emotion is defined as a complex motivational phenome-non, with characteristic neurophysiological, expressive, and experiential components. No single component of the three suffices as a description of an emotion; all three are essential to the concept. At the neurophysio-logical level, a fundamental emotion is defined as a particular, innately programmed pattern of electrochemical activity in the nervous system. The expressive component consists mainly of a characteristic pattern of facial activity, but may also include bodily responses (postural-gestural, visceral-glandular) and vocal expressions. At the experiential level, each fundamental emotion is a unique quality of consciousness. (p. 167.)

In the last 2 decades, scientists have learned a great deal about the nature of emotion. In this paper we are only able to present a scattering of this voluminous research. For a more complete review, see Carlson and Hatfield (in press). Scientific discoveries make it clear that: (a) people do, in part, speak a universal language of emotion. Many aspects of emotional experience and expression are genetically "hard-wired" into humans. (b) However, peoples' emotional socialization and emotional experiences are very different. The historical era in which people live, the cultural and social groups to which they belong, and the type of family in which they are raised, insure that, in part, the language of emotion that they speak must be their own.

## THE NATURE OF EMOTION

Darwin (1872/1965) proposed an evolutionary model for understand-ing emotional expression. In prehistory, animals (including man) were confronted again and again with certain problems of survival. Those animals that best fitted their environments survived. In *The Expression of the Emotions in Man and Animals,* Darwin proposed that, as a conse-quence of their shared evolutionary history, animals and man came to experience and express emotions in much the same way. The facial, postural, physiological, and behavioral reactions associated with emotion evolved because they "worked", that is, they increased the species' chances of survival. In recent years, scientists have begun to make some impressive strides in detailing just how these basic inherited emotional systems operate.

## Cognitive Aspects of Emotion

A variety of cognitive psychologists have attempted to spell out how cognitive factors shape intimates' emotional experiences. For example, Lazarus (Lazarus, Kanner, & Folkman, 1980) argued that the first step in an emotional sequence is a "cognitive appraisal." In the process of "primary appraisal," people try to decide what consequences impending events are likely to have for their well-being. Once they have assessed the situation they must proceed to a "secondary appraisal." What *should* they do about the situation? What *can* they do? Finally, "reappraisal" highlights the interactive nature of peoples' encounters with other persons and with the world. Individuals perceive and react; the environment counterreacts. Individuals, in turn, must appraise these reactions. People never stop making evaluative judgments about themselves and the world around them.

Cognitive theorists such as Lazarus attempt to provide a sort of universal framework, which outlines how all people at all times will analyze challenging situations. Theorists from a variety of related disciplines add complexity and variability to this picture.

For example, anthropologists (see Lutz & White, 1986), sociologists (see Kemper, 1986), and historians (see Degler, 1980; Gay, 1984; Stearns & Stearns, 1985; or Stone, 1979) have begun to document the profound impact of culture in shaping peoples' perceptions of how they are supposed to feel about various events and how they can legitimately express those feelings. This work makes it clear that the historical and cultural contexts play a mighty role in determining how emotions ultimately take shape and gain expression in real life.

Social psychologists have also documented the impact that families have on family members' emotional experiences, and on: (a) their ability to express their emotions with clarity; (b) the intensity with which they express their emotions; and (c) their ability to read others' most subtle emotional expressions, (see, for example, Buck, 1979; Ekman & Friesen, 1969; Izard, 1971; or Jones, 1960). Obviously, people possess very different interests and skills in dealing with emotion. For example, someone with a literary, theatrical, artistic, or psychological bent may well find it rewarding to spend a great deal of time in analyzing the minute details of their *own feelings,* and may also enjoy looking at portraits, watching Masterpiece Theater (where the dramatists are often deeply concerned with the subtleties and contradictions of character), and talking with friends and acquaintances about their personal problems. Such people are likely to know exactly what they feel in a given situation. Others, "macho men" for example, convinced that masculinity equals *lack* of emotional responsiveness, might find their rewards in insisting, in even the most trying of situations, that for them it is "no sweat." They may indeed turn things off to such an extent that they are totally unaware of their feelings. The same holds true with regard to emotional *expression.* Some of my colleagues try very hard to convey, in measured, precise, verbal expression, the nuances of their inner lives. Others think that to express emotions means to shout, cry, pound pillows, and hit one another over the head with batakas (or worse). Finally, people have learned to be differentially attentive to others' emotional displays. Some people are sharply attuned to the tiniest movement of another's eyebrow. The most minute change in facial expression throws them into a panic. "Is he angry?" "Have they hurt her feelings; is she going to cry?" Social psychologists have begun to explore the ways in which families socialize children in these areas. For example, some social psychologists find a strong correlation between parental expressiveness and the expressiveness of infants as young as 3 months old. (Malatesta & Haviland, 1982). Lanzetta and Kleck, 1970, proposed that individuals who have been punished by socializing agents for engaging in overt displays of emotionality learn to inhibit their own emotional expression. At the same time, however, they become unusually sensitive to the displays of others. Halberstadt (1986) observed: "When the family environment is low in expressiveness, individuals must become sensitive to the most subtle displays of emotion in order to relate effectively with other family members." (p. 827).

Interestingly, then, some researchers have proposed that often there is a negative relationship between peoples' sending and receiving skills: The people who send the clearest, most intense emotional messages themselves are often the poorest at recognizing other, more subtle, forms of expression. Those whose own emotional responses are muted and difficult to fathom are often expert readers of the emotions of others (Buck, 1979; Halberstadt, 1986; Izard, 1971; Morency & Krauss, 1982; Zuckerman, Hall, DeFrank, & Rosenthal, 1976). Obviously, there is no reason a person would have to be either a poor sender or receiver. It would seem that people who are taught to be comfortable with a variety of forms of emotional expression—to carefully analyze emotion-laden situations, sometimes; to be spontaneous, sometimes; to express emotions softly when that is appropriate and more fiercely when that is necessary; and to be capable of reading subtle and powerful expressions of emotion—would do best in close relationships.

The research of historians, anthropologists, sociologists, social psychologists, and developmentalists, then, makes it clear that there will be both universality and idiosyncracy in emotional expression.

## Biological Aspects of Emotion

From evolutionary biology, we are learning *when* the various layers of the brain evolved. From neuroanatomy, we are discovering how the brain is structured. From neurophysiology, we are beginning to understand how the brain functions chemically.

### The Anatomy of Emotion

MacLean (1986) argued that, in the course of evolution, humans have ended up with a brain that has a triune structure. In a sense, the brain consists of three different types of brains, with different anatomical structures and chemical processes layered one upon the other. The oldest type of brain is basically reptilian. The second is inherited from the early mammals. The third is from the late mammals/primates. MacLean pointed out that the reptilian brain was primarily concerned with preservation of self and species. Its primitive structures were designed to guide the reptile in the processes required for obtaining food (search, angry attacks, self-defense, feeding, and mates).

In the neo-mammalian brain three new patterns of behavior, which were primarily designed to facilitate mother–child relationships, emerged through evolution. These included nursing of the young, "audiovocal communication" for facilitating mother–child contact, and play behavior. MacLean contended that such affects as desire, fear, anger, dejection and depression, ecstasy and affection, all derive from activities in the limbic system.

It was not until the neo-cortex evolved in the late mammalian/primate period that symbolic or verbal information became important in shaping primate emotional experience and expression. MacLean (1986) reviewed over 40 years of clinical and experimental findings in support of his contention that it is not cognition alone, but emotions, that guide the behavior required for self-preservation and preservation of the species.

### The Physiology of Emotion

Psychologists are beginning to learn more about the chemistry of emotions and the way various emotions interact. Liebowitz (1983), for example, offered some speculations about the chemistry of the "highs" and the "lows" that crisscross people's consciousness. These include the highs of euphoria, excitement, relaxation, spiritual feelings, and relief, as well as the lows of anxiety, terrifying panic attacks, the pain of separation, and the fear of punishment.

Liebowitz proposed that naturally occurring brain chemicals produce emotions. *Joy and excitement:* Chemicals resembling stimulants (such as amphetamine and cocaine) produce the "rush" felt by joyous people, lovers, and those engaging in exciting activities. *Relaxation:* Chemicals related to the narcotics (such as heroin, opium, and morphine), tranquilizers (such as Librium and Valium), sedatives (such as barbiturates, Quaaludes, and other "downers"), alcohol, and marijuana all produce a mellow state and wipe out loneliness, panic attacks, and depression. *Spiritual peak experiences:* Chemicals similar to the psychedelics (such as LSD, mescaline, and psilocybin) produce a sense of beauty, meaningfulness, and timelessness.

Physiologists do not usually try to produce painful experiences in the laboratory. Thus, we know a bit less about the chemistry of pain. Such painful feelings may, however, arise from two sources: (a) withdrawal from the chemicals that produce the highs; (b) the infusion of chemicals which, in and of themselves, produce anxiety, pain, or depression. (A great deal is known about the physiology and chemistry of emotion. For a review of relevant sources see Carlson and Hatfield, in press.)

The basic emotions, then, are associated with chemical neurotransmitters or with chemicals that increase/decrease the receptors' sensitivity. The basic emotions may well be, in part, chemically distinct. Yet, at the same time, emotions have more similarities than differences. Chemically, joy, love, sexual desire, and excitement, as well as anger, hate, fear, jealousy, and anxiety have much in common: for example, they are all intensely arousing. They all produce a sympathetic response in the automatic nervous system (ANS). This is evidenced by the symptoms associated with all of these emotions—a flushed face, sweaty palms, weak knees, butterflies in the stomach, dizziness, a pounding heart, trembling hands, and accelerated breathing. Lacey (1967) made a surprising discovery. In emotional situations people seemed to react in stereotyped, *but very different,* ways. For example, Person A's heart might start to beat wildly in response to feeling frightened *or* excited *or* joyous—and that would be the only ANS

reaction manifested. Person B might start to breathe heavily and per-
spire whenever becoming emotional, and those would be the only
reactions visible. Lacey pointed out that it was therefore misleading to
speak of ANS "arousal," as if all people at all times showed a uniform
ANS reaction, one in which the various indicants of ANS arousal were
perfectly correlated. Different people experience different patterns
of ANS arousal. The reactions shown by one person will not be strongly
correlated with those shown by others in the same emotional situation,
and the various indicants of ANS arousal themselves will not be correlated. Once again we see that people seem to share *some* emotional
experiences (most show some type of ANS arousal), but that some
aspects of their experiences are unique.

There are other factors that contribute to the difficulty people have
both in articulating their own emotional experiences with precision
much less making assumptions about what other people might be
experiencing. Recent neuroanatomical/neurophysiological research
suggests that the various emotions probably are more tightly interrelated than psychologists once thought. Hatfield (1970) and Hatfield
and Walster (1978) pointed out that when people are caught up in an
intensely emotional situation, "chemical spill-over" is likely to occur—
that is, peoples' feelings get all mixed up. Everything gets intensified.
People can move from elation through terror into the depths of despair and back again in a matter of seconds. They know that they are
feeling intensely but it is difficult to disentangle their complicated
interlocking feelings. They literally do not know whether to laugh or
to cry.

### Skeletomotor Reactions

A variety of researchers have studied the impact of emotional experiences on facial reactions (For recent reviews, see Cacioppo, Petty, &
Tassinary, in press).

*The Facial Response System.* When we think about things (as evidenced in the anecdote that began this chapter) our bodies play out
our thoughts. As we think about what we will say next, the *orbicularis
oris* (the muscle around the mouth; see Fig. 2.1) invisibly sounds out
the words. When we think about writing, small muscle movements
occur in our fingers and arms. Although these movements are invisible
to the naked eye, scientists can easily detect them via EMG (electromyographic) recordings. Scientists have demonstrated that facial EMG
activity is capable of distinguishing positive from negative emotional
states, even when there are no changes in overt facial action or auto-

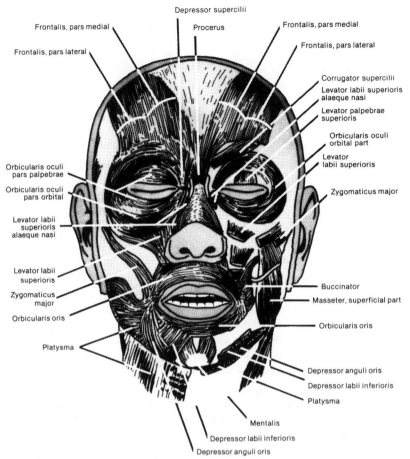

Depressor supercilii

Frontalis, pars medial · Procerus · Frontalis, pars medial

Frontalis, pars lateral · Frontalis, pars lateral

Corrugator supercilii
Levator labii superioris alaeque nasi
Levator palpebrae superioris
Orbicularis oculi orbital part
Levator labii superioris
Zygomaticus major

Orbicularis oculi pars palpebrae
Orbicularis oculi pars orbital
Levator labii superioris alaeque nasi
Levator labii superioris
Zygomaticus major
Orbicularis oris
Platysma

Buccinator
Masseter, superficial part
Orbicularis oris
Depressor anguli oris
Depressor labii inferioris
Platysma

Mentalis
Depressor labii inferioris
Depressor anguli oris

FIG. 2.1. Schematic representation of selected facial muscles. Overt facial expressions of emotion are based on contractions of the underlying musculature that are sufficiently intense to result in visibly perceptible dislocations of the skin and landmarks. The more common visible effects of strong contractions of the depicted facial muscles include the following.

*Muscles of the lower face: Depressor anguli oris*—pulls the lip corners downward; *Depressor labii inferioris*—depresses the lower lip; *Orbicularis oris*—tightens, compresses, protrudes, and/or inverts the lips; *Mentalis*—raises the chin and protrudes the lower lip; *Platysma*—wrinkles the skin of the neck and may draw down both the lower lip and the lip corners.

*Muscles of the mid-face: Buccinator*—compresses and tightens the cheek, forming a "dimple", *Levator labii superioris alaeque nasi*—raises the center of the upper lip and flares the nostrils; *Levator labii superioris*—raises the upper lip and flares the nostrils, exposing the canine teeth; *Masseter*—adducts the lower jaw; *Zygomaticus major*—pulls the lip corners up and back.

*Muscles of the upper face: corrugator supercilii*—draws the brows together and downward, producing vertical furrows between the brows; *Depressor supercilii/procerus*—pulls the medial part of the brows downward and may wrinkle the skin over the bridge of the nose; *Frontalis, pars lateral*—raises the outer brows, producing horizontal furrows in the lateral regions of the forehead; *Frontalis, pars medial*—raises the inner brows, producing horizontal furrows in the medial region of the forehead; *Levator palpebrae superioris*—raises the upper eyelid; *Orbicularis oculi, pars orbital*—tightens the skin surrounding the eye causing "crows-feet" wrinkles; *Orbicularis oculi, pars palpebrae*—tightens the skin surrounding the eye causing the lower eyelid to raise. (From Cacioppo, Martzke, Petty, & Tassinary, 1987).

Cacioppo, J. T. Mahtzke, J. S., Petty, R. E., & Tassinary, L. G. (1988). Specific forms of facial EMG response index emotions during an interview: from Darwin to the continuous flow hypothesis of affect-laden information processing. *Journal of Personality and Social Psychology, 54*, 592–603. Permission obtained from: Dr. John Cacioppo Department of Psychology, Ohio State University, Columbus, Ohio.

nomic activity (Cacioppo et al., in press, or Fridlund & Izard, 1983). Since this research is just in its infancy, researchers are optimistic that they may be able to distinguish the basic emotions via their EMG signatures.

Perhaps the most powerful way we communicate with one another is via visible facial expressions. Ekman (1972) and Izard (1971) have argued that the face speaks a universally understood language. Recently, psychologists have uncovered some compelling evidence that the basic emotions *are* expressed in much the same way in all cultures. (Of course, every culture also possesses its own display rules). Recent research illustrates how both these processes operate. Scientists studying infants, children, and adults from a variety of cultures have linked happiness, sadness, fear, anger, disgust, and surprise to a series of distinctive facial displays (Ekman, 1972; Izard, 1977; Scherer & Ekman, 1982; Steiner, 1979). Figure 2.2, for example, illustrates how a

FIG. 2.2.    Basic emotions posed by the Fore of New Guinea. Copyright © 1972 by Paul Ekman. Permission received from: Dr. Paul Ekman, Human Interaction Laboratory, University of California San Francisco, 401 Parnassus Avenue, San Francisco, California 94943.

sampling of emotions are expressed among the Fore of New Guinea, who have never been exposed to Western man.

These same studies, however, show that peoples' emotional reactions are most similar when observed in private. In public, powerful "display rules" partially shape our responses. (For example, we try to look happy at weddings and sad at funerals, regardless of how we might really feel.)


## Behavioral Aspects of Emotion


Many eminent learning theorists have explored the link between emotion and motivation, and the link between both those factors and behavior. For example, Skinner (1953) argued that emotional patterns of responding may arise from two very different sources. First, the evolutionary history of the species may favor certain unlearned or unconditioned responses. "For example, in some species biting, striking and clawing appear to be strengthened during anger before conditioning (that is, learning) can have taken place" (Skinner, 1953, p. 164). In short, we may strike out in anger simply because we are "wired" that way. Second, some emotional behaviors are learned. For example, an angry child may have been conditioned to "teasing the other child, taking toys away from him, destroying his work, or calling him names" (Skinner, 1953, p. 164). Such children have learned that such irritating behavior causes their enemies to suffer.

In the case of innate behaviors, such as instinctive anger, the history of the species may have insured that certain behavioral consequences are rewarding or punishing. That is, those patterns of angry behavior that fostered survival (such as biting or clawing one's enemies) came to be wired in. Reactions that were ineffective dropped out. Learned emotional behavior continues because it is reinforcing. People soon learn that an angry outburst "works." They cause the timid to give them what they want (a positive reinforcer) or at least to quit causing trouble (a negative reinforcer).

More recently, theorists such as Baron and Byrne (1981) and Berscheid and Hatfield (1969) attempted to explain why people are attracted to some people and repelled by others by citing the principle of reinforcement. They contend that people come to like and love those who reward them and dislike and hate those who punish them. Baron and Byrne's (1981) argument goes as follows:

1. Most stimuli can be identified as either rewarding or punishing.
2. Rewarding stimuli arouse positive feelings; punishing stimuli

2. Rewarding stimuli arouse positive feelings; punishing stimuli arouse negative feelings. These feelings, or affective responses, fall along a continuum from extremely positive to extremely negative.

3. The evaluation of any given stimulus as good or bad, enjoyable or unenjoyable, depends on whether it arouses positive or negative feelings. How positively or negatively a person evaluates another depends on the strength of the aroused effect. They illustrate their theory with this example:

> To take an obvious example, if a stranger were to walk up to you on the street and give you a swift kick in the shins, negative feelings would be aroused. If asked to evaluate the experience, you would no doubt say you also learned to associate negative feelings with the person, you would also indicate dislike for him in the future, but that is not all you learned in the situation. It may be less obvious, but your negative feelings aroused by a kick would also be likely to extend to any innocent bystander who happened to be there, . . . to the street where the kicking took place, and to anything else that was associated with the unpleasant interaction. In an analogous way, if on the following day, another passing stranger gave you a year's supply of free movie passes, your feelings would be positive and you would probably express liking toward your surroundings. (p. 212)

In this view, the human mind functions like a giant computer. The mind tallies up how emotionally pleasurable versus painful a lifetime of intimate encounters with Person X have proved to be, sums, and "spits out" an emotional reaction. A very handy tally indeed. Byrne (1971) even proposed a simple formula, a "law of attraction" to predict how people will evaluate others (See Fig. 2.3).

FIG. 2.3. Byrne's "Law of Attraction."

$$Y = \left[\frac{\Sigma PR}{(\Sigma PR + \Sigma NR)}\right] + k$$

The Y in Byrne's formula stands for attraction. On the other side of the equation the only symbols that really matter are PR (which stands for positive reinforcement—i.e., reward) and NR (which stands for negative reinforcement—which Byrne equates with punishment). Y (attraction) is greatest when there is a great deal of PR and very little NR. In *The Attraction Paradigm*, Byrne (1971) provided an encyclopedic review of evidence in support of these propositions.

Learning theorists make it clear that people may learn very different things about what is appropriate to feel, express, and observe in social situations.

What rewards seem most critical in love relationships? Hatfield and men and women, and 400 elderly women as to the rewards (or lack thereof) the interviewees found to be most critical in their love relationships (Hatfield, Traupmann, Sprecher, Utne, & Hay, 1984). Their answers were surprisingly similar. The following rewards were critically important to almost everyone:

PERSONAL REWARDS

1. *Social grace.*
   Having a partner who is sociable, friendly, and relaxed in social settings.

2. *Intellect.*
   Having a partner who is intelligent and informed.

3. *Appearance.*
   Having a physically attractive partner.
   Having a partner who takes care of his or her appearance and conditioning; who attends to such things as personal cleanliness, dress, exercise, and good eating habits.

EMOTIONAL REWARDS

1. *Liking and loving.*
   Being liked by your partner.
   Being loved by your partner.

2. *Understanding and concern.*
   Having your personal concerns and emotional needs understood and responded to.

3. *Acceptance.*
   Because of your partner's acceptance and encouragement, being free to try out different roles occasionally—for example, being a baby sometimes, a mother, a colleague or a friend, an aggressive as well as a passive lover, and so on.

4. *Appreciation.*
   Being appreciated for contributions to the relationship; not being taken for granted by your partner.

5. *Physical affection.*
   Receiving open affection—touching, hugging, kissing.

6. *Sex.*
   Experiencing a sexually fulfilling and pleasurable relationship with your partner.
   Sexual fidelity; having a partner who is faithful to your agreements about extramarital relations.

7. *Security.*
   Being secure in your partner's commitment to you and to the future of your relationship together.

8. *Plans and goals for the future.*
Planning for and dreaming about your future together.

DAY-TO-DAY REWARDS

1. *Day-to-day operations.*
Having a smoothly operating household, because of the way you two have organized your household responsibilities.

2. *Finances.*
The amount of income and other financial resources that you may gain through your "joint account."

3. *Sociability.*
Having a pleasant living together situation, because your partner is easy to live with on a day-to-day basis.
Having a good companion, who suggests enjoyable things to do and who also goes along with your ideas for what you might do together.
Knowing your partner is interested in hearing about your day and what is on your mind, and in turn will share concerns and events with you.
Having a partner who is compatible with your friends and relatives; who is able to fit in.

4. *Decision making.*
Having a partner who takes a fair share of the responsibility for making and carrying out decisions that affect both of you.

5. *Remembering special occasions.*
Having a partner who is thoughtful about sentimental things; who remembers, for example, birthdays and other special occasions.

OPPORTUNITIES GAINED AND LOST

1. *Opportunities gained.*
Having the opportunity to partake of the many life experiences that depend on being married—for example, the chance to become a parent and even grandparent, the chance to be included in "married couple" social events, and, finally, having someone to count on in old age.

2. *Opportunities foregone.*
Necessarily giving up certain opportunities in order to be in this relationship. The opportunities could have been other possible mates, a career, travel, etc.

### Summary

To understand emotion, scientists have found it necessary to acknowledge that emotions are a complex system, with multiple components. In part, the three components of the emotional trinity interact with one another. Candland (1977) proposed that emotional stimuli quickly elicit a response in the cognitive and physiological systems. The two elements combine to produce an emotional experience and then to generate appropriate emotional behavior. Each of the three elements is an indispensable part of a continuous emotional feedback loop. Each element modifies and is modified by the others. Each is both a stimulus and a response. Cognitive appraisals shape and are shaped by physiological reactions. The experience feeds back and shapes the perception of the eliciting stimuli. The various aspects of emotion continually feed back on one another, affecting the course of an emotional experience (see Figure A).

Nonetheless, each component of the emotional trinity provides unique information. This information is not redundant. For example, Lazarus (1977) pointed out that the various aspects of emotion are not always in sync:

> ". . . the three components correlate very poorly with each other. An individual might report no distress yet exhibit strong physiological reactions, or the behavioral responses signifying anger or fear might be inhibited as a result of social or internal pressures. . . . In short, the somatic changes connected with an emotion usually appear in a complex pattern of end-organ responses rather than in a simple, highly correlated one." (pp. 69–70)

To truly understand an intimate's inner life, one ideally would have some glimmering of how they *thought* about emotional events, and *felt* (physiologically) in addition to how they *behaved*. In the next section, we argue that intimates would do well to broaden their skills at speaking their mates' and families' emotional languages. We think Skinners' advice (chapter 1) is misleading because he suggests that intimates narrow the way they speak about their feelings and that they rule out entire forms of discourse. We think people will do better if they expand their skills at emotional communication, adding those of Skinner and others to their existing repertoire, rather than trying to force themselves and those they love into a narrow, artificial form of expression. This richer repertoire fits with the more complex view of emotions derived from recent research. Let us begin our discussion of techniques for imple-

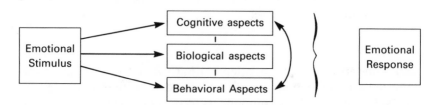

FIG. A.   An emotional sequence.

menting these suggestions, by discussing how the authors try to communicate with their clients in psychotherapy about their inner lives.

## IN THERAPY

In addition to our academic careers, Drs. Rapson and Hatfield work as family therapists in Honolulu, Hawaii. In Hawaii, couples come from a wide array of educational and occupational backgrounds and ethnic groups—Caucasian, Japanese, Chinese, Filipino, Hawaiian. (Surprisingly, in Hawaii, more than 60% of relationships are interethnic. See Rapson, 1980). It is no surprise, therefore, to discover that couples often speak a wide variety of emotional "languages." Thus, the first step in therapy is to find out how clients think and feel. That is no easy feat. Some clients speak in poetic metaphors. For example, one English teacher spoke of sexual passion as akin to holding grapes, cool and tart, in her mouth; touching the fruit's stiff skin with her tongue. Others are singularly direct. "My problem started when my mother croaked" said one man, with tears in his eyes. Some clients have *no* verbal language for expressing feelings. They may be unaware that they ever feel anything like an emotion. With them, we may well use the very techniques Skinner recommends: "Feel under your arms; Are you sweating? Do you have a lump in your throat? Cramps?" Sometimes, clients' perceptions seem at variance with ours. An example: A woman's eyes *seem* to flash with anger, as she describes her mother-in-law's impending visit. "How do you feel"? we ask. "I've always loved her," she replies. To unravel the mystery we have to talk some more. Often she will finally admit in a rush, after long denials, that: "Well, wouldn't you be angry, too, if she never lifted a finger? You just stand there like a piece of luggage while she and my husband go off hand-in-hand for a walk on Sunday. On Monday, he has to go to work, but she expects me to sit around entertaining her all day, and I can't stand her. . . . I guess."

In deciphering emotion, we sometimes use a second clue that therapists rarely talk about: *We observe our own emotional reactions as a clue to what our clients are feeling!* For example, on occasion we will start to feel very anxious as we listen to the client. What is going on? At first glance, the client *looks* calm. But we are still anxious. We begin a little detective work. What is the client thinking about? What is she feeling? After a time, clients will usually recognize their own feelings of anxiety. Had we not probed, we might have missed it. Scientific work into the nature of emotions gives us some insights into how such "contagion" might work. Ekman (1985) observed that when people are feeling strong emotions, but are suppressing them, nearly indiscernible "micromove-ments," which signal their true feelings (but are completely at variance with their displayed feelings), often flicker across their face for a quarter of a second. Perhaps that is what we are picking up. Or perhaps we are merely sensitive to subtle cues of shifting posture or alerted tone. It is also possible that therapists tend to mimic their clients' tones, postures, and facial expression, and that the feedback from these pseudo-emotional expressions feeds back and produces the same emo-tional reaction the client feels. However it works, the therapists' own emotional reactions are often an indispensable guide to the emotions that flicker across the clients' consciousness.

Why is it so important to know what our clients are thinking and feeling, rather than limiting ourselves to observing how they are acting?

1. A knowledge of our own and others' inner lives is one of the delights of life. It is the stuff of poetry, literature, dance, music, and the arts.

2. The mind is a giant computer. We get a great deal of informa-tion from rational analysis. We get even more by looking at a "print-out" of our feelings. For example, if you wish to know how things can be expected to go with your Great Aunt Ethel, you can often gain some information by noticing how you *feel* when you go to the mailbox and find a letter from her. Consciously, you may *think* she is a fine person who wishes you the best. You should let her visit you for the two weeks she proposes. But if your heart sinks when you spot her purple ink and scented card, you might think again. Think through those interactions with her again. Something must be going on to make receipt of her letters so depressing. The emotions seem to be an accurate summary of how things have gone during the years you have interacted with Ethel.

3. One does better if one is using all one's faculties—cognitive *and* emotional—to make decisions.

4. Others don't always know or want to tell you what they feel. If you have a knowledge of many emotional languages, you can make some rough estimates. One gains by listening to what people say, as well as observing their physiological and behavioral responses. One gains by tuning into as many subtle cues as possible in addition to observing more obvious responses. Even behavior often expresses itself in a variety of disguises.

We have reviewed why we think emotional detective work is so important in therapy. How can intimates learn to communicate about their emotions? Researchers have formulated some suggestions, discussed in the following section.

## Developing Intimacy Skills

Before we begin, let us define two terms we will be using—companionate love and intimacy.

### Companionate Love

Companionate love (sometimes called "true love") has been defined as "the affection we feel for those with whom our lives are deeply entwined." (Hatfield & Walster, 1978, p. 9).

Rubin (1970) developed a scale to measure such love. He sifted through a jumble of lovers', novelists', and scientists' descriptions of love. He concluded that love includes such elements as idealization of the other, tenderness, responsibility, the longing to serve and be served by the loved one, intimacy, the desire to share emotions and experiences, sexual attraction, the exclusive and absorptive nature of the relationship, and finally, a relative lack of concern with social norms and constraints. Sternberg (1988) proposed a triangular theory of love. He argued that, potentially, love may involve three different components.

1. Passion: This component embraces the drives that lead to romance, physical attraction, and sexual consummation.
2. Intimacy: This component embraces close, connected, and bonded feelings.
3. Decision/commitment: In the short term, this encompasses the decision that one loves another. In the long term, it involves the commitment to maintain that love.

### Intimacy

What about intimacy? The word intimacy is derived from the Latin *intimus*, meaning "inner" or "inmost." To be intimate means to be close to another. Hatfield (1984) defined intimacy as "A process in which people attempt to get close to another; to explore similarities (and differences) in the way they think, feel, and behave." (p. 207).

Intimate relationships have a number of characteristics:

*Cognitive Characteristics.*    Intimates are willing to reveal themselves to one another. They disclose information about themselves and listen to their partners' confidences. In deeply intimate relationships, friends and lovers feel free to reveal most facets of themselves. As a result, intimates share profound information about one another's histories, values, strengths, weaknesses, idiosyncracies, hopes, and fears. (Altman & Taylor, 1973; Huesmann & Levinger, 1976; Jourard, 1964).

*Emotional Characteristics.*    Intimates care deeply about one another. People generally feel more intense love for intimates than for anyone else. Yet, because intimates care so much about one another, they have the power to hurt one another as well. The dark side of love is jealousy, loneliness, depression, and anger. It is this powerful interplay of conflicting emotions that gives vibrancy to the most intimate of relationships. (See Berscheid, 1983; Hatfield & Walster, 1978). Basic to all intimate relationships, of course, is trust.

*Behavioral Characteristics.*    Intimates are comfortable in close physical proximity. They gaze at one another (Argyle, 1967), stand close to one another (Allgeier & Byrne, 1973), lean on one another (Galton, 1884; Hatfield, Roberts, & Schmidt, 1980), and perhaps touch.

   Now that we have defined what we mean by companionate love and intimacy, let us see what scientists and therapists have learned about how to get it (see Figure B).

### Intimacy Skills

*Encouraging People to Accept Themselves as They Are.*    Many people are determined to be perfect (at the least!). They find it hard to settle for less in themselves. Perfectionists are bound to have trouble in their intimate encounters. Intimates rarely assume their partners are

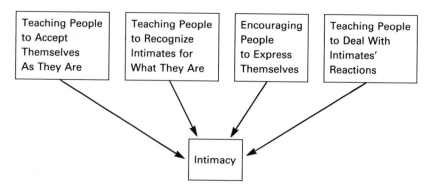

FIG. B.   Developing intimacy skills.

perfect; soon enough they begin to think tart thoughts about their "Beloved One." The first step in learning to be intimate, then, is to accept the fact that you are entitled to be what you are—to have the ideas you have and the feelings you feel—and to accept the fact that after you've done the best you can, there is not much more you can do, that your best is good enough.

In therapy, we try to move people away from the notion that one should come into the world perfect and stay that way, toward a more modest realization that one can usually gain wisdom only in small steps. People must pick one small goal and work to accomplish that. When that is accomplished, they can move on to another. In that way change becomes possible and manageable (Watson & Tharp, 1985). The American notion that "you can be whatever to want to be" is an exaggeration—sometimes charming, often harmful (See Rapson, 1988).

***Encouraging People to Recognize Their Intimates for What They Are.*** People may be hard on themselves, but they are generally even harder on their partners. Most people have the idea that everyone is entitled to a perfect partner, or at least one a little bit better than the one available (See Hatfield, 1984). If people are going to have an intimate relationship, they have to learn to enjoy others as they are, without hoping to fix them.

It is extraordinarily difficult for people to accept that their friends are entitled to be the people that they are. People long for their mate to be the person they want him to be. It would take so little for him to change his entire personality. Why is she so stubborn? Why is he so mean? What is wrong with me that I can't change her?

If we can come to the realization that our lover or friend is the person who exists right now, not the person we wish he was, not the person he could be, but what he is—once that realization occurs, intimacy becomes possible.

***Encouraging People to Express Themselves.*** Next, intimates have to learn to be more comfortable about expressing ideas and feelings. This is harder than one might think. Intimate relationships spring forth with powerful hopes. When passions are so intense, consequences so momentous, people are often hesitant to speak the truth. From moment to moment, it is tempting to present a consistent picture. In the throes of passionate love, people are hesitant to admit having residual niggling doubts. (What if the person they love is hurt? What if revelations destroy the relationship?) When they are angry, they don't want to speak about their complicated love or their self-doubts, and their wish to lash out. Dependent persons are particularly loathe to express inner doubts for fear of losing the person without whom they think survival is not possible.

To be intimate, people have to push toward a more honest, graceful, complete, and patient communication. They must understand that ideas and feelings are necessarily complex, with many nuances, shadings, and inconsistencies. In love, there is time to clear things up.

One interesting thing that people often discover is that their affection increases when they begin to admit their irritations. People are often surprised to discover that when they think that they have fallen out of love—they are "bored" with their affair—that as they begin to express their anger and ambivalence, they feel their love come back in a rush.

In *The Family Crucible* Napier and Whitaker (1978) described just such a confrontation:

> What followed was a classic confrontation. If John's affair was a kind of reawakening, so now was this marital encounter, though of a very different sort. Eleanor was enraged, hurt, confused, and racked with a sense of failure. John was guilty, also confused, but not apologetic. The two partners fought and cried, talked and searched for an entire night. The next evening, more exhausting encounters. Feelings that had been hidden for years emerged; doubts and accusations that they had never expected to admit articulated.
>
> Eleanor had to find out everything, and the more she discovered, the more insatiable her curiosity became. The more she heard, the guiltier her husband became and the angrier she grew, until he finally cried for a halt. It was his cry for mercy that finally led to a temporary reconciliation of the couple. They cried together for the first time either of them could remember.
>
> For a while they were elated; they had achieved a breakthrough in their silent and dreary marriage. They felt alive together for the first time in years. Somewhat mysteriously, they found themselves going to bed together in the midst of a great tangle of emotions—continuing anger, and hurt, and guilt, and this new quality: abandon. The lovemaking was, they were to admit to each other, 'the best it had ever been.' How could they have moved through hatred into caring so quickly?" (p. 153)

***Teaching People to Deal with Their Intimate's Reactions.***   To say that you should communicate your ideas and feelings, *must* communicate them if you are to have an intimate affair, does not mean your partner is always going to like it. You can expect that when you try to express your deepest feelings, it will sometimes hurt. Your lovers and friends may tell you frankly how deeply you have hurt them and that may make you feel extremely guilty. Or they may react with intense anger. Intimates have to learn to stop responding in automatic fashion to such emotional outbursts—backing up, apologizing for what they have said, measuring their words. They have to learn to stay calm, remind themselves that they are entitled to say what they think and what they feel, and to listen to what their partners think and feel—and keep on trying. Only then is there a chance of an emotionally intimate encounter.

*In sum.* It appears that a multifaceted approach to emotional communication will likely yield better results than a more limited approach. This is because emotions themselves are a multifaceted phenomenon.

## REFERENCES

Allgeier, A. R., & Byrne, D. (1973). Attraction toward the opposite sex as a determinant of physical proximity. *Journal of Social Psychology, 90,* 213–219.

Altman, I., & Taylor, D. A. (1973). *Social penetration: The development of interpersonal relationships.* New York: Holt.

Argyle, M. (1967). *The psychology of interpersonal behavior.* Baltimore, MD: Penguin Books.

Baron, R. A., & Byrne, D. (1981). *Social psychology: Understanding human interaction. (3rd ed.).* Boston: Allyn and Bacon.

Berscheid, E. (1983). Emotion. In H. H. Kelley, E. Berscheid, A. Christensen, J. H. Harvey, T. L. Huston, G. Levinger, E. McClintock, L. A. Peplau, & D. R. Peterson (Eds.), *Close relationships.* (pp. 110–168). New York: Freeman.

Berscheid, E., & Hatfield, E. (1969). *Interpersonal attraction.* Reading, MA: Addison-Wesley.

Buck, R. (1979). Individual differences in nonverbal sending accuracy and electrodermal responding: The externalizing–internalizing dimension. In R. Rosenthal (Ed.), *Skill in nonverbal communication: Individual differences.* (pp. 140–170). Cambridge, MA: Oelgeschlager, Gunn, & Hain.

Byrne, D. (1971). *The attraction paradigm.* New York: Academic Press.

Cacioppo, J. T., Petty, R. E., & Tassinary, L. G. (in press). Social psychophysiology: A new look. To appear in L. Berkowitz (Ed.) *Advances in experimental social psychology.*

Candland, D. K. (1977). The persistent problems of emotion. In D. K. Candland, J. P. Fell, E. Keen, A. I. Leshner, R. Plutchik, & R. M. Tarpy (Eds.), *Emotion.* (pp. 1–84). Monterey, CA: Brooks-Cole.

Carlson, J., & Hatfield, E. (in press). *The psychology of emotions.* Lanham, MD: University Press of America.

Darwin, C. (1965). *The expression of the emotions in man and animals.* Chicago, IL: University of Chicago Press. (Original work published 1872)

Degler, C. N. (1980). *At odds: Women and the family in America from the revolution to the present.* New York: Oxford University Press.

Ekman, P. (1972). Universals and cultural differences in facial expressions of emotion. In J. Cole (Ed.), *Nebraska Symposium on Motivation, 19,* (pp. 207–282) Lincoln: University of Nebraska Press.

Ekman, P. (1985). *Telling lies.* New York: Berkley Books.

Ekman, P., & Friesen, W. V. (1969). Nonverbal leakage and clues to deception. *Psychiatry, 32,* 88–106.

Fridlund, A. J., & Izard, C. E. (1983). Electromyographic studies of facial expressions of emotions and patterns of emotions. In J. T. Cacioppo & R. E. Petty (Eds.), *Social psychophysiology: A sourcebook.* (pp. 243–286). New York: Guilford Press.

Galton, F. (1884). Measurement of character. *Fortnightly Review, 36,* 179–185.

Gay, P. (1984). *The bourgeois experience: Victoria to Freud. Vol. 1: Education of the senses.* New York: Oxford University Press.

Halberstadt, A. G. (1986). Family socialization of emotional expression and nonverbal communication styles and skills. *Journal of Personality and Social Psychology, 51,* 827–836.

Hatfield, E. (1970). Studies testing a theory of positive affect. National Science Foundation Grant GS 30822X, Washington, DC.

Hatfield, E. (1984). The dangers of intimacy. In V. Derlaga (Ed.), *Communication, intimacy, and close relationships.* (pp. 207–220.) New York: Academic Press.

Hatfield, E., Roberts, D., & Schmidt, L. (1980). The impact of sex and physical attractiveness on an initial social encounter. *Recherches de psychologie sociale, 2,* 27–40.

Hatfield, E., Traupmann, J., Sprecher, S., Utne, M., & Hay, J. (1984). Equity and intimate relations: recent research. In W. Ickes (Ed.), *Compatible and incompatible relationships.* (pp. 1–27). New York: Springer-Verlag.

Hatfield, E., & Walster, G. W. (1978). *A new look at love.* Lanham, MD: University Press of America.

Huesmann, L. R., & Levinger, G. (1976). Incremental exchange theory: A formal model for progression in dyadic social interaction. In L. Berkowitz & E. Hatfield (Eds.), *Advances in experimental social psychology. Equity theory: Toward a general theory of social interaction. 9,* (pp. 192–230). New York: Academic Press.

Izard, C. E. (1971). *The face of emotion.* New York: Appleton-Century-Crofts.

Izard, C. E. (1977). *Human emotions.* New York: Plenum Press.

Izard, C. E., & Buechler, S. (1986). Aspects of consciousness and personality in terms of differential emotions theory. In R. Plutchik & H. Kellerman (Eds.), *Emotion: Theory, research and experience. Vol. 1* (pp. 165–188). New York: Academic Press.

Jones, H. E. (1960). The longitudinal method in the study of personality. In I. Iscoe & H. W. Stevenson (Eds.), *Personality development in children.* (pp. 3–27). Austin, TX: University of Texas Press.

Jourard, S. M. (1964). *The transparent self.* Princeton, NJ: Van Nostrand.

Kemper, T. (1986). *A social interaction theory of emotions.* New York: John Wiley and Sons.

Lacey, J. I. (1967). Somatic response patterning and stress: Some revisions of activation theory. In M. H. Appley & R. Trumbull (Eds.), *Psychological stress: Issues in research* (pp. 14–42). New York: Appleton-Century-Crofts.

Lanzetta, J. T., & Kleck, R. E. (1970). Encoding and decoding of nonverbal affect in humans. *Journal of Personality and Social Psychology, 16,* 12–19.

Lazarus, R. S. (1977). A cognitive analysis of biofeedback control. In G. E. Schwartz & G. Beatty (Eds.), *Biofeedback: Theory and research* (pp. 69–71). New York: Academic Press.)

Lazarus, R. S., Kanner, A. D., & Folkman, S. (1980). Emotions: A cognitive phenomenological analysis: In R. Plutchik & H. Kellerman (Eds.), *Emotion: Theory, research and experience. Vol. I.* (pp. 189–218). New York: Academic Press.

Liebowitz, M. R. (1983). *The chemistry of love.* Boston, Little, Brown, and Co.

Lutz, C., & White, G. M. (1986). The anthropology of emotions. *Annual Review of Anthropology, 15,* 405–436.

MacLean, P. D. (1986). Ictal symptoms relating to the nature of affects and their cerebral substrate. In R. Plutchik & H. Kellerman (Eds.), *Emotion: theory, research, and experience. Vol. 3. Biological foundations of emotion.* (pp. 61–90) New York: Academic Press.

Malatesta, C. Z., & Haviland, J. M. (1982). Learning display rules: The socialization of emotion expression in infancy. *Child Development, 53,* 991–1003.

Morency, N. L., & Krauss, R. M. (1982). Children's nonverbal encoding and decoding of affect. In R. Feldman (Ed.), *Development of non-verbal behavior in children.* (pp. 181–199). New York: Springer-Verlag.

Napier, A. V., & Whitaker, C. (1978). *The family crucible.* New York: Harper & Rowe.

Rapson, R. (1980). *Fairly lucky you live Hawaii.* Lanham, MD: University Press of America.

Rapson, R. (1988). *American yearnings: Love, money, and endless possibility.* Lanham, MD: University Press of America.

Rubin, Z. (1970). Measurement of romantic love. *Journal of Personality and Social Psychology, 16,* 265–273.

Scherer, K. R., & Ekman, P. (1982). *Handbook of methods in nonverbal behavior research.* Cambridge: Cambridge University Press.

Skinner, B. (1953). *Science and human behavior.* New York: The Macmillan Co.

Stearns, P. N., & Stearns, C. Z. (1985). Emotionology: Clarifying the history of emotions and emotional standards: *American Historical Review, 90: 4,* 813–836.

Steiner, J. E. (1979). Human facial expression in response to taste and smell stimulation. Advances in Child Development and Behavior, 13, 257–295.

Sternberg, R. J. (1988). Triangulating love. In R. J. Sternberg & M. L. Barnes (Eds.), *The psychology of love.* (pp. 119–138). New Haven: Yale University Press.

Stone, L. (1979). *The family, sex, and marriage: In England 1500–1800.* New York: Harper Torchbooks.

Watson, D. L., & Tharp, R. G. (1985). *Self-directed behavior: Self-modification for personal adjustment.* Monterey, CA: Brooks-Cole.

Zuckerman, M., Hall, J. A., DeFrank, R. S., & Rosenthal, R. (1976). Encoding and decoding of spontaneous and posed facial expressions. *Journal of Personality and Social Psychology, 34,* 966–977.

# CHAPTER 3

# Communication and Coping in Families

**Robert Plutchik**
Albert Einstein College of Medicine
**Anita Plutchik**
New York Medical College

While waiting on a cashier's line in a department store, we overheard an interaction between a mother and her 6- or 7-year-old son. The mother was waiting to pay for some merchandise and the boy was restlessly walking along the nearby aisle, touching everything he passed. The mother became increasingly agitated and finally began to talk loudly to her son. She began with the following remark: "Stop touching everything."

Her son ignored her and continued to touch the merchandise. She then said. "You're stupid. I can't wait for you to go back to school. Boy, am I going to go out and celebrate."

The son said nothing, but continued to touch things on the counters. The mother then said, "If you don't stop touching things I'm going to hit you so hard your teeth will rattle."

The boy ignored the mother, made no remarks, and continued to wander along the aisles. After a brief hesitation the mother said, "When we get home, if your room is clean I may let you go out and play."

This threat finally roused the son to respond. He looked at his mother and said, "But my room is clean."

The mother answered, "Well, it didn't look clean to me. When we get back I'll look at it and decide if I want to let you go out and play."

This was as much of the conversation as we heard, but in retrospect it seemed to reveal some important ideas. First, the conversation reflects the very basic fact that much of the communication between people expresses needs to influence one another and to accomplish certain implicit (or explicit) goals. The mother in this scene clearly used her communications to express her need to control her son's behavior. However, implied in this situation is the fact that the mother also has power over the child and is clearly the dominant one in the relationship. Because she was the dominant one she was able to use humiliation, threats of physical punishment, and control over his anticipated pleasure of playing with his friends.

A second idea that the conversation suggests is that all communications between people have consequences; some are desirable and some are not. The attempt to influence the child's behavior by calling him "stupid" may or may not change his behavior, but it is very likely to have a negative impact on his image of himself and his self-esteem. The threat to hit the child may possibly change his behavior, but it is also likely to reinforce the idea of his weakness or vulnerability. The threat to prevent the boy from playing with his friends might change his behavior, but it also communicates the arbitrary use of parental power.

Assuming that this mother was very distressed by her son's behavior, it seemed to us that she had many alternatives to the way she dealt with it.

Some possibilities were:

1. Hold the child by the hand.
2. Distract or amuse the child with a story.
3. Offer a reward for good behavior.
4. Ask him to change his behavior as a favor.
5. Explain why his behavior was unacceptable and reason with him to change.
6. Leave the store.
7. Let him buy a snack or toy for good behavior.
8. Ignore him even if she is troubled.

One very important lesson that this story reveals is that for every problem, however small or large, there are many possible solutions. In this case all the solutions involved different kinds of communications. Although much of this seems obvious when pointed out, it has been our experience that most people tend to use one style of communication most of the time. When this particular style does not work, they become angry and frustrated rather than simply switching to an alternative approach. A second implication is that some solutions probably work better than others. A third is that each solution has its own consequences, some good and some bad. The optimum solution is one through which both parties feel that their needs have been met to a reasonable degree.

## COMMUNICATION STYLES

An extensive literature has developed over the past few years dealing with various aspects of communication in families. It has been pointed out that all relationships involve some degree of conflict and that such conflicts are expressed, subtly, or overtly, in communications (Hatfield, 1984; Langs, 1983; Rausch, Barry, Hertel, & Swain, 1974; Watzlawick, Beavin, & Jackson, 1967). It has been noted that there are relatively few styles of communicating, and that people are often unaware of their own particular styles. Some examples of communication styles are: placating, blaming, being unusually reasonable, and being congruent (Satir, Stachowiak, & Taschman, 1975), or being dramatic, attentive, dominant, relaxed, or open (Norton, 1983).

In recent years a number of studies concerned with family education or enrichment have focused on teaching communication styles and problem-solving approaches (Day, Bosworth, Gustafson, Chewing, & Hawkins, 1985; Giblin, 1986; Markman, Jamieson, & Floyd, 1983; Rabin, Blechman, Kahn, & Carel, 1985; Raue & Spence, 1985). These studies have generally reported that enrichment programs had positive long-term effects (Lai, 1983; Giblin, 1986).

An area that has been relatively neglected is the relation between communication style or content and emotional response. The point was made in the anecdote that began this chapter that the content of the mother's communications influence the feelings of the child, just as the child's communications influence the mother's feelings. It is this connection that requires more research.

An interesting approach to communication styles has been presented by Wahlroos (1974). He presents 20 "rules of communication" that he believes make for good interpersonal involvement and indirectly define emotional health. Some examples of his rules are:

1. Define what is important and stress it; define what is unimportant and ignore it.
2. Make your communication positive.
3. Recognize that each event can be seen from different points of view.

4. Be tactful, considerate, and courteous.

5. Do not preach, nag, yell, or whine.

6. Do not use unfair communication techniques.

Illustrations of this last point would be such things as bringing up irrelevant events that happened a long time ago, calling the other person names, being sarcastic, and deliberately distorting facts to make a point. Wahlroos documents with many examples how direct training in communication skills greatly increases the capacity of individuals to exhibit signs of emotional health.

### An Example of Poor Communication: "Why" Questions

The point has been made that communications often have multiple meanings (Langs, 1983), that not all communication is intentional, conscious, or successful (Watzlawick, et al., 1967), and that context determines how messages are to be interpreted (Norton, 1983). These ideas are especially relevant to a simple communicative act that most people engage in quite frequently, and that is the act of asking "why?"

"Why" questions can divided into two general categories, those that are concerned with scientific or technical issues and those that are concerned with personal feelings and motivations. An example of the former type would be: "Why did the car break down?", and the answer would be given in such terms as unpaved roads, heavy snow, or worn spark plugs. An example of the latter type would be: "Why can't you lose weight?" and the expected answer would presumably be given in terms of lack of willpower, poor habits of eating, or unconscious wishes to punish someone. The comments to follow are solely about the second type of why questions.

One of the things we have discovered is that why questions concerned with personal feelings and motivations tend to make most individuals to whom they are directed feel defensive or uncomfortable. Think of your own reactions if someone asked you such questions as: "Why don't you lose weight?", "Why are you late?", "Why can't you eat alone in a restaurant?", or "Why are you afraid of insects?". What is it about such questions that make people feel uncomfortable?

We may understand such questions better if we recognize the settings in which they typically occur. Parents feel free to ask their children why questions ("Why didn't you call"?) whereas children rarely ask such questions of their parents. Teachers normally ask their students why questions ("Why didn't you do your homework?"), whereas students rarely ask their teachers such questions. Bosses feel free to ask their employees why questions ("Why were you late?"), but employees rarely ask such questions of their bosses.

What this suggests is that people who are in higher positions of power or authority usually ask why questions of those who are in lower positions. Implicitly, the asking of a why question of this type is an indirect expression of dominance. When one finds why questions typically being asked by one spouse to another or one friend to another, this is an indirect indication of who feels more dominant or powerful in the relationship. Similarly, dominance is being expressed when psychotherapists ask patients why they felt certain emotions or carried out certain acts.

There is another important aspect to why questions. Most people are so well socialized and polite that their immediate thought when asked a personal why question is to begin a sentence with the word "Because." We have a strong tendency to want to answer such questions, and this creates problems for us. One problem is that we do not always know the reason we do things. If a mother says to a child "Why did you knock over my favorite lamp while playing in the living room?", what can the child say? If the child says it was an accident, this does not really answer the mother's question. The child might have a number of other thoughts about it. For example, he might think; "Because I'm clumsy," or "Because I'm stupid," or "Because I'm mad at you for making me go to bed early." None of these responses, even if true, are acceptable either to the mother or the child. More likely, the child is simply unaware of any plausible reason for his action.

This point can be illustrated by an incident we observed involving a 5-or 6-year-old girl. Her grandmother had just bought her a large teddy bear that was almost as large as she was. They walked out of the store and down a flight of steps with the little girl holding the large teddy bear in her arms so that she was hardly able to see in front of her. Near the bottom of the stairs the child slipped and fell.

The grandmother turned and angrily shouted "Look what that doll caused."

The child looked up and said, "No."

The grandmother then said, "Then why did you fall?"

The child answered "Because. . . I don't know."

Both adults and children feel defensive and uncomfortable when asked why questions. For the most part such questions are put downs and the implied response is a negative one. Asking an adult "Why didn't you get that promotion?" leads to the feeling "Because I'm not competent." "Why is your room always so sloppy?" implies the response "Because I'm a slob." Thus, why questions often seem to press people to supply an internal stable attribute (or trait) to account for implicitly undesirable actions.

The point being made is that these why questions have no truly adequate answers. Someone may have to lie to get around them gracefully; often there is an implied insult. The real reason for the behaviors or feelings being asked about are often unknown to the person involved.

Let us summarize the points that have been made. Why questions imply an hierarchical dominance relation between the questioner and the one being questioned. It is also likely that the person asking the question is not really interested in the answer but rather in the implied right to ask the question. Because of normal social expectations, most people who are asked why questions try to answer them in some way. However, because motives are not often clear, this may lead to exaggerations or lies. For these reasons we believe that good communication requires that we not ask personal why questions of the people with whom we interact. There still remains the problem, however, of how we should respond to why questions directed at us by other people.

## Answering Why Questions

We assume that everyone is confronted by why questions from time to time and would like to be able to deal with them in a friendly, nonconfrontational way, without responding directly to the question. This means, for example, that a response like "It's none of your business" would not be appropriate.

Probably the easiest answer to a valid criticism (in the form of a why question) is "I'm sorry." Therefore, in the example of the boss asking the question "Why were you late?" the response of "I'm sorry" acknowledges awareness of the lateness and offers an apology. It is not a lie and is not apt to lead to further discussion.

There are a number of other responses that can be used in many situations where a personal why question is asked. Here are some illustrations:

Why did you forget my birthday?
  I wish I knew.
Why don't you like opera?
  That's a good question.
Why are you biting your nails?
  Yes, I am doing that, aren't I?

Why did you cut your hair so short?
　Isn't it nice?
Why are you always losing your temper?
　I give up.
Why do you smoke?
　I don't answer why questions.

Sometimes if one cannot think of a suitable response to a why question that will not generate antagonism, it may be appropriate simply to say nothing and to change the topic. The value of these approaches is that they provide an individual with a series of options or choices that allow him or her to maintain communication between equals, without hostility or confrontation.

It is important to emphasize that why questions tend to generate feelings of anger, guilt, or irritation in individuals to whom they are addressed. Such feelings reflect the often unexpressed sense of being put down by the questioner or of being put in an inferior position. The result is that it is often difficult to think of a calm, nonhostile response in such a setting. We have found that the major solution to this problem is to become aware of the significance of why questions, listen for the occasions of their occurrence in oneself and in others, and deliberately practice a variety of nonhostile responses of the type cited above.

Effectively handling why questions is only one communication problem among many. Because most problems in life are related to our interactions with other people, is there a general approach to problem-solving that will apply to a wide variety of problems? We believe there is. The next section introduces a theory of coping styles.

## EMOTIONS AND COPING

During the past several decades the senior author of this chapter has been developing a general psychoevolutionary theory of emotions (Plutchik, 1970, 1980a, 1984). This theory has many interrelated concepts, but only two are described here.

The theory assumes that emotions are more than feeling states, facial expressions, or physiological changes. Emotions are complex chains of events triggered by certain stimuli as shown in Fig. 3.1. They involve cognitive interpretations, feeling states, physiological changes, impulses to action, display behavior, and overt action designed to affect the initial triggering stimuli. Because emotions are complex,

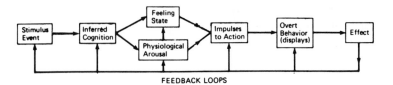

FIG. 3.1.   The Complex Chain of Events Defining an Emotion.

there is no way to completely describe an emotion by knowing only
some of its components. Verbal reports of feelings are often inaccurate
because people may not know exactly what they feel, or they may feel
several different emotions at the same time. There are also situations
that arise in which individuals attempt to hide their feelings.

In some ways, this view is like Skinner's (chapter 1). We both believe
that public and private events seldom coincide exactly, and that words
for feelings are generally more ambiguous than are words for objects
or events. We both believe that a number of different life scenarios
and contingencies of reinforcement create the ambiguities of the affect
language (Plutchik, 1980a). And we both acknowledge that theories
constructed primarily in terms of memories and feelings ignore important realities of contemporary behaviors and their sensitivity to environmental events.

There are some differences, however. The psychoevolutionary theory assumes that emotions are always inferences (hypothetical constructs) based on various classes of evidence. It does not assume that
overt behavior is necessarily a "better" source of information than are
other classes of indicators. And the theory offers an explicit structural
model that describes specific relations among all emotions as well as
between emotions and other conceptual domains such as personality.

The psychoevolutionary theory of emotion is based upon a number
of explicit postulates. Some of the more important ones are:

1. Emotions are communication and survival mechanisms based
   on evolutionary adaptations.

2. Emotions have a genetic basis.

3. Emotions are hypothetical constructs based on various classes
   of evidence.

4. Emotions are complex chains of events with stabilizing feedback
   loops that produce some kind of behavioral homeostasis.

5. The relations among emotions can be represented by a 3-dimen-
   sional structural model.

6. Emotions are related to a number of derivative conceptual domains.

A detailed elaboration of these postulates may be found in Plutchik (1980a, 1980b, 1984, 1989). The postulate that is most relevant to the concept of coping styles presented later in this chapter is number 6. This assumes that there are several different "languages" that one may use to describe aspects of emotion, and that these languages are related to one another in systematic ways. This is illustrated in Table 3.1.

One may focus on feeling states such as joy, sadness, surprise, and curiosity (The Subjective Language). Or one may focus on associated behaviors; that is, flight instead of fear, threat instead of anger, distress signals instead of sadness (The Behavioral Language). If, however, emotional states persist for a long time, or occur in many different situations, then a new descriptive language becomes appropriate. For example, someone who frequently expresses fear in social situations is usually called timid. Someone who frequently expresses anger is quarrelsome, and someone who is frequently sad is likely to be described as gloomy. These terms are part of the language of personality traits, and it is reasonable to assume that personality traits reflect frequent expressions of particular emotions or combinations of emotions (The Trait Language).

The idea of derivatives can be extended further. Diagnostic terms represent extreme manifestations of certain personality traits. Thus the trait of gloominess in extreme form is recognized as depression; the trait of hostility in an extreme form might be diagnosed as paranoid; and methodical planning, in extreme form, is described by the label of obsessive–compulsive (The Diagnostic Language).

Still another derivative language refers to ego defenses, which have been conceptualized as ways to regulate emotions (The Ego Defense Language). For example, displacement can be conceptualized as an unconscious way to deal with anger that cannot be directly expressed without punishment. Similarly, projection can be conceptualized as an unconscious way to deal with feelings of disgust about oneself by expressing this feeling to other people. Parallels of this sort have been made for each primary emotion and are described in detail in Kellerman (1979) and in Plutchik, Kellerman, and Conte (1979).

Another domain of related languages is that of coping styles. According to the psycho-evolutionary theory, coping styles are the conscious derivatives of the unconscious ego defenses. A new set of terms has been suggested to reflect the parallels. For example, the defense of denial is assumed to correspond to the conscious coping style of "minimization." The ego defense of displacement is assumed to corre-

TABLE 3.1
Emotions and Their Derivatives

| Subjective Language | Behavioral Language | Functional Language | Trait Language | Diagnostic Language | Ego-defense Language | Coping-style Language |
|---|---|---|---|---|---|---|
| Fear | Escape | Protection | Timid | Passive | Repression | Supression |
| Anger | Attack | Destruction | Quarrelsome | Antisocial | Displacement | Substitution |
| Joy | Mate | Reproduction | Sociable | Manic | Reaction-formation | Reversal |
| Sadness | Cry | Reintegration | Gloomy | Depressed | Compensation | Replacement |
| Acceptance | Groom | Incorporation | Trusting | Histrionic | Denial | Minimization |
| Disgust | Vomit | Rejection | Hostile | Paranoid | Projection | Fault-finding |
| Expectation | Map | Exploration | Demanding | Obsessive-Compulsive | Intellectual-ization | Mapping |
| Surprise | Stop | Orientation | Indecisive | Borderline | Regression | Help-seeking |

spond to the coping style of "substitution," and the defense of intellectualization corresponds to the coping style of "mapping." These coping styles, because they are central to the point of this chapter, are described in detail in the following section.

## Basic Coping Styles

Based on the concepts briefly outlined in the previous section, it is possible to define a small number of basic coping styles that are related to the basic emotions and that have applicability to life problems. The eight basic coping styles will be described and illustrated.

*Mapping.* One way that individuals deal with problems is by using their innate curiosity and intelligence to get more information about the problem. If a person went to a physician and described headaches, a rash, and a slight fever, the physician would probably ask for more information about feelings and symptoms, and do blood tests, x-rays, and other evaluations. In a sense, the doctor expands his understanding of an illness by making a map of the territory, by getting to know as much as possible about the situation as he can. Only then is he in a position to make an educated judgment designed to diagnose the problem and begin to arrive at the best solution.

In the same sense, everyone needs to get as much information as possible about a problem before taking actions to deal with it. If a mother were to discover some marijuana in her son's room, mapping would imply that she find out (a) if it is actually marijuana, (b) if it really belongs to her son, (c) if he is holding it for someone else, and (d) if he is actually using it. Only after obtaining such information would she be in a position to act appropriately. Mapping means trying to cope with a problem by getting more information about it.

*Avoidance.* Another possible way to deal with a problem is by avoiding the situation that gives rise to the problem. People do this every day. If there is someone who is difficult to get along with it may be possible to avoid any contact with that person. If someone is very uncomfortable in a plane he may decide to avoid planes. Many people who hate cold weather relocate to warmer climates. If an individual cannot get along with a boss he might request a transfer to another department or he might resign. When people get a divorce they have decided to avoid further marital conflict. Obviously some forms of avoidance are more extreme than others but all people occasionally use avoidance as a coping style. In short, avoidance is a way of coping with a problem by removing oneself from the situation that tends to trigger the problem.

*Help-Seeking.*   Another way to solve problems is to ask for help. Sometimes help-seeking is carried out on a very informal basis. For example, people call their friends to get opinions and advice about various life problems. Relatives may take turns helping someone who is ill. Neighbors frequently do errands and favors for each other. These are all ways in which people seek help.

Sometimes difficult life problems may require help-seeking from an expert. For example, going to a doctor, taking a car to a service station, consulting a therapist or clergyman, writing to an "advice column," dealing with a financial advisor, or joining a support group, all may be considered ways in which people seek help.

*Minimizing.*   Many situations are ambiguous in terms of their implications for any individual and different people can interpret the same situation in different or even opposite ways. It is possible to see a glass as half full (the optimist) or half empty (the pessimist). The objective facts are the same, but the emotion an individual feels depends on how he or she interprets the facts. Minimization refers to the idea that one can minimize the importance or seriousness of events in one's life, and that one can choose this method of coping as a conscious strategy.

In studies of middle managers in a large national corporation, it was found that those managers who tended to minimize problems experienced less stress on the job and were still rated as good managers (Bunker et al., 1982). It is important to emphasize that minimization is not the same as denial, but is, in fact, a useful coping style for handling problems.

*Reversal.*   This idea refers to the coping style that leads individuals to do the opposite of what they feel. Such behavior is not a sign of hypocrisy but is a frequent, and socially effective, way of handling certain problems. If someone asks how an individual is feeling, one does not generally expect a catalog of current aches and pains.

In many ways a large part of acceptable and social behavior is dependent upon people acting in ways opposite to the way they feel. The ideas of politeness, tact, graciousness, and diplomacy, all relate to people acting differently than they feel. When politicians are interviewed they generally seem friendly and gracious and tend to suppress the anger and irritation they are likely to feel to some of the questions asked of them. Similarly, many people undertake arduous training programs to lose weight or develop skills, or engage in dangerous sports such as hang gliding, sky diving, or mountain climbing. They do this despite feelings of anxiety, or boredom, or insecurity; they act determined, secure, or courageous—that is, the opposite of what they feel. People such as nurses or surgeons, who deal with unpleasant or painful life problems generally act the opposite of what they feel in order to solve problems effectively.

Reversal is a very important coping style that nearly everyone uses to a greater or lesser degree. It would be nearly impossible to have successful relationships without it. In fact, many family conflicts arise because people act exactly the way they feel when they are home.

The coping style of reversal is evidently related to the general issue of the extent to which deception, of others or oneself, occurs in everyday life. This has been discussed by the sociobiologists and is summarized in Plutchik (1989).

**Blame.** Some people cope with problems by blaming other people. This method works well under certain conditions, at least for a while. It makes the person doing the blaming feel good because he or she does not take responsibility for the problem. If the blamer is in a position of authority he or she may be able to get away with it. For example, if an error is found in a company's books the manager may say his subordinate made the mistake and will thereby be himself absolved from responsibility.

Placing blame on a person or situation helps one feel a little better but it does not solve the problem. One of the problems with blaming is that it makes the person being blamed feel bad, and there is a strong likelihood that the blamed person will develop resentment. Resentment, in turn, tends to lead to a desire for revenge and the vicious cycle of blame–resentment–revenge is started. Therefore, although blaming others helps cope with a problem in the short run, it has some undesirable consequences in the long run.

**Substitution.** Sometimes life creates problems for which there are no direct solutions. Substitution refers to methods of coping which are indirect. For example, someone who has a very unpleasant job but for various reasons cannot leave it might make an effort to do enjoyable things such as hobbies, travel, or exercise during hours when he is not working. Couples who cannot have children frequently adopt or take foster children into their home. Sometimes people turn to alcohol and drugs as a form of substitution. What all these approaches have in common is the fact that they represent indirect substitute solutions to problems.

*Improving Shortcomings.*   Sometimes a problem is created by a weakness in oneself. When there is a problem, many people tend to look at how others are handling things poorly. However, it is also possible to look at oneself more closely and consider one's own contribution to the problem. Assume for example that someone has been passed over for a promotion and that the advancement has been given to someone else. Clearly, many coping styles may be necessary to handle the disappointment, embarrassment, and resentment that may result from this. One important possibility is to improve one's own shortcomings. The individual might evaluate himself with regard to the qualifications he knows are necessary for advancement; for example, leadership skills, formal training, speech ability, manner of dress, willingness to travel or work late, et cetera, and decide to change or modify some of these skills.

Improving shortcomings may also include changing a situation. For example, if a child does poorly in school he may need to have a tutor, have his classes or teacher changed, or he may even need a special school. He might have an undetected learning or physical problem which would be improved by exercises, glasses, or by special training.

Shortcomings may sometimes be in one's own personality or attitudes. Arguments with a spouse may reflect a lack of tolerance or acceptance of other's idiosyncracies. Developing an enlarged sense of acceptance may go a long way toward overcoming the friction. It is thus evident that an important way to cope with problems is to identify shortcomings in the situation or in oneself, and to take steps to reduce the shortcomings.

## How to Choose a Coping Style

It was noted earlier that each solution of a problem has its own particular implications. For example, if one copes with a problem by blaming others, it is likely that the long-term effect will be to get these other people angry and desirous of revenge. Similarly, if an individual does the opposite of what he feels in every problem situation, it is possible that others will begin to think of him as dishonest or as a hypocrite. To the extent that people consider an individual phony, the long-term consequence may be a reduction in self-esteem.

These examples illustrate the point that there should be some guidelines to influence the choice of particular coping styles in the various problem situations that people face. We have found that there are a number of guidelines for the choice of problem solving styles. Two general ones are:

1. Choose the coping style that produces results that are in one's own best long-term interests.

2. Choose a coping style that does not make the situation worse.

There are other factors to consider when making choices designed to try to solve important life problems. These are aspects of a personal philosophy. They include the assumption that each person would like certain freedoms and opportunities; for example, the freedom to express his or her opinions without threat or intimidation, and the opportunity to work at a meaningful and productive job. Most people want to be free to exercise choices in religion and education, and to have the opportunity to choose a style of life that is congenial. But since each person is unique, what is congenial to one person may not be to another.

Given such considerations, we have gradually evolved what we call a "Personal Bill of Rights", as follows:

### Your Personal Bill of Rights

You have a right to your own opinions without having to explain or justify them.

You have the right to feel whatever you feel.

You have a right to make your own mistakes.

You have a right to be less than perfect.

You have a right to be different from other people.

You have a right to choose your own style of life.

You have a right to be responsible only for your own behavior.

You have a right not to be responsible for others who are able to be responsible for themselves.

You have a right to prevent yourself from being manipulated by other people.

You have a right to negotiate problems in your own best interests.

This Personal Bill of Rights suggests that each person has the right to be him (or her)self, even if that self is different from everyone else. It also implies that people who are competent have to be responsible for themselves, yet they do bear a responsibility in relation to people who are incapable of handling life's problems, for example, the young, the very old, the sick, and the dying.

Another implication of this Personal Bill of Rights is that exercising each right always has consequences. If an individual chooses to exercise the right to be different from other people, this may lead to criticism or ostracism. If an individual claims to be responsible for his own behavior, others may accuse him of selfishness. If an individual tries to prevent himself from being manipulated, others may feel hurt, disappointed, or angry that they no longer have a scapegoat. Choices have consequences. Our suggestions are designed to help individuals be more conscious of the choices they make, and more rational in judging their implications.

## CONCLUSIONS

This chapter has examined some aspects of communication and coping. It recognizes that coping in families is simply part of coping with any life problem, and that each solution has its own consequences.

The literature in the field clearly implies that all relationships involve some degree of subtle or overt conflict between individuals, and that coping with such conflict requires communications. Research has shown that there are a limited number of styles of communication and that such styles have effects on others that are pleasant or unpleasant, desirable or undesirable, short-term or long-term. An illustration of a poor form of communication was given: the use of "why" questions about feelings and motivations. It was noted that some "why" questions imply hierarchical relationships, tend to create defensive feelings, and increase the chances of distortions or lies.

A conceptualization of coping styles was then presented based on a general theory of emotions. It assumes that a few types of coping styles are used in a wide variety of situations. These coping styles have been labeled as follows: mapping, avoidance, help-seeking, minimizing, reversal, substitution, blame, and improving shortcomings. Illustrations of their use was also presented. In order to rationally and effectively decide on what coping styles to use and in what settings, certain guidelines were suggested. These concern the long-term consequences of decisions and they concern our personal beliefs about what is right and wrong.

## REFERENCES

Bunker, K. A. (1982). Comparisons of marketing subjects high and low in psychological symptoms. Report No. CA 2059, 114 from the Assessment Center of American Telephone and Telegraph Co., New York, NY.

Day, T., Bosworth, K., Gustafson, D. H., Chewing, B., & Hawkins, R., (1985). A computer system to help family members talk to one another. *Marriage & Family Review, 8*, 111–120.

Giblin, P. (1986). Research and assessment in marriage and family enrichment: A metaanalysis study. *Journal of Psychotherapy & The Family, 2,* 79–86.

Hatfield, E. (1984). The dangers of intimacy. In V. J. Derlega (Ed.), *Communication, intimacy, and close relationships* (pp. 207–220). New York: Academic Press.

Kellerman, H. (1979). *Group psychotherapy and personality. Intersecting structures.* New York: Grune and Stratton.

Lai, P. (1983). A study of the parent–child relations of delinquents in Taiwan. *Japanese Journal of Criminal Psychology, 20,* 33–43.

Langs, R. (1983). *Unconscious communication in everyday life.* New York: Jason Aronson.

Markman, H. J., Jamieson, K. J., & Floyd, F. J. (1983). The assessment and modification of premarital relationships: Preliminary findings on the etiology and prevention of marital and family distress. *Advances in Family Intervention, Assessment and Theory, 3,* 41–90.

Norton, R., (1983). *Communication style.* Beverly Hills, CA: Sage.

Plutchik, R. (1970). Emotions, evolution and adaptive processes. In M. Arnold (Ed.), *Feelings and emotions: The Loyola Symposium* (pp. 3–24). New York: Academic Press.

Plutchik, R. (1980a). *Emotions: A psychoevolutionary synthesis.* New York: Harper & Row.

Plutchik, R. (1980b). A psychoevolutionary theory of emotion. In R. Plutchik and H. Kellerman (Eds.), *Theories of emotion Vol. 1* (pp. 3–33). New York: Academic Press.

Plutchik, R. (1984). Emotions: A general psychoevolutionary theory. In K. R. Scherer and P. Ekman (Eds.), *Approaches to emotion* (pp. 197–219). Hillsdale, NJ: Lawrence Erlbaum Associates.

Plutchik, R. (1989). Emotions and psychotherapy: A psychoevolutionary perspective. In R. Plutchik and H. Kellerman (Eds.), *Emotions, psychotherapy and psychopathology, Vol. 5* (pp. 3–41). New York: Academic Press.

Plutchik, R., Kellerman, H., & Conte, H. R. (1979). A structural theory of ego defenses. In C. E. Izard (Ed.), *Emotions, personality and psychopathology* (pp. 229–257). New York: Plenum.

Raue, J., & Spence, S. H. (1985). Group versus individual applications of reciprocity training for parent–youth conflict. *Behavior Research and Theory, 23,* 177–186.

Raush, H. L., Barry, W. A., Hertel, R. K., & Swain, M. A. (1974). *Communication, conflict, and marriage.* San Francisco: Jossey-Bass.

Rabin, C., Blechman, E. A., Kahn, D., & Carel, C. H. (1985). Refocusing from child to marital problems using the marriage contract game. *Journal of Marital and Family Therapy, 11,* 75–85.

Satir, V., Stachowiak, J., & Taschman, H. A. (1975). *Helping families to change.* New York: Jason Aronson.

Wahlroos, S. (1974). *Family communication: A guide to emotional health.* New York: Macmillan.

Watzlawick, P., Beavin, J. H., & Jackson, D. D. (1967). *Pragmatics of human communication.* New York: W. W. Norton.

# CHAPTER 4

# The Development of Emotion Regulation: Effects on Emotional State and Expression

**Carolyn Saarni**
Sonoma State University, California
**Michael Crowley**
University of Oregon

Emotion regulation may be defined as behavior aimed at changing feelings in a desired direction. That the change is in a desired direction is inferred from the term *regulation,* which implies purposeful action of a regulator or governing mechanism. Behavior, in this context, should be broadly defined to include not only easily observed actions but also physiological changes and cognitions. We use the term "feelings" here to refer to a similarly broad class of responses: Feelings may be either physiological states or the subjective awareness and experience of emotion that is influenced by both physiological response and personal interpretation (Schacter & Singer, 1962).

The process of changing feelings may include replacing one emotional state with another or altering the intensity of a feeling. An example of the former is when we feel rejected and deeply hurt we change our vulnerable feeling state into a less vulnerable one by shifting our attention to the "bad" intentions of the rejector and replace our former emotional state of hurt with anger—an emotion that reduces feelings of vulnerability. An example of the second sort of change, altering the intensity of emotional state, is when we experience a loss and attempt to reduce the intensity of grief associated with the loss through reappraisal of the situation; for example, the death of an ill relative engenders sadness and loss, yet we may try to focus on the relief of suffering that death brought to the deceased so as to ameliorate our own sadness.

Regulation of emotional state begins with inborn, homeostatic mechanisms or reflexes; thus, it can be considered to be a biological drive toward adaptation to environmental change. Emotion regulation may also occur through effortful behaviors, including changes in cognition, which may function as attempts at adaptation. This latter sort of adaptation is most commonly employed in later childhood and adulthood as a way of coping with negative feelings or stress. Because adaptation is essential to survival and growth (and an increasing body of research links successful coping with emotional and physical health), processes of emotion regulation deserve serious attention. As developmental psychologists we are interested in examining how the process of emotion regulation changes through growth and development of the individual and in exploring the factors that influence such change.

In the first section we present some examples of emotion regulation and comment briefly on several major factors that appear to influence emotion regulation to varying degrees in different situations and at different developmental stages. These major factors are temperament, cognitive development, and socialization, and they are viewed from a systems perspective, that is, the factors themselves are mutually interactive. In the second section of this chapter we introduce two basic premises that guide our thinking on emotion regulation as it affects the *expression* of emotion, especially within interpersonal transactions. Lastly, we conclude with a brief discussion of how our ideas on the development of emotion regulation can be coordinated with those put forward by Skinner in his chapter in this volume.

## EMOTION REGULATION IN INFANCY AND CHILDHOOD

The development of emotion regulation begins virtually at birth and possibly before. The neonate, when distressed, will solicit relief from caregivers, and the caregivers, usually the parents, will characteristically respond quickly to try to change the distress into comfort. Thus, what begins as a biological response on the part of the newborn, for example, crying, rapidly becomes embedded in a social context that facilitates a reciprocal reinforcement of emotional responses. *Both* infant and parent are soothed when emotion regulation is effective and comfort restored. In addition, the neonate has at its disposal self-soothing strategies for regulating emotional arousal; thumb-sucking is the best known example and has thus been observed prenatally.

Let us assume that this young infant is a normal, healthy little girl with a clean diaper and a full belly. Knowing all this, and what has immediately preceded the distress cry, the parents develop and enact certain strategies aimed at changing her emotional state. Whether they acquire these strategies consciously or unconsciously is not the issue here; most likely, parents' interventions are a mixture of both. But one of the most obvious influences on the parents' strategic attempts to ameliorate their baby's distress is their perception of her temperament.

## Temperament

Temperament may be thought of as biologically based and as reflecting relatively stable individual differences in emotional reactivity and self-regulation (Campos, Barrett, Lamb, Goldsmith, & Stenberg, 1983; Rothbart & Posner, 1985). Thus, for example, if the infant in our example tends to be highly reactive to stimuli and low in self-regulating, self-soothing capacities, the parents will frequently be solicited by her intense and frequent expressions of distress to assist in her coping attempts. Increasing awareness of their infant's temperament will influence the parents' responses. They may attempt to relieve their baby's distress by drastically reducing environmental stimulation, perhaps by turning off the television, talking in whispers, dimming several lights, and covering the telephone with a pillow. They may attempt to provide a level of stimulation that is moderate but also curiously monotonous: While holding the baby, they inhibit their own emotional-expressive behavior; they might maintain a tuneless humming, walk her constantly, or drive the baby endlessly around the block in order to put her to sleep. (We understand that there is now a product that, when attached to the crib, simulates the vibration of a car's motion and provides a low level of "white noise" similar to that of a car engine.) Not only does the infant's temperament influence her or his own emotion regulatory processes, but it may also modify emotions and behaviors in other family members (Brazelton, Koslowski, & Main, 1974; Emde, Gaensbauer, & Harmon, 1976; Frodi, Lamb, Leavitt, & Donovan, 1978).

If we visit this same family periodically over the years, we will probably find that the child increasingly applies emotion regulation strategies effectively. Temperament influences this development by affecting thresholds for reactivity to stress and coping styles (e.g., Kagan, 1983; Rutter, 1981). In the late preschool years we may find this little girl still to be quite sensitive and reactive to stimulation, change, or stress; however, she may have developed effective coping strategies, such as burying her face in her mother's lap as a way of shutting out excess stimulation and reassuring herself of a secure emotional base. When mother's lap is not available, she may develop strategies for blunting stimulation or for outright withdrawal. She may also spend more time relative to her peers in quieter environments and involved in activities such as reading, art work, and creating elaborate scenarios with her toys in her bedroom. Family responses to these behaviors and how the child's temperament meshes with the family style and values in general will further influence the development of emotion regulation abilities, which are integrated within the overall trajectory of emotional development (e.g., Thomas & Chess, 1977).

## Cognitive Development

The influence of cognitive development on emotion regulation is evident in both the expression of emotion and in the experience of emotion. The development of symbolic thought, shared emotion concepts, and comprehension of perceptual transformations are just a few of the cognitive advances in the preschool years that facilitate more subtle strategies for emotion regulation. Symbolic thought, for example, allows the child to realize that others look to one's face as a sign of what one is feeling even when one is not actually feeling the emotion suggested by the facial expression. Children also begin to intentionally manipulate facial expressions of emotion in pretend play and in interaction with others. Lewis and Michalson (1985) present evidence for this sort of symbolic manipulation of emotional-expressive behavior as early as 2 to 3 years. Some children by age 4 years, according to Harris and Gross (1988), are able to recognize that one can mislead another to have a false belief about one's emotional state by presenting a misleading facial expression.

This distinction between appearance (the facial expression) and reality (the internal emotional state) in understanding emotional experience is fairly well established by the time children are 6 years old. It is a development that also requires children to be able to take into account perceptual transformations and to dissociate such a transformation (i.e., in emotional expression) from some other factor or variable, in this case, emotional state. Emotion concepts that are common to one's community also become well-established in the preschool years, and, indeed, even 2-year-olds demonstrate communicatively effective use of the emotional coping language of their family or subculture (see, for example, the ethnographic study by Miller & Sperry, 1987; for relevant reviews see Lewis & Michalson, 1983, or Saarni & Harris, 1989).

Intriguing to us is how cognitive development allows children beyond the preschool years to change how they feel, particularly if they are feeling badly. Harris, Olthof, and Meerum Terwogt (1981) interviewed 6-, 11-, and 15-year-old children about how they thought they could change from feeling unhappy to feeling happy. The most common response was to change the situation in which one was feeling unhappy, but the two older groups also nominated what might be called "mentalistic" strategies for helping oneself to overcome unhappy feelings. For example, they might say that one could change the situation, but they would accompany that suggestion with a statement as to *why* merely changing the situation or an activity had any bearing on changing one's emotion.

In a subsequent study (reviewed in Harris & Lipian, 1989) children (boys only, age 8) who had just arrived for the first time at boarding school in England were interviewed about how they coped with sadness, homesickness, and the like. The children said that they tried to boost their morale by looking at the situation they were in as a positive one, or they suggested distraction by absorbing one's attention elsewhere, or they noted that one could reduce the intensity of an aversive emotion by getting into an activity that facilitated intervening emotions of a more positive sort. What we see in these intentional cognitive strategies is how increasing cognitive development in middle childhood also allows one to think about one's thought and thus maneuver one's emotional experience.

It seems to us that for such cognitive strategies to be available to an individual he or she must also believe that how one thinks is related to how one feels. A further dilemma lies in the discrepancy between belief and action: Probably the majority of North American adults would subscribe to the belief that how one makes sense of some situation is highly related to how one then feels in or about that situation (see D'Andrade, 1987). Yet, in the midst of an intensely negative emotional experience, such "rationality" appears to play a reduced role in coping with an immediate crisis. On the other hand, if one is involved in a particular ongoing or recurrent emotion-eliciting situation, one may more readily begin to cope with one's negative emotion with these rational or mentalistic strategies for regulating and diminishing aversive emotions.

Harris and Lipian (1989) also discussed a study done with hospitalized children, who, in fact, demonstrated exactly this sort of cognitive regression, or "slippage" as the authors referred to it, relative to their matched nonhospitalized peers. Harris and Lipian proposed that when a negative emotional state is intensely engaged, cognitive biases emerge that prevent access to alternative viewpoints or perspectives from which to make sense of one's emotional experience. Thus, they argue, depression maintains its grip through these self-defeating cog-

nitive biases that often reflect a sense of helplessness and self-depre-
cation.

***Controllability.***    This study on hospitalized children raises the issue
of perceived control over a situation and the influence of such a
perception or belief on how people make sense of the situation they
are in. Attribution theorists have long posited the importance of controllability in influencing how we are likely to feel (e.g., Weiner &
Graham, 1984). Weiner and Graham maintain that helplessness is the
likely outcome when individuals attribute the cause of their experience
as beyond their control and as based in some external source (e.g., "I
can't help how I feel," "She made me feel this way"). When people do
feel themselves to be in control of emotion-eliciting events and believe
that they are the source of influence, then they are more likely to feel
positive emotions and a sense of self-efficacy.

When we apply attribution theory's concepts of controllability,
source of influence, and likelihood of recurrence to children's efforts
to cope with negative emotions, we are examining emotion regulation
from the standpoint of how cognitive development interacts with attribution of causality. We list below some of the ways that this admixture
of cognitive development and attribution of causality can affect children's coping efforts (adapted from Saarni, 1988a).

1. The child endures the negative emotion for a short time and
then distracts himself or herself by attending to another situation.
(The child is in control, the source of influence is external, and the
child seeks to minimize the recurrence of the negative emotion by
leaving the negative emotion-eliciting situation.)

2. The child attempts to redefine the emotion-eliciting *situation*
and thereby feel a less intensely negative emotion. For example, fear
is reduced to apprehension by focusing on thoughts such as "well,
this shot will keep me from getting a terrible disease." Sometimes an
altogether different emotion is experienced; for example, one feels
hurt or scared and then becomes angry upon further reflection. (The
child is in control, the source of influence is internal, namely, self-
reflection, and recurrence is limited.)

3. The child redefines the *emotion* he or she is experiencing; for
example, "I'm not scared, I'm mad!". (The child is in control, the
source of influence is internal, and recurrence is limited.)

4. The child attempts to ameliorate the intensity of the negative
emotion by managing her or his emotional-expressive *behavior* in a
more positive way; for instance, "whistling in the dark" when afraid,

smiling through tears. (The child is in control, the source of influence may be both internal and external, and recurrence may be problematic.)

5. The child endures the negative emotion for a short time but copes by ventilating on a safe target; for example, the family dog gets hit when the child actually wants to hit the parent. (The child has only limited control, the source of influence is mostly external, and recurrence is unknown.)

6. The child sublimates the negative emotion either through psychosomatic illness, dissociation, or by means of another compensating activity; imaginary playmates of early childhood are, in a sense, a dissociative compensating activity for not experiencing desired events and their attendant emotions. (The child is for the most part not in control, the source of influence is external, and recurrence is problematic.)

*Cognitive Blunting.* Lastly, Miller and Green's (1985) work on cognitive blunting is relevant here as well. They examined research on children facing dental or medical procedures where the child's personal control was low or altogether absent. They found that children who could avoid thinking about the threatening situation or could emotionally withdraw from the situation through intellectualization coped better, that is, they were less distressed than those children who were vigilant and monitored the medical situation throughout. Vigilance produced greater arousal, which, if one had no control or influence over the situation, intensified negative affect. However, if one did have control over the emotion-eliciting events, then vigilance would be instrumental, even if one experienced considerable negative emotion, because one could then presumably alter those features of the situation that were most distressing.

## Socialization

This last factor to be considered influences emotion regulation in ways that developmental psychologists are eagerly still investigating and describing. What we sketch out here about the role of socialization in emotion regulation should be viewed as a working model. Elsewhere one of us has elaborated on the effects of communication on the socialization of emotional development (Saarni, 1985) and on the development of emotional competence (Saarni, 1988a), and the reader is referred to those sources for additional discussion.

There are several modes in which socialization of emotion can take place. The most obvious is what we call *direct socialization,* which in the present context refers to a caregiver's response reinforcing the emotional behavior of an infant or child. Illustrating this contingency paradigm particularly well for emotion regulation is a study carried out by Malatesta and Haviland (1982). They videotaped mothers interacting with their young infants and found that during the period of a few months, mothers' positive expressive responses were reinforcing the display of positive behavior in their infants, whereas the display of negative expressive behavior declined during this period. Malatesta and Haviland also found an interesting sex difference: Baby boys received more expressive matching behavior from their mothers, and daughters received a greater variety of expressive reactions from their mothers. While this study is provocative for how emotion regulation may be directly socialized, what we cannot determine is whether the infants' emotional state was affected or whether only their expressive behavior was "dampened" in its intensity.

Another broad category of socialization that has implications for emotion regulation is that which uses *indirect influence.* By "indirect" we are referring to those processes of influence that include temporal or situational factors, which intervene between the initial stimulus and subsequent emotional experience. Imitation, identification, and social referencing are all examples of indirect socialization. Social referencing in particular has attracted considerable attention in recent years in investigations of emotional development. It refers to the process whereby an infant derives the "appropriate" emotional meaning of an otherwise ambiguous situation through observing how the caregiver expressively responds in the situation (Feinman & Lewis, 1983; Sorce, Emde, Campos, & Klinnert, 1985). It is likely that, for older children and adults, social referencing is used more often in an imitative fashion: We may mimic the emotional-expressive behavior of others when we are in an emotionally ambiguous situation, but we may not necessarily recreate internally the corresponding emotional state. However, for infants there does appear to be more of a correspondence between the subsequent expressive behavior displayed and the internal emotional state.

The last sort of socialization influence to be mentioned here is that of expectancy communication (see also Saarni, 1985). Emotion regulation may be influenced by others' communicated beliefs or expectations about how one is likely to feel in some situation. The communication can be verbal or nonverbal. The process begins with a suggestion being offered (again, verbally or nonverbally) about the anticipated emotional reaction, and to the degree to which that suggested emotional response appears credible to the listener, he or she will be more likely to scan his or her subsequent emotional experience for features that match this suggestion. When there is a good match between the prior suggestion and the subsequent emotional response, then the suggestion is validated and begins to be used by the listener as a personal expectancy. In other words, what was once "outside" the listener begins to be internalized as an "inside" expectancy for how one is likely to feel in similar future situations.

Readers may notice that this expectancy communication process bears considerable similarity to hypnotic communication, and one could also contend that parents are the "original hypnotists" in terms of how emotion beliefs and expectancies are passed on to children. Media also plays a similarly hypnotic role in suggesting how one will feel in a particular situation, with advertising perhaps being the most blatant purveyor of such emotion suggestions.

In wrapping up this first section on influences on the regulation of emotional state, we have implicitly adopted a components approach to emotion. We have found Lewis and Michalson's (1983) structural approach to emotion most useful, and their description of the five components of emotion (i.e., elicitors, receptors, state, expression, and experience) permits an analytical approach to discussing regulation of emotion. For, of course, one must ask, which aspect of emotion are we talking about that is subject to regulation. We have used in this first section the terms emotional state and emotional experience, which are taken from Lewis and Michalson's structural approach, and in the next section we go on to consider in greater detail emotional expression and its regulation.

## REGULATION AND ORGANIZATION
## OF EMOTIONAL-EXPRESSIVE BEHAVIOR

We begin by presenting two basic premises that have guided our work on emotional development. Then, with those assumptions made explicit, we describe relevant research. We also make connections between that research and how the development of emotional organization appears to differentiate in conjunction with children's maturing social skills for negotiating their way through interpersonal transactions.

### Basic Premises

#### Emotional Development Occurs Because We Exist
#### Within Interpersonal Systems.

Although most of us would probably agree with this statement as relevant to infancy and the pervasiveness of the attachment experience in the emotional life of the infant, allow us to illustrate what we are interested in by giving a few examples from older children:

1. Four-year-old John jumped down from a low wall onto a cement path, landing on his feet with a more solid "thud" than he had anticipated. Then he noticed his mother had stepped outside into the yard; he "fell" backwards and screwed up his face into a grimace, let out a moan, and peered in her direction with abject agony. Mother ran over to comfort John.

2. Cynthia, age 9, knew there was going to be trouble when she heard her father shouting outside; he was probably drunk again. She knew she must not let him see her upset or tearful: He had turned on her, hitting her on the side of her head too many times before, just because he could not stand to see anybody upset around him. She stiffened her mouth, blinked hard, and tightened her face and body into a rigid stance. Her father came indoors and ignored her.

3. Jack, 13 years old, was new at the junior high. He felt self-conscious and at the same time really wanted the other kids to like him. During class a note was passed to him that said, "The new boy is really cute and sexy." Jack felt embarrassed and wished he could just disappear. Instead, he managed to smile, scrawled on the note, "And my phone number is 525-5430" and passed it back in the direction it had come from. At lunchtime several kids called him over to their table.

These vignettes illustrate the complex interplay of emotional state and emotional expression as we interact with others. Young John knows how to get his mother's attention; Cynthia has figured out a way to avoid family troubles, and Jack can project a self-confident image to his peers. Each of these examples illustrates how we feel (our emotional state) need not be congruent with what we express verbally or nonverbally. Our implicit and explicit relationships with others are a powerful tool in influencing what we express. This essentially reflects the process of emotion socialization, which leaves its mark in the patterns we demonstrate behaviorally or in the expectancies we hold about when, how, and what to *express* emotionally.

In the last few years we have seen more research that substantiates the *social contextualization* of emotion (e.g., Dunn, 1988; Lewis & Saarni, 1985; Saarni & Harris, 1989; Thompson, 1988). This is not to say that emotion does not have a biological substrate; obviously it does—our facial musculature and central nervous system are testimony to that. But when it comes to refining our theories of emotional *development*, we need to examine the social context in which emotion is experienced by a subjective self. One of the examples cited earlier, Cynthia, who inhibits her emotional distress in order to avoid her father's alcoholic wrath, may represent one sort of pattern of social context that when chronically experienced leads to a set of expectancies about how to cope with unhappiness. The pattern found among many children growing up with alcoholic parents is one of avoidance and even denial of negative emotional states (Ackerman, 1983).

Research undertaken by Camras, Grow, and Ribordy (1983) with children of abusive parents also shows us a pattern of emotional expectancies that differs from children who have not been abused; the former appear to discriminate negative emotions similarly to children who have not been abused but do not discriminate positive emotions as well—perhaps because the social precursors and consequences of "happiness" in their parents are not contingently experienced. Subsequent research showed that abusing mothers pose less recognizable emotional facial expressions, suggesting that their children may have less adequate exposure to facial expression meaning (Camras, Ribordy, Hill, Martino, Spaccarelli, & Stefani, 1988).

### Coping with Stress Involves Strategies for Regulating Emotions.

If we go back to our definition of emotion regulation, which was presented as behavior aimed at changing feelings in a desired direction, then coping is directly involved in emotion regulation. For when one copes, it means that one is attempting to resolve a problematic situation (whether internally or externally generated) and emerge with a resolution that also allows one *to feel better*. This second premise is also one that is widely shared, but it has become more salient in our own investigations of the development of strategies for emotion management. In addition, a recent study on children's coping with stress (Compas, 1987) and Folkman and Lazarus' study (1988) on coping as mediator, emphasize the variability of the coping strategies according to the nature of the stressful situation.

What neither of these two papers address directly is how we learn to *manage* our emotional-expressive behavior as a way to cope with *interpersonal* stress, stress being the problematic situation needing resolution for us to feel better. These expressive management strategies are both diverse and flexible, making them particularly useful for coping with interpersonal stress. Effective coping with interpersonal stress appears to yield the following outcomes: One feels better, one's self-esteem remains resilient, the interpersonal situation is adaptively resolved, and one's expectations for future relations with the person involved are viewed as adequate to one's needs and values.

Although the nature of interpersonal stress may change with development, once a child enters school there seems to be a convergence (at least in North American culture) toward a common theme suggesting conflict between the emotion-experiencing individual and what he or she believes to be a more effective emotional presentation of the self.

The theme that children themselves talk about is that one could more readily satisfy one's wants, reach one's goals, or avoid some social fiasco if one could *strategically* manage one's emotional-expressive behavior. Thus, they tell us that there are social situations where it is important to dissemble one's genuine feelings, but they are also adamant that there are situations where it is similarly important to express one's real feelings, as in friendships or with one's parents. The point to make here is that, as children mature, they view the display of genuine emotion as a regulated act: There are certain kinds of relationships where it is expected that one reveal one's real feelings—although there is one big exception, which will be discussed later. They are also in agreement that very strong or intense emotions are the likeliest to be truthfully expressed, and it especially helps if one also happens to be bleeding or quite obviously injured at the time.

What continues to impress us is that children and young adolescents are remarkably insightful and articulate about the process of coping with interpersonal stress through managing strategically their emotional-expressive behavior—and maintaining a sense of self-respect or dignity on top of it all. Perhaps it is because during middle childhood and early adolescence we acquire relationships with the social world beyond the family and as a result, young people demonstrate such astuteness. By the time we reach adulthood, many of these coping strategies have become habitual behaviors that may no longer have much awareness associated with their use (see also Goffman, 1967).

Next we discuss research that is directly related to how children and young adolescents use emotion management strategies to regulate their social transactions.

## DISSEMBLANCE AND DISPLAY RULES

Much of our work has been concerned with display rules, which are social expectations commonly held about appropriate or conventionally acceptable ways to express emotions in certain situations. For example, a common cultural display rule in North America is that one should look pleased when receiving a gift, even if it is a disappointing one. Cultural display rules are conventions for making interpersonal coping predictable (e.g., Goffman, 1967). Distress may be reduced by (a) allowing another to save face (as when we do not pointedly tell the gift-giver that he or she has insensitively selected an inappropriate gift) or (b) by facilitating the emotion-experiencing person to retain some semblance of civility or maintenance of social approval (by not appearing ungrateful). Interestingly, negative emotional states are not necessarily alleviated by using cultural display rules, rather it is the *illusion* of positive emotional response that is brought about by using display rules. Thus, it is the expression, for example, of pleasure upon receiving a gift, not one's actual internal emotional state, that permits the smooth operation of social interaction, despite an internal conflict occurring, namely, one did not get what one wanted.

In addition to cultural display rules, children also acquire personal display rules, which function as internalized guides for regulating degree of "emotional equilibrium" or one's individual comfort level with emotional experience. Trying to stay in control, for example, may manifest itself in emotional-expressive behavior as a "poker-face" response to some intense emotion-eliciting situation.

Lastly, there is strategic use of dissemblance, which is simply dissimulating one's emotional state so as to gain some advantage or avoid some disadvantage in a particular situation. There is little of the obligatory rule quality to strategic expressive dissemblance, although it is often commonplace and predictable. Examples include not revealing one's fear to a bully, feigning surprise at the consequence of some misdeed, not revealing one's hurt after injuring oneself after showing off, and the three vignettes cited earlier would fit this category as well.

Our recent research with children has focused on how children use these three general, at times overlapping, categories of emotion management in their social negotiation maneuvers when there is some sort of interpersonal stress involved. These recent studies with children are all interview-based, not observational, and thus limitations to generalizability should be noted.

## Vulnerability: Who Is at Risk?

Two recent studies, one of them replicated with an adult sample as well (Saarni, 1989), have indicated that one of the most salient social context features used by children as young as 6 years is an appraisal of who is more likely to feel worse or get their feelings hurt if genuine feelings are expressed. Little in the way of age differences occurred in this determination of who was more vulnerable; 6-year-olds and adults made very similar judgments. The way this appraisal of vulnerability affects emotion management is straightforward: If someone else is likely to get their feelings hurt or becomes vulnerable in some way if one expresses one's genuine emotional state to them, then social pressure is increased to dissemble one's emotion and substitute for how one feels other emotional-expressive behavior. Children readily report that one had better not show how one really feels under such circumstances.

In greater detail, what was done was to present to children, ages 6 to 13, seven cartoon scenarios in which a child reveals genuine emotion with a parent present. In the interview, children were asked to choose from four options how the parent was likely to react to the child; these four options ranged from an extremely controlling, restrictive reaction by the parent to the child's genuine display of emotion to a very accepting, empathic parent reaction. Four of the cartoon vignettes featured social situations in which someone other than the child was at risk for having their feelings hurt by the child revealing how he or she really felt. The remaining three cartoon stories featured situations in which the child-protagonist was potentially more vulnerable by revealing his or her genuine feelings. The children were also asked to justify their choice of parent reaction.

The overall pattern of results was that the majority of children at all ages were quite convinced that rather controlling parent reactions could be expected if one showed how one really felt in interpersonal transactions where it could negatively affect someone else's feelings. The adult sample, who were also parents, confirmed this expectation. From the standpoint of emotion socialization, children and parents alike seem to be in agreement that making someone else vulnerable by truthfully expressing one's own feelings was not desirable. Children justified this strict parent reaction by appealing to conventionality ("You shouldn't be so rude.") or that the child should change her or his behavior ("She should look sad at the funeral and think about the dead person.").

A different picture emerged with the cartoon scenarios in which the protagonist was at risk for feeling badly. In these sorts of interpersonal transactions children were more likely to expect the parent to respond in an accepting fashion toward the child's display of genuine feeling. However, the pattern was not as strong as for the "vulnerable other" stories, and there was somewhat less consistency in the adult sample as well. Children justified their responses most often by saying the parent was concerned about how the child felt. Interestingly, there were no sex differences among the children's responses, but the adult data did reveal a significant sex difference. They believed that boys in these stories were less likely to receive accepting parental reactions than girls when revealing genuine feelings of distress, fear, anxiety, and the like.

Relative to coping in social contexts, we may derive from this research that by 6 years of age children are quite aware that they are expected to regulate their emotional-expressive behavior in order to reduce the likelihood of any interpersonal stress that could come about by revealing their genuine feelings. Children believe that in close relationships, as with their parents, generally it is acceptable to reveal genuine feelings of distress. However, this expectation is a more tempered one in the sense that children typically were more variable in their choice of degree of parental acceptance or control than when someone else was at risk for having their feelings hurt. It may be concluded from this pattern of variability that many children believe that parents do expect them to moderate the degree of distress they show, that is, that one "ought" not to become *so* vulnerable by revealing distress in a completely unmanaged fashion. What may be embedded in these expectancies is an implicit belief about the use of personal display rules as facilitating the reduction of negative emotional states, that is, "if I don't show the full intensity of how badly I feel, then I won't feel quite so badly."

## Children's Views on the Relative Adaptiveness of "Emotional Fronts" vs. Genuine Displays of Emotion

"Emotional front" is a term useful for describing the sort of *image* one may wish to project to others about oneself, in particular about one's emotional experience. In a recent study (Saarni, 1988b) children were interviewed about what they thought would happen to a child, same age and same sex as themselves, who almost never expressed his or her real feelings to others. The majority of children, across ages 6 to 13 years, thought the outcome would be maladaptive. The most frequent responses were that such a child would be disliked, would be perceived as maladjusted, and as hard to get to know. No child had anything to say that was especially positive about what would happen to a child who presented an emotional front most of the time; the possible exception was that such a child might be able to avoid getting into trouble. An example from a 13-year-old girl suggests the reaction such an emotionally closed youngster might expect from his or her peers: "If she kept everything inside her all the time, she'd consume all her anger, jealousy, whatever, and then one day she'd explode, commit suicide, and get emotionally disturbed."

The opposite question, namely, what would happen to children who almost always showed their real feelings, elicited the following sorts of expectations: A substantial majority of the children thought such children would be rejected, would be vulnerable, would get into trouble more often, or would hurt the feelings of others. On the other hand, about a quarter of the children did believe that such children would be perceived as honest, as being able to get "emotional relief," would be popular, or would be able to get help from others.

Clearly children view either extreme as maladaptive for coping with social relations. But it is also important to note that for this particular sample of children from Northern California we may infer that if one were to choose one sort of child over the other, the likely preference would be for the child who almost always did indeed reveal how he or she genuinely felt. An early study substantiates this (Saarni, 1979): When children were asked when would they reveal their real feelings, a significant proportion said it would be when they were with friends or family. The point here is that school-age children view the nature of the relationship one has with another as the "pivot" around which genuine or dissembled expression of emotion varies.

## Variation in Social Contexts

Children are also very sensitive to contextual nuances when predicting whether an interactant will detect emotional fronts or take them at face value (Saarni, 1988b). Children were presented with photo-accompanied vignettes in which the protagonist dealt with a social conflict by dissembling how he or she actually felt. School-age children were then asked whether the person interacting with the protagonist would detect the dissemblance or not and what the interactant would think or feel about the protagonist, given the emotional front presented. The developmental trend was for the youngest children (6–7 years) to believe the interactant would take at face value the emotional front; the oldest children (13–14 years) were more likely to think that the interactant would see through the emotional front.

*Sex Differences.* Interesting sex differences occurred among the older children: In contrast to boys and younger children, the adolescent girls were much more likely to believe that an adult *male* could be misled by dissembling when one had behaved wrongly and did not want to get in trouble. On the other hand, the oldest girls were more likely than boys or younger children to believe that other *females* would see through the emotional front presented but would not do anything negative about it. Indeed, the consequences among females for dissembling were viewed by the oldest girls as desirable: Smooth social interaction was facilitated by such dissimulation of genuine feelings. Just as children from an early age are strongly convinced that they ought not to reveal their real feelings to another if that person might get their feelings hurt as a result, likewise, these adolescent girls are also saying that if it would make someone vulnerable if one pointed out to her that one was aware that she was trying to put forward an emotional front, then one ought not to do so and instead should respond in a sensitively protective fashion.

## SOCIAL CONTEXT AND COPING

The preceding research shows us the sensitivity and awareness that children bring to bear on issues of emotion management and social conflict. They are also telling us that any given emotional experience that does not occur in some complete social vacuum (and few do) is organized around the sort of relationship one has with the other, whether that individual is physically or symbolically present. Insofar as coping with negative emotion in social situations (i.e., interpersonal stress) necessitates regulating one's emotions. children are readily able to articulate that whoever is at risk for becoming vulnerable is a major contextual feature that is taken into account when working out the strategies of emotion management.

*Naive Theories of Emotion.*    In many respects what we have described here is what child subjects use as an implicit theory of emotion that functions pragmatically as a way to regulate both emotion *and* interpersonal transactions. Especially fitting here is Catherine Lutz's (1987) definition of ethnotheories of emotion: [They are] "a fundamental and ubiquitous aspect of *psychosocial* [italics ours] functioning. They are used to explain why, when, and how emotion occurs, and they are embedded in more general theories of the person, internal processes, and social life" (p. 291). She also emphasizes that ethnotheories of emotion are ambiguous, not shared by all members of a community, and often undergo modification. What we would add further is that naive (or ethno-) theories of emotion provide us with guidelines for how to cope with interpersonal stress and thus regulate dysphoric emotion. When children say one ought to manage one's emotional-expressive behavior so as not to hurt another, or not be impolite, or to help reduce one's own distressed emotional state, they are drawing upon our culture's notions of how emotion "works" and how to make it work so that stress in one's transactions with another is ameliorated.

Perhaps the most important task of emotion socialization in middle childhood and beyond is facilitating the child's use of the culture's naive theory of emotion, which then also allows the child to figure out how to promote social bonds and mitigate against their disruption. Obviously as the child moves out from the protective family, knowing

how to regulate one's emotional experience vis-à-vis others will critically affect that child's well-being and sense of emotional competence.

## CONCLUSION

Our final remarks are intended to highlight how our ideas can be
coordinated with those put forward by Skinner in his contribution to
this volume. We do not perceive that our thinking is incompatible with
his notions of reinforcement. Emotions are obviously instrumental
phenomena—whether one examines individual emotion components
or the whole complex configuration called "emotion." Individual components may be responsive to contingent influences, and, indeed,
we have indicated that this occurs in our discussion of socialization
influence on emotion regulation.

Where we begin to diverge from a narrow reinforcement model for
emotion regulation is in our use of a systems perspective on emotional
development. Thus, temperament, cognitive development, socialization patterns, and the idiosyncracies of one's family or subculture are
mutually interactive in non-linear ways. As an example, the temperament of a highly reactive/low self-soothing infant may "disproportionately" affect the process of emotion regulation in the early months of
life. Similarly, the naive or ethnotheory of emotion that is implicitly
held within a family or community is only understood to the degree
to which a child's cognitive developmental level can assimilate the
features of such a naive theory of emotion and apply it to her or his
working knowledge of how to regulate her or his emotional state,
expression, and experience. Access to different sorts of socialization
processes further complicates the development of emotion regulation;
recall what Camras and colleagues (1988) determined that abused
children learn about emotion. Lastly, what we find in the emotional
crises of hospitalized children is a temporary regression in cognitive
complexity in understanding how to manage their emotional distress.
When they needed it most, these children found it extremely difficult
to consider what they could do to feel better. Thus, simple contingency
paradigms do not seem sufficient to describe the vagaries and nuances
of the development of emotion regulation. On the other hand, the
recent increased attention to the social contextualization of emotion
suggests that we need to look at more specific contingencies in how
emotion expression in particular is managed relative to sources of
reinforcement. To sum up, if one views emotion regulation (regardless
of whether the regulatory processes are directed at emotional state,
expression, or subjective experience) as an interactive process, then

one will need to look beyond a contingency paradigm. If one's aims include both the development of adequate theory for explaining emotional development and further empirical inquiry that addresses with depth the kinds of complex emotion systems we are seeking to understand, then one needs multifaceted models that include contingency paradigms, social constructionist views, biological data, and anthropological/historical perspectives. Contingency explanations are very useful, but they are only part of the picture.

## ACKNOWLEDGMENTS

Portions of this chapter were presented as part of the symposium, "The Development of Emotional Organization," at the meeting of the International Society for Research on Emotions, Paris, March 15–18, 1989.

The preparation of this chapter was supported in part by a grant from the National Science Foundation.

## REFERENCES

Ackerman, R. (1983). *Children of alcoholics: A guidebook for educators, therapists, and parents.* (2nd ed.) Holmes Beach, FL: Learning Publications.

Brazelton, T., Koslowski, B., & Main, M. (1974). The origin of reciprocity: The early mother–infant interaction. In M. Lewis & L. Rosenblum (Eds.), *The effect of the infant on its caregiver* (pp. 49–76). New York: Wiley.

Campos, J., Barrett, K., Lamb, M., Goldsmith, H., & Stenberg, C. (1983). Socioemotional development. In M. Haith & J. Campos (Eds.), *Handbook of child psychology: Vol. 2. Infancy and developmental psychobiology* (pp. 783–915). New York: Wiley.

Camras, L., Grow, G., & Ribordy, S. (1983). Recognition of emotion expressions by abused children. *Journal of Clinical and Child Psychology, 12,* 325–328.

Camras, L., Ribordy, S., Hill, J., Martino, S., Spaccarelli, S., & Stefani, R. (1988). Recognition and posing of emotional expressions by abused children and their mothers. *Developmental Psychology, 24,* 776–781.

Compas, B. (1987). Coping with stress during childhood and adolescence. *Psychological Bulletin, 101,* 393–403.

D'Andrade, R. (1987). A folk model of the mind. In D. Holland & N. Quinn (Eds.), *Cultural models in language and thought* (pp. 112–148). New York: Cambridge University Press.

Dunn, J. (1988). *The beginnings of social understanding.* London: Basil Blackwell.

Emde, R., Gaensbauer, T., & Harmon, R. (1976). Emotional expression in infancy: A biobehavioral study. *Psychological Issues Monograph Series, 10,* Monograph 37.

Feinman, S., & Lewis, M. (1983). Social referencing and second order effects in ten-month-old infants. *Child Development, 54,* 878–887.

Folkman, S., & Lazarus, R. (1988). Coping as a mediator of emotion. *Journal of Personality and Social Psychology, 54,* 466–475.

Frodi, A., Lamb, M., Leavitt, L., & Donovan, W. (1978). Fathers' and mothers' responses to infant smiles and cries. *Infant Behavior and Development, 1,* 187–198.

Goffman, E. (1967). *Interaction ritual.* Garden City, NY: Doubleday.

Harris, P. L., & Gross, D. (1988). Children's understanding of real and apparent emotion. In J. Astington, P. L. Harris, & D. R. Olson (Eds.), *Developing theories of mind* (pp. 295–314). Cambridge, England: Cambridge University Press.

Harris, P. L., & Lipian, M. (1989). Understanding emotion and experiencing emotion. In C. Saarni & P. L. Harris (Eds.), *Children's understanding of emotion* (pp. 241–258). New York: Cambridge University Press.

Harris, P. L., Olthof, T., & Meerum Terwogt, M. (1981). Children's knowledge of emotion. *Journal of Child Psychology and Psychiatry, 22,* 247–261.

Kagan, J. (1983). Stress and coping in early development. In N. Garmezy & M. Rutter (Eds.), *Stress, coping, and development in children* (pp. 191–216). New York: McGraw-Hill.

Lewis, M., & Michalson, L. (1983). *Children's emotions and moods: Development theory and measurement.* New York: Plenum.

Lewis, M., & Michalson, L. (1985). Faces as signs and symbols. In G. Zivin (Ed.), *The development of expressive behavior* (pp. 155–180). New York: Academic Press.

Lewis, M., & Saarni, C. (1985). Culture and emotions. In M. Lewis & C. Saarni (Eds.), *The socialization of emotions* (pp. 1–17). New York: Plenum.

Lutz, C. (1987). Goals, events, and understanding in Ifaluk emotion theory. In D. Holland & N. Quinn (Eds.), *Cultural models in language and thought* (pp. 290–312). New York: Cambridge University Press.

Malatesta, C., & Haviland, J. (1982). Learning display rules: The socialization of emotion expression in infancy. *Child Development, 53,* 991–1003.

Miller, P., & Sperry, P. (1987). The socialization of anger and aggression. *Merrill-Palmer Quarterly, 33,* 1–31.

Miller, S., & Green, M. L. (1985). Coping with stress and frustration: Origins, nature, and development. In M. Lewis & C. Saarni (Eds.), *The socialization of emotions* (pp. 263–314). New York: Plenum.

Rothbart, M., & Posner, M. (1985). Temperament and the development of self-regulation. In L. Hartlage & C. Telzrow (Eds.), *The neuropsychology of individual differences: A developmental perspective* (pp. 93–123). New York: Plenum.

Rutter, M. (1981). Stress, coping, and development: Some issues and some questions. *Journal of Child Psychology and Psychiatry, 22,* 323–356.

Saarni, C. (1979). When *not* to show what you think you feel: Children's understanding of relations between emotional experience and expressive behavior. Paper presented at the meeting of the Society for Research in Child Development, San Francisco.

Saarni, C. (1985). Indirect processes in affect socialization. In M. Lewis & C. Saarni (Eds.), *The socialization of emotions.* (pp. 187–209). New York: Plenum.

Saarni, C. (1988a). Emotional competence: How emotions and relationships become integrated. In R. Thompson (Ed.), *Socioemotional development, Nebraska Symposium on Motivation,* Vol. 36, 131–198. Lincoln, NE: University of Nebraska Press.

Saarni, C. (1988b). Children's understanding of the interpersonal consequences of dissemblance of nonverbal emotional–expressive behavior. *Journal of Nonverbal Behavior, 12,* (4), 275–294.

Saarni, C. (1989). Children's beliefs about emotion. In M. Luszcz & T. Nettlebeck (Eds.), *Developmental Psychology: Proceedings from the XXIV International Congress, Vol. 6.* Sydney: Elsevier Science Publishers.

Saarni, C., & Harris, P. L. (Eds.). (1980). *Children's understanding of emotion.* New York: Cambridge University Press.

Schachter, S., & Singer, J. (1962). Cognitive, social, and physiological determinants of emotional states. *Psychological Review, 69,* 379–399.

Sorce, J., Emde, R., Campos, J., & Klinnert, M. (1985). Maternal emotional signalling: Its effect on the visual cliff behavior of one-year-olds. *Developmental Psychology, 21,* 195–200.

Thomas, A., & Chess, S. (1977). *Temperament and development.* New York: Brunner/ Mazel.

Thompson, R. (Ed.). (1988). *Socioemotional development, Nebraska Symposium on Motivation, Vol. 36.* Lincoln, NE: University of Nebraska Press.

Weiner, B., & Graham, S. (1984). An attributional approach to emotional development. In C. Izard, J. Kagan, & R. Zajonc (Eds.), *Emotion, cognition, and behavior.* (pp. 167–191). New York: Cambridge University Press.

# CHAPTER 5

# Social Support
# and the Family

**Thomas Ashby Wills**
Ferkauf Graduate School of Psychology
Albert Einstein College of Medicine

This chapter considers the family as a social support system. I discuss how supportive relationships among family members can serve to influence the emotional states of adults and children, and how this may relate to the health status of family members. My discussion is based on a functional model of social support processes (Wills, 1985), which proposes specific functions of social networks that may help to reduce negative affect and increase positive affect. I consider how interpersonal relationships may have a stress-reducing function through mechanisms that operate primarily in times of distress, a process termed *stress-buffering* (Cohen & Wills, 1985). I also consider mechanisms through which family support may improve general coping ability, such that well-being would be enhanced irrespective of current stress level, a process usually termed the *main-effect model* (Kessler & McLeod, 1985; Thoits, 1986). From what is currently known about the relation of social networks to health status, I try to draw some links between family support and variables that mediate health outcomes.

The study of family support involves some intriguing complexity because parents and children have to some extent different social networks, which may have different implications for coping and health. Adolescents in particular have connections with both peer and adult networks, which may have differential influences on their emotions and behavior (cf. Kandel & Lesser, 1972). Although peer networks may provide supportive functions, they may have some influences that are not health-promoting, for example with respect to substance use (Glynn, 1981; Kandel, Kessler, & Margulies, 1978). This chapter considers the differential effects of peer and adult support on adolescents' health behavior and self-efficacy, and discusses implications for relationships between emotions and behavior.

This chapter begins with a summary of epidemiological research on social support and health. Then I propose some mechanisms through which social support may relate to health status, and suggest ways that family interaction could involve such mechanisms. The subsequent section reports some recent data concerning effects of family support on adolescents. Finally, a general discussion considers directions for research on family interaction and health.

## SOCIAL SUPPORT AND HEALTH

Research on social support and health has focused on the role of interpersonal relationships as a protective factor in resistance to illness (Antonovsky, 1979; Cohen & Syme, 1985). In this research, social factors have been assessed in several different ways. *Structural* measures focus on descriptive characteristics of social networks, obtaining counts of variables such as marital status, number of friends, connections with neighbors or relatives in the community, and membership in formal organizations (e.g., Hall & Wellman, 1985). *Functional* measures tap the availability of relevant resources that may be provided by other people, such as availability of persons to talk with about problems (emotional or esteem support), persons who can provide useful information and advice (informational support), and persons who can provide needed material goods and services (tangible or instrumental support) (Wills, 1985). *Satisfaction* measures tap respondents' perceptions about the adequacy of the support they have from other persons (e.g., Blazer, 1982). These measures are by no means identical: structural and functional measures typically are not highly correlated, and support satisfaction measures account for some variance not accounted for by functional measures (e.g., Henderson, Byrne, Duncan-Jones, Scott, & Adcock, 1980). Each measure indexes a different aspect of the structure, function, and perception of social resources. For example, a relatively small network can provide a high level of functional support if members support each others' esteem, are good at listening to others' problems, and are skilled at providing guidance for defining and solving problems.

## The Relationship of Support and Illness

Extending from theoretical work by social epidemiologists (Cassel, 1976; Cobb, 1976), prospective studies of community samples of adults examined the connection between social networks and health status, following initially healthy samples over time to investigate the relation between social connections and disease onset. The primary epidemiological studies, employing mortality as the endpoint measure, are a 9-year follow-up of the Alameda County cohort of 6,928 adults (Berkman & Syme, 1979), a 10-year follow-up of a community sample of 2,754 persons in Tecumseh County, Michigan (House, Robbins, & Metzner, 1982), a 30-month follow-up of a sample of 331 elderly men and women in Durham County, North Carolina (Blazer, 1982), and a 12-year follow-up of a community sample of 2,059 adults in Evans County, Georgia (Schoenbach, Kaplan, Fredman, & Kleinbaum, 1986). Support was indexed in these studies by structural measures utilizing various combinations of social network variables. In all four samples, persons with a higher level of social support were found to have a lower risk of mortality over the prospective interval; in other words, support is a protective factor. Relative risks for mortality ranged from 2.0 to 3.4, all substantial effect sizes; analyses of causes of death showed no disease-specific effect of social support, but rather a general effect on all-causes mortality. The available data generally indicated independent contributions by several dimensions of social network variables including close relationships (marriage), social activity (extended family and friends), and formal organizational involvements (churches, clubs, and community organizations). In most cases the effect of social support on mortality remained in multivariate analyses after controlling for baseline health status and health-related behavior patterns.

Although long-term prospective studies have shown an overall main effect of support on mortality, they do not necessarily indicate whether support acts by reducing the impact of life stressors (Dohrenwend & Dohrenwend, 1981). The hypothesis that support acts through a stress-buffering mechanism has been tested in a number of concurrent and prospective studies that included an index of life stress, measures of social network structure or functional support availability, and criterion measures of depression/anxiety (Cohen & Wills, 1985).[1] The buff-

---

[1] The concordance of evidence from concurrent and prospective studies indicates that support is antecedent to changes in well-being. The suggestion that low support may be a consequence of negative psychological states has been ruled out in the prospective studies.

ering model has been confirmed in several studies, showing that the relationship between life stressors and symptomatology is reduced, or in some cases eliminated, among persons with a high level of social support. Stress-buffering effects have been found with community samples of adults (e.g., Cohen & Hoberman, 1983; Fleming, Baum, Gisriel, & Gatchel, 1982; Henderson et al., 1980; Pearlin, Menaghan, Lieberman, & Mullan, 1981), with worksite samples (e.g., LaRocco, House, & French, 1980), and with samples of adolescents (Sandler, 1980).

## Specific Effects of Support on Illness

Evidence for stress-buffering is found primarily in studies where the support measure assesses the availability of specific support functions such as emotional support and confiding. This may include support from close relationships (Brown & Harris, 1978; Husaini, Neff, Newbrough, & Moore, 1982; Linn & McGranahan, 1980) or from a more diffuse set of connections with workmates and community friends (Henderson et al., 1980; Miller & Ingham, 1979). Buffering effects are particularly evident when the support measure is functionally matched to specific life stressors, such as economic stress (Kessler & Essex, 1982; Pearlin et al., 1981), chronic illness of children (Frydman, 1981), or pregnancy and postpartum stress (Barrera, 1981; Paykel, Emms, Fletcher, & Rassaby, 1980). In contrast, structural measures of support typically show main effects, but no buffering effects. From this, Cohen and Wills (1985) concluded that integration in a large social network is conducive to well-being, but not necessary useful for coping with a high level of negative events. Structural and functional aspects of social relationships apparently involve different mechanisms of action.[2]

There is some evidence of individual differences in support needs and effects. Studies with structural measures provide mixed evidence, some suggesting that social connections decrease risk primarily for men (House et al., 1982; Schoenbach et al., 1986), whereas others have

---

[2]It has been suggested by some investigators that social support is simply a proxy for personality variables that are the real causal factors in support-health relationships (e.g., Sarason, Sarason, & Shearin, 1986). Evidence for this proposition is based on laboratory studies showing correlations of personality variables to interaction behavior; field studies that control for personality variables have generally found these did not account for the effect of social support (e.g., Cohen, Sherrod, & Clark, 1986). However, the hypothesis remains an open one, and the role of personality factors in support formation and maintenance should not be discounted.

found protective effects for both men and women (Berkman & Syme, 1979). Studies of psychological symptomatology indicate that marital satisfaction and confidant support show buffering effects consistently for women (Cleary & Mechanic, 1983; Henderson et al., 1980; Husaini et al., 1982). In contrast, measures of worksite support and community-based social integration consistently show buffering effects for men (Henderson et al., 1980; Holahan & Moos, 1981). For employed women, measures of worksite support from supervisor or co-workers may also have a protective effect (Haynes & Feinleib, 1980; Holahan & Moos, 1981).

## Social Support and Adolescents

A few studies have examined the effects of peer and parental support on the well-being of adolescents (Burke & Weir, 1978, 1979; Greenberg, Siegel, & Leitch, 1983; Hoelter & Harper, 1987; Larson, 1983; Wright & Keple, 1981). An exemplary study by Burke and Weir surveyed a sample of 274 adolescents in the Toronto metropolitan area aged 13–18 years, obtaining measures of helping relationships with peers and parents and relating these in concurrent analyses to measures of psychological well-being. Measures termed Emotional Support and Concrete (i.e., informational) Support both were positively related to adolescents' well-being. In contrast, measures indicating that respondents tried to deny the existence of adolescents' problems were inversely related to well-being. In absolute terms, respondents indicated they were somewhat more likely to talk to peers (versus mothers or fathers) when they had a problem; but cross-sectional analyses controlling for stress level indicated that the influence of mother's, father's, and peers' help on adolescents' well-being was approximately the same.

In multivariate analyses of data from a sample of 213 adolescents, Greenberg, Siegel, and Leitch (1983) tested the simultaneous contributions of peer relationships and parental relationships for criterion measures of self-concept and life satisfaction. Here the measures tapped the affective quality of relationships, indexing the extent to which peers or parents were perceived as understanding the respondent's problems and could be trusted to talk with; so these are more like measures of support satisfaction. In this concurrent study the measures of peer and parental relationships both showed independent contributions to adolescents' well-being. The unique effect of parental support was considerably larger than the effect of peer support, approximating 10% versus 3% of the explained variance.[3] Buffering effects were tested through Life Events X Support interactions; these analyses indicated a significant buffering effect of parental support, but no buffer effect for peer support.

## MECHANISMS OF ACTION FOR SOCIAL SUPPORT

Although there is considerable evidence on the beneficial effects of social support on psychological and physical health, there is relatively little knowledge about the mechanism(s) that mediate this effect. Linkages of support to health may occur through influences on emotional factors, through influences on behavior factors, or both (Cohen, 1988; Cohen & Wills, 1985). Following, I discuss some of the theoretical possibilities suggested by current social support research. Several mechanisms are suggested, because pathways to health are multidetermined.

This discussion is guided by two assumptions about the role of psychological factors in health. One is that negative affective states (depression, anxiety, tension, hostility), if sustained over time, constitute a risk factor for illness. This is suggested by studies of the relation between personality variables and disease states (Friedman & Booth-Kewley, 1987; Vaillant, 1979) and the impact of life stressors on immune function and physical illness (Calabrese, Kling, & Gold, 1987; Jemmott & Locke, 1984). This suggests a linkage of social support to health through emotional factors. Second, social networks may be related to health because of behavioral factors, which include effects on preventive health behaviors and medical service utilization (Kirscht, 1983; Ostrove & Baum, 1983).

### Social Support May Reduce Negative Affect

Social support may influence health status because it reduces long-term levels of negative affect. Support may relate to negative affect through an appraisal process because the knowledge that network members can provide needed support may have an impact on the way persons perceive and react to potential stressors (Cohen & McKay, 1984). Knowing that support is available, persons may perceive negative occurrences as less severe, or spend less time worrying about the

---

[3]Note that this is a conservative analytic approach, because any shared variance is apportioned to the peer support variable. Thus this analysis provides a strong test of the role of parental support.

consequences of the event, that is, less time in self-generated negative affect. Having available confidant support from close relationships may also reduce negative affect because a person is available to talk to about worries and concerns. Emotional support could relate to long-term affective states through enhancement of self-perceptions such as self-esteem and self-efficacy, with effects on coping persistence generated by having available persons who express confidence in a person's eventual success in dealing with problematic situations (Wills, 1985). Alternatively, there may be a cathartic effect provided by talking about a traumatic event (Pennebaker & Beall, 1986; Pennebaker, Hughes, & O'Heeron, 1987).

## Social Support May Promote
## Health-protective Behavior

Social networks could relate to health because of effects on preventive health behaviors, including (a) recognition of symptoms, and (b) seeking of medical consultation when a disease condition is suspected. This model derives from epidemiological studies suggesting that low support leads to a greater probability of sudden death from myocardial infarction (MI) (Ruberman, Weinblatt, Goldberg, & Chaudhary, 1984), through a lessened tendency to seek treatment. The available data on social networks and medical help-seeking are complex. There are some grounds for believing that social support reduces stress levels and thereby reduces the frequency of medical service utilization (Ostrove & Baum, 1983; Pilisuk, Boylan, & Acredolo, 1987). People with high support may detect more early disease symptomatology because they talk more with other persons about physical health, or engage in more preventive and help-seeking behavior (Langlie, 1977; Taylor, Falke, Shoptaw, & Lichtman, 1986; Wills, 1983). There is some complexity to this issue because persons may be less likely to use medical services if the network is dense and kin-centered (McKinlay, 1973; Seeman, Seeman, & Sayles, 1985; Wilcox & Birkel, 1983). In high-density networks there may be more self-treatment or referral to alternative healers for services that otherwise would be obtained from medical professionals.

## Low Support May Lead to Health-damaging Behavior

Low support may lead to smoking, alcohol use, or relapse to either of these. There is some evidence that persons with minimal social networks are more susceptible to substance abuse (Umberson, 1987) or more vulnerable to relapse (Billings & Moos, 1983; Mermelstein,

Cohen, Lichtenstein, Kamarck, & Baer, 1986). Whether this occurs through affective or normative mechanisms is unclear. There may be a link to affective mechanisms if low support is linked to sustained levels of negative affect, which is a risk factor for alcohol abuse (Hull & Bond, 1986; Wills & Shiffman, 1985). Alternatively, persons with normative role obligations (e.g., marriage, parenthood) may be more susceptible to social control processes (Umberson, 1987). In this context it must be recognized that smoking or alcohol use by network members is itself a risk factor for substance use or relapse (Cronkite & Moos, 1984; Fondacaro & Heller, 1983; Mermelstein et al., 1986; Tucker, 1985), so the role of social networks in substance use cannot be assumed always to be a protective one.[4]

## Support May Promote Positive Affect

Positive affect and negative affect represent independent domains of emotion in the general population, and positive affect is strongly linked to social interaction (Campbell, 1981; Diener, 1984). Positive and negative daily events show independent relationships to subjective well-being (Rehm, 1978; Stone, 1981; Stone & Neale, 1984a; Wills, Weiss, & Patterson, 1974), and positive affect is strongly linked to social activity (Beiser, 1974; Diener, Larsen, & Emmons, 1984). Evidence from epidemiological studies suggests that positive affect may be enhanced both through formal social interaction (e.g., clubs, churches, community organizations) and through informal social activity with friends and relatives (House et al., 1982; Okun, Stock, Haring, & Witter, 1984). Recent research suggests that high functional support is related to higher levels of positive affect (Bryant & Veroff, 1984; Eckenrode, Kruger, & Cerkovnik, 1986). Additionally, recent studies of daily events have shown that positive affect is related to improved levels of immune system function, and negative affect is independently related to decrements in immune function (Stone, Cox, Valdimarsdottir, Jandorf, & Neale, 1987).

The exact process through which social support is linked to positive affect remains unclear. It could derive from predictable, regularized social interaction, from leisure activities where the focus is on relaxation and positive mood, or from the enjoyment of shared activities. Positive affect could also be linked to better sleep patterns, better appetite, or stronger motivation for preventive health behaviors.

---

[4]Relationships to other health behaviors, such as eating or exercise, are unknown. This is an interesting area for further investigation. One could hypothesize that larger social networks would be related to greater frequency of exercise.

## HOW DOES FAMILY SOCIAL SUPPORT OPERATE?

How does family interaction provide the functions previously discussed? In the following section I suggest several aspects of family systems that may relate to support–health relationships in the family context.

### Support Through Confiding About Problems

Parents' perceived availability to talk about problems and worries may influence adolescents' emotional regulation. Although in common mythology, adolescents are exclusively involved with peer groups, the available data in fact indicate that most adolescents maintain important connections to both peers and parents (Greenberg, Siegel, & Leitch, 1983; Wills & Vaughan, 1989). The perceived availability of parents for emotional support depends, of course, on the history of previous occasions when the teen tried to talk about a problem with his/her mother or father. If parents respond by reassuring the child, showing that they are interested in his/her situation, trying to understand it from his/her point of view, and showing that they respect the adolescent as a person, then perceived supportiveness is likely to be high. These supportive responses are essentially similar to the patterns of responding that seem to be "therapeutic" in professional helping relationships (Elliott, Stiles, Shiffman, Barker, Burstein, & Goodman, 1982; Wills, 1987), and it seems that they are just as important for adolescents as for adults. The presumed mechanism of action for confiding would be through reducing negative affect in times of stress.

This is not to imply that any family interaction must necessarily be supportive (cf. Rook, 1984). If parents respond by criticizing or blaming the adolescent; ordering or commanding him/her to do something; denying the existence of the problem; or lecturing the teenager about how they should have done things differently, then subsequently the adolescent is likely to take problems elsewhere when he or she wants to talk with someone (Burke & Weir, 1979).

### Support Through Development of Problem Solving

Parents' help in generating solutions to problems, and exploring alternative courses of action in problematic situations, may be of considerable benefit to adolescents' well-being. In the Burke and Weir (1979) study a dimension termed "Concrete Support," reflecting the perception that parents provide useful advice and suggestions about how to solve problems, was a significant correlate of life satisfaction. (It should be noted that this factor did not include items that reflected parents' blaming or lecturing the adolescent about the problem.) Communication style may promote adolescents' learning, if parents wait for adolescents to begin describing their problems and wait for them to generate solutions, before providing feedback or suggesting alternatives. It may be that some component of problem-solving support is derived also from observational modeling. Adolescents may be influenced over the long term by how they see their parents reacting to problems: whether situations are approached with a cooperative, problem-solving attitude, or whether parents respond to problematic situations by blaming and criticizing each other. The presumed mechanism of action for problem solving would be through decreasing the number of problematic situations that adolescents experience, thus reducing long-term negative affect.

### Support Through Development of Coping Competency

Coping skills include both specific abilities and generalized efficacy— one's perception of ability to control the environment and probable effectiveness of efforts at coping (Scheier & Carver, 1985; Compas, 1987). The more specific efficacies a person develops during the early adolescent period, the higher their self-esteem and the more likely they are to develop an attitude of optimism (Harter, 1986; Wills, 1988). Parents are typically not the agents of direct instruction for some skills, for example, academic skills for math or reading, physical skills at athletics, cultural skills at art or music. For the most part, these skills are learned by adolescents either "on their own," or with formal instruction. Parents, however, can be supportive of adolescents' initial efforts at acquiring such skills, can be reassuring about initial difficulties, and can encourage persistence in practicing skills. They may provide instrumental resources that help children develop skills, for example, dance or music lessons, buying equipment so that a child can be on a team, or helping with transportation so that the child can attend meetings. Parents may be more important for indirectly teaching social skills, through their interactions with children both at home and away from home.

Because adolescents' esteem is correlated with academic performance, the extent to which parents are perceived as helpful and encouraging for problems with schoolwork may also be a significant influence on adolescents' well-being. Moreover, their modeling of general attitudes about coping (e.g., the attitude that one has control over the environment) may be another aspect of family relationships that helps to build adolescents' competency. The presumed mechanism of action for coping development is that it increases the adolescent's level of efficacy and esteem, thus increasing long-term positive affect.

## Support Through Development of Multiple Community Roles

Parents' social networks become relevant when considering how parents help children become integrated into the larger community. To some extent, children can benefit from the formal organizational memberships of parents such as community organizations, sports teams, and churches or temples. These often include components relevant for teens such as athletic teams, youth organizations, and cultural groups. Adolescents' involvement in such activities provides opportunities for development of specific competencies, and for increased self-esteem from the social status acquired through some types of memberships; so this aspect includes some elements of instrumental skills and social skills.

This aspect of social support could involve multiple functions, analogous to the role of diffuse networks or social integration in other support studies. Adolescents could gain increased information about a variety of available resources and enhanced emotional support through friendships that are developed, as well as increased instrumental skills. Conversely, when parents have minimal social networks, then children are unlikely to gain much benefit in this respect (cf. Belsky, 1980; Wahler, 1980). The presumed mechanism of action for community integration is complex, probably involving effects on instrumental competency and social esteem, increased feelings of predictability, and possible increases in positive affect through involvement in leisure and recreational activities.

## Support Through Counteracting Adverse Peer Influences

The effects of peer activity are by no means wholly positive. For various reasons, teens may experience rejection from adolescent social groups or individual peer relationships, which raises doubts about self-esteem. In peer networks, adolescents may encounter instances of deviant behavior, ranging from smoking or alcohol use to various forms of

illegal activity (Patterson & Dishion, 1986). Positive relationships with
parents may reduce the psychological impact of negative experiences
with peers and the modeling impact of peers' antisocial behavior.
Whether or not an adolescent feels explicit pressure to engage in these
activities, the fact remains that when relationships with parents are
not positive, the importance of peer networks may increase because
teens have few alternative sources of reinforcement. Teens who have
positive relationships with parents may be generally less susceptible to
explicit influence attempts, for example to use drugs, or may perceive
antisocial peers as not being attractive targets for modeling. It should
also be noted that when parents themselves are smokers or substance
abusers, then the impact of peers' behavior is increased (Wills &
Vaughan, 1989). The presumed mechanism of action for this aspect
of family interaction is not clear. This type of family support could
influence assertiveness skills and self-confidence, and thus influence
positive affect through changes in self-perception and self-efficacy (cf.
Wills, Baker, & Botvin, 1989). Alternatively, parents could influence
long-term skill development through modeling processes.

## COPING AND SOCIAL SUPPORT
## AMONG URBAN ADOLESCENTS

My recent research has focused on the role of stress and coping processes in the health-related behavior of urban adolescents.[5] This research developed measures that tap social and nonsocial coping processes used for dealing with life stressors, and related these to indices
of self-efficacy and substance use. Here I focus on the overall predictors of positive health behavior (Wills, 1986; Wills & Vaughan, 1989)
and the differential role of peer versus adult support in contributing
to adolescents' adjustment and self-efficacy (Wills, 1988).

The subjects in these studies were adolescents in junior high schools
in New York City. The student population was drawn from varying
socioeconomic levels, being middle class on the average and including
substantial proportions of White (50%), Black (20%), and Hispanic
(20%) students. Students were surveyed four times from the beginning
of 7th grade through the end of 8th grade (ages 12–14 years), with
completion rates of 82%–84%. An initial panel was based on 675
students from three junior high schools; a replication panel, started a
year after the first cohort, was based on 901 students from four schools.

---

[5]This work was done with the assistance of Stephen Ramirez, Donna Spitzhoff, Roger
Vaughan, and Aaron Warshawsky.

Two types of coping measures were used in this study. In the first cohort, a behavior-based inventory was used (Bugen & Hawkins, 1981). In this 54-item instrument, subjects were presented with a number of specific behaviors and asked to indicate how often they do each one when they have a problem at school or at home. The responses were factor analyzed and the inventory was scored for orthogonal coping dimensions. The inventory used with the first cohort included scores for behavioral coping and cognitive coping (cf. Billings & Moos, 1981; Lazarus & Folkman, 1984), and separate scores for peer support and adult support. The support items indexed the tendency to talk with someone who will understand the problem and can be trusted to share things with, so this dimension is similar to what is termed confidant support or emotional support.

In the second cohort, an intention-based inventory was used, based on the method of Stone and Neale (1984b). In this approach, subjects were presented with a coping goal (e.g., "something to solve the problem") and asked to indicate how frequently they pursue this type of goal when they have a problem. This instrument included scales for several dimensions of coping and for separate measures of peer-support-seeking and adult-support-seeking. The two measures produced comparable results (see Wills, 1986), and the findings presented here are based on a composite of results from both cohorts.

## Predictors of Adolescent Substance Use

I first note some general relationships that the stress and coping measures showed for predicting adolescent substance use. Significant prospective as well as cross-sectional analyses indicated that stress–coping processes precede increases in smoking and alcohol use (Wills, 1986). Stress was indexed through measures of major life events and daily negative events, and through a scale indexing subjective perceptions of stress. A high level of stress was consistently related to smoking and alcohol use, both for negative life events and for subjective stress. While there was considerable commonality in predictive patterns, the events measures generally were better predictors for cigarette smoking, whereas the subjective stress measure was a better predictor for alcohol use.

High levels of several coping dimensions were consistently related to reduced likelihood of substance use. Problem-solving or behavioral coping was inversely related to smoking and alcohol use; cognitive coping was related primarily to alcohol use. A tendency to respond to stress by relaxation was inversely related to substance use in several replications. Conversely, distraction and aggression as ways of responding to stress were positively related to substance use.

## Peer Versus Family Social Support

When the support measures differentiated between support from peers and support from adults, consistently significant relationships between support and substance use were found. The results indicated that peer support was related to *higher* levels of substance use, whereas parental and other adult support was related to *lower* levels of substance use. This was found both for cigarette smoking and for alcohol use. The absolute levels of the support measures indicated that support from peers and support from parents were used with comparable frequency (Wills & Vaughan, 1989).

It should be noted that the findings reported here are maintained in multivariate analyses with simultaneous entry of stress measures and other coping measures. Thus, the effects of peer and adult support cannot be attributed to effects of life stress (in fact, correlations between stress and support measures were quite low) or to correlations of social support with other coping mechanisms. Although having an extensive social network may have an influence on coping ability (Fondacaro & Moos, 1987), the results reported here all represent unique contributions of support variables, independent of other stress-coping processes.

*Adult Support.* Measures of support from parents and other adults were consistently inversely related to substance use; that is, teens with high adult support were less likely to be current smokers or drinkers. This was found both with the behavior based coping inventory (first cohort) and with the intention based coping inventory (second cohort). In two waves, it was possible to test the unique effects of support from parents versus support from other adults in professional helping roles (e.g., teacher, counselor, doctor). These tests suggested that support from parents had the greatest effect.

*Peer Support.* Support from peers was consistently positively related to smoking and alcohol use; that is, adolescents with high peer support were more likely to be current substance users. This finding was replicated with both coping inventories, and in prospective as well as concurrent analyses. The effect of peer support tended to be stronger for Whites (vs. Blacks or Hispanics), and for females (vs. males).

*Interaction of Support and Substance Use.* Peer support had little relationship to substance use when the teen had no friends who smoked/drank, but had an increasingly stronger effect as the number of smoking/drinking peers increased. Parental or adult support had little relationship to substance use when the teen had no friends who smoked/drank, but had an increasingly stronger (inverse) effect as the number of smoking/drinking peers increased. Also, the effect of peer smoking on teens' smoking was particularly strong when the parents of the index subject smoked. Thus, social networks act in some way to moderate (positively or negatively) the impact of substance use cues.

*Interaction of Support Variables.* Significant interactions of Adult Support X Peer Support were found in several tests, such that the effect of peer support on substance use was increasingly stronger for teens with lower levels of adult support. In other words, a teen with low adult support and high peer support is disproportionately at risk for adverse health behaviors.

## Support and Self-efficacy

I investigated the relationship of stress and coping variables to psychological outcomes using measures of self-esteem (Rosenberg, 1965) and self-efficacy (Ilfeld, 1978). Both concurrent and prospective analyses were performed to rule out reverse causation explanations—that is, higher efficacy leading to increased efforts at coping. The patterning of results for outcomes of self-esteem and self-efficacy was similar (Wills, 1988), and the following discussion focuses on self-efficacy as the outcome of interest.

*Adverse Impact of Stress.* A high level of life stress was related to adverse psychological outcomes such as low self-esteem and low self-efficacy. Results for coping measures indicated that the dimensions of behavioral coping, relaxation, and physical exercise were consistently related to higher levels of self-efficacy; these measures also were related to decreased levels of negative events over time. Measures of cognitive coping showed few significant relationships to the self-esteem or self-efficacy measures, but it was found that cognitive coping was related to reduced level of subjective stress. Inverse relationships were found consistently for measures of aggression, withdrawal, and distraction as coping mechanisms; that is, persons who responded in any of these ways to stressors were lower in self-efficacy. These measures also tended to relate to increased levels of negative events over time.

*Adult Support.* Support from parents or other adults was consistently related to higher self-esteem and self-efficacy, with parental support making a significant unique contribution when entered with other adult support. Parental support also predicted lower subjective stress and fewer negative events.

*Peer Support.* Peer support was not consistently related to self-esteem and self-efficacy. However, high peer support predicted increased subjective stress and more negative events, representing a mirror image of the impact of adult support.

*Stress-Buffering.* I found buffering-type interactions (i.e., coping related to better outcomes primarily at a high level of stress) only for physical exercise, and marginally for behavioral coping. A different type of interaction was found for the other measures. For example, adult support was related to efficacy primarily at a low level of stress, with little relationship at a high level of stress. It may be that for desirable outcomes such as self-esteem, buffering effects are generally not relevant; most tests of buffering have been based on measures of undesirable outcomes such as anxiety or depression.

## CONCLUSION

I have considered the mechanisms of support–health relationships among adults, the mechanisms through which family support may influence adolescents' well-being, and relevant data from a general population sample of teenagers. The major points can be summarized as follows:

1. Social networks may affect health status through multiple pathways. Both emotional and behavioral mechanisms may be involved; affective mechanisms may include both positive and negative affect.

2. Close relationships and community integration make independent contributions to health. There is evidence of protective value both for emotional support from confidant relationships and for involvement in a more diffuse network of community relationships and formal organizations.

3. Females are more influenced by emotional support and confidant relationships, males by instrumental support and involvement in activity-oriented relationships.

4. Adolescents gain support both from parents and from peers.

Through middle adolescence, teens maintain important relationships with family members and with peer groups.

5. Parental support buffers stress and promotes adolescents' well-being, protecting against negative life events. Peer support is not consistently related to well-being, and does not show buffering effects.

6. Low parental support makes adolescents more susceptible to adverse influences from peer networks, and parental substance use increases the adverse impact of peer substance use.

7. Adolescents' well-being is inversely related to negative life events and positively related to behavioral coping, cognitive coping, relaxation, and physical exercise.

Many parents believe that they are powerless in the face of peer pressures toward adolescent deviance. To the contrary, my findings indicate that parents, through the support they provide to teens, can have considerable favorable influence. Not all parents' behavior is supportive, and some is nonsupportive (Burke & Weir, 1978, 1979; cf. Henderson, 1981; Rook, 1984); but my data show that parents protect their teens by being interested in and available to talk about problems. Conversely, negative parental behavior can be harmful to adolescents through decreasing perceived support and self-efficacy, and increasing the tendency of teenagers to gravitate toward deviant peer groups that provide support which is lacking in the home. Peers may exercise both adverse influences (e.g., low interest in academic pursuits, modeling of antisocial behavior), and positive influences (e.g., companionship, emotional support). Parents can combat adverse peer effects by providing social support of the type that teens prefer.

### Functions of Peer and Adult Networks

From the data on peer and adult support, we know that these have different effects on adolescents' emotions and behavior. The question is, how does this occur. Several possibilities need further investigation. One is that having positive relationships with parents provides a general stress-buffering effect which is valuable for adolescents in times of adversity; this implies a mechanism based on reduction of negative affect (Cohen & Wills, 1985). Another possibility is that having good relationships with adults strengthens general commitment to normative societal values, such as attitudes toward school, family, and work; this implies that a general orientation of commitment and coherence may have health-protective effects (Antonovsky, 1979; Kobasa, Maddi,

& Kahn, 1982). A third possibility is essentially a third-variable explanation: parents whose general coping style is positive provide useful models for adolescents and also generate positive relationships with their children. This could be based on common temperamental characteristics of parents and children, such as easy-going disposition and absence of depressive/anxiety symptoms (Friedman & Booth-Kewley, 1987; Holahan & Moos, 1986), or an overall effect on adolescents' optimism and sense of control (Scheier & Carver, 1985).

One route for investigating these questions is to get more data on the psychosocial attributes of adolescents with low versus high parental support, to determine whether they differ in the predicted ways on a main-effect basis, and to determine whether there is an interaction with recent history of negative events. It would also be interesting to study how teens with different types of support respond in specific temptation or coping situations such as dealing with offers of substances, dealing with anger or depression, dealing with task failure (cf. Shiffman, 1985). It would be informative to understand better the characteristics of interpersonal transactions that occur in peer networks, conversations with parents, and occurrences in everyday community settings (Larson, Czikszentmihalyi, & Freeman, 1984). It is known, for instance, that interactions with peers are more hedonically positive whereas interactions with parents have more instrumental utility; and that time spent with peers is negatively correlated with academic performance (Larson, 1983; Wright & Keple, 1981). One could ask what kinds of supportive interactions occur in the daily life of adolescents, how these are related to the kinds of daily situations that adolescents experience, and how they are related to affective states and mood variability.

### Implications for Labeling of Emotions

The constructs discussed in this chapter may have implications for emotional labeling, which depend strongly on the age of the child. My perspective would suggest that for very young children (say 4–7 years), parents may serve an important role for teaching the child to label emotions that he/she is experiencing. In this respect, I agree with Skinner (this volume). Parents may facilitate learning of emotional labeling by providing an appropriate language for describing emotional states, teaching the meaning of concepts like "tired," "happy," "sad," "worried," and using emotional language appropriately so that the child can learn appropriate context cues. For older children (8–

11 years), parents may be more important for discrimination training, through making statements such as, "You look like you're feeling sad this afternoon." For adolescents (12–15 years) the functional support model suggests that family members are more important for helping adolescents to directly reduce negative emotional states (e.g., talking about personal problems to reduce depressive feelings and restore self-esteem, helping the teen to feel better after failure experiences, and build efficacy for future coping efforts). Skinner (chapter 1) does not take this parental function into account.

## Implications for Prevention

The research reported here adds to a line of thinking in prevention research that holds that family relationships can be a factor in primary prevention programs (Baranowski & Nader, 1986; Bry, 1983; Dishion, Reid, & Patterson, 1989; Glynn, 1981). The implication of the work reported here is that adolescents' risk for adverse outcomes can be reduced by increasing the level of adult support that they experience. This derives from the fact that adult support is clearly a protective factor, plus the consideration that, for several reasons, it may be unadvisable to propose reducing peer support. The knowledge base for this work could be broadened by analytical research to determine which specific functions of parental support (emotional, informational, instrumental, companionship) show significant relationships to various program outcomes. Dimensions for investigation should include normative psychological outcomes (life satisfaction, self-efficacy), nonnormative psychological outcomes (depression, anxiety), normative behavioral patterns (preventive health behaviors, positive coping mechanisms) and nonnormative behavioral patterns (substance abuse).

The work reported here also suggests approaches through which parental support could be strengthened in intervention programs. Some data suggest specific parental behaviors that are perceived as supportive and nonsupportive by adolescents; these responses could be taught to parents in formal educational programs, either directly or through media presentations (print or videodisk). Programs aimed at adolescents could emphasize the benefits and costs of peer support, and aim at teaching ways in which beneficial aspects of peer support could be derived without becoming subject to adverse influences from peer networks.

## REFERENCES

Antonovsky, A. (1979). *Health, stress and coping.* San Francisco: Jossey-Bass.

Baranowski, T., & Nader, P. (1986). The role of the family in health behavior change programs. In D. Turk & C. Kerns (Eds.), *The family in health and illness* (pp. 51–80). New York: Wiley.

Barrera, M. (1981). Social support in the adjustment of pregnant adolescents. In B. H. Gottlieb (Ed.), *Social networks and social support* (pp. 69–96). Beverly Hills, CA: Sage.

Beiser, M. (1974). Components and correlates of mental well-being. *Journal of Health and Social Behavior, 15,* 320–327.

Belsky, J. (1980). Child maltreatment: An ecological integration. *American Psychologist, 35,* 320–335.

Berkman, L. F., & Syme, S. L. (1979). Social networks, host resistance, and mortality. *American Journal of Epidemiology, 109,* 186–204.

Billings, A. G., & Moos, R. H. (1981). The role of coping responses and social resources in attenuating the stress of life events. *Journal of Behavioral Medicine, 4,* 139–157.

Billings, A. G., & Moos, R. H. (1983). Psychosocial processes of recovery among alcoholics and their families. *Addictive Behaviors, 8,* 205–218.

Blazer, D. G. (1982). Social support and mortality in an elderly community population. *American Journal of Epidemiology, 115,* 684–694.

Brown, G. W., & Harris, T. (1978). *Social origins of depression: a study of psychiatric disorders in women.* London: Tavistock.

Bry, B. H. (1983). Family-based approaches to adolescent substance abuse prevention. In T. J. Glynn, C. G. Leukefeld, & J. P. Ludford (Eds.), *Preventing adolescent drug abuse* (pp. 154–171). Rockville, MD: National Institute on Drug Abuse.

Bryant, F. B., & Veroff, J. (1984). Dimensions of subjective mental health in American men and women. *Journal of Health and Social Behavior, 25,* 116–135.

Bugen, L. A., & Hawkins, R. C. (1981, August). *The Coping Assessment Battery: Theoretical and empirical foundations.* Paper presented at the meeting of the American Psychological Association, Los Angeles.

Burke, R. J., & Weir, T. (1978). Benefits to adolescents of informal helping relationships with their parents and peers. *Psychological Reports, 42,* 1175–1184.

Burke, R. J., & Weir, T. (1979). Helping responses of parents and peers and adolescent well-being. *Journal of Psychology, 102,* 49–62.

Calabrese, J. R., Kling, M. A., & Gold, P. W. (1987). Alterations in immunocompetence during stress: Focus on neuroendocrine regulation. *American Journal of Psychiatry, 144,* 1123–1134.

Campbell, A. (1981). *The sense of well-being in America: Recent patterns and trends.* New York: McGraw-Hill.

Cassel, J. C. (1976). Contribution of the social environment to host resistance. *American Journal of Epidemiology, 104,* 107–123.

Cleary, P. D., & Mechanic, D. (1983). Sex differences in psychological distress among married women. *Journal of Health and Social Behavior, 24,* 111–121.

Cobb, S. (1976). Social support as a moderator of life stress. *Psychosomatic Medicine, 38,* 300–314.

Cohen, S. (1988). Psychosocial models of the role of social support in the etiology of physical disease. *Health Psychology, 7,* 269–297.

Cohen, S., & Hoberman, H. (1983). Positive events and social supports as buffers of life change stress. *Journal of Applied Social Psychology, 13,* 99–125.

Cohen, S., & McKay, G. (1984). Social support and the buffering hypothesis: A theoretical analysis. In A. Baum, S. E. Taylor, & J. E. Singer (Eds.), *Handbook of psychology and health (Vol. 4*, pp. 253–267). Hillsdale, NJ: Lawrence Erlbaum Associates.

Cohen, S., Sherrod, D. R., & Clark, M. S. (1986). Social skills and the stress-protective role of social support. *Journal of Personality and Social Psychology, 50*, 963–973.

Cohen, S., & Syme, S. L. (Eds.) (1985). *Social support and health*. Orlando: Academic Press.

Cohen, S., & Wills, T. A. (1985). Stress, social support, and the buffering hypothesis. *Psychological Bulletin, 98*, 310–357.

Compas, B. E. (1987). Coping with stress during childhood and adolescence. *Psychological Bulletin, 101*, 393–403.

Cronkite, R. C., & Moos, R. H. (1984). The role of predisposing and moderating factors in the stress–illness relationship. *Journal of Health and Social Behavior, 25*, 372–393.

Diener, E. (1984). Subjective well-being. *Psychological Bulletin, 95*, 542–575.

Diener, E., Larsen, R. J., & Emmons, R. A. (1984). Person X Situation interactions: Choice of situations and congruence response models. *Journal of Personality and Social Psychology, 47*, 580–592.

Dishion, T. J., Reid, J. B., & Patterson, G. R. (1989). Empirical guidelines for a family intervention for adolescent drug use. In R. H. Coombs (Ed.), *The family context of adolescent drug use*. New York: Haworth Press.

Dohrenwend, B. S., & Dohrenwend, B. P. (Eds.). *Stressful life events and their contexts*. New York: Prodist.

Eckenrode, J., Kruger, G., & Cerkovnik, M. (1986, August). Positive and negative affect: Life events and social support as predictors. Paper presented at the meeting of the American Psychological Association, Washington, DC.

Elliott, R., Stiles, W. B., Shiffman, S., Barker, C. B., Burstein, B., & Goodman, G. (1982). The empirical analysis of help-intended communications. In T. A. Wills (Ed.), *Basic processes in helping relationships* (pp. 333–356). New York: Academic Press.

Fleming, R., Baum, A., Gisriel, M., & Gatchel, R. (1982). Mediating influences of social support on stress at Three Mile Island. *Journal of Human Stress, 8*, 14–22.

Fondacaro, M. R., & Heller, K. (1983). Social support factors and drinking among college student males. *Journal of Youth and Adolescence, 12*, 285–299.

Fondacaro, M. R., & Moos, R. H. (1987). Social support and coping: A longitudinal analysis. *American Journal of Community Psychology, 15*, 653–673.

Friedman, H. S., & Booth-Kewley, S. (1987). The "Disease-prone personality": A meta-analytic view of the construct. *American Psychologist, 42*, 539–555.

Frydman, M. I. (1981). Social support, life events and psychiatric symptoms: A study of direct, conditional and interaction effects. *Social Psychiatry, 16*, 69–78.

Glynn, T. J. (1981). From family to peer: Transitions of influence among drug-using youth. *Journal of Youth and Adolescence, 10*, 363–383.

Greenberg, M. T., Siegel, J. M., & Leitch, C. J. (1983). The nature and importance of attachment relationships to parents and peers during adolescence. *Journal of Youth and Adolescence, 12*, 373–386.

Hall, A., & Wellman, B. (1985). Social networks and social support. In S. Cohen & S. L. Syme (Eds.), *Social support and health* (pp. 23–41). Orlando, FL: Academic Press.

Harter, S. (1986). Processes underlying the construction, maintenance, and enhancement of the self-concept in children. In J. Suls & A. G. Greenwald (Eds.), *Psychological perspectives on the self* (vol. 3, pp. 136–132). Hillsdale, NJ: Lawrence Erlbaum Associates.

Haynes, S., & Feinleib, M. (1980). Women, work and coronary heart disease: Prospective findings from the Framingham heart study. *American Journal of Public Health, 70*, 133–141.

Henderson, S. (1981). Social relationships, adversity and neurosis: An analysis of prospective observations. *British Journal of Psychiatry, 138,* 391–398.

Henderson, S., Byrne, D. G., Duncan-Jones, P., Scott, R., & Adcock, S. (1980). Social relationships, adversity and neurosis: A study of associations in a general population sample. *British Journal of Psychiatry, 136,* 574–583.

Hoelter, J., & Harper, L. (1987). Structural and interpersonal family influences on adolescent self-conception. *Journal of Marriage and the Family, 49,* 129–139.

Holahan, C. J., & Moos, R. H. (1981). Social support and psychological distress: A longitudinal analysis. *Journal of Abnormal Psychology, 90,* 365–370.

Holahan, C. J., & Moos, R. H. (1986). Personality, coping, and family resources in stress resistance. *Journal of Personality and Social Psychology, 51,* 389–395.

House, J. S., Robbins, C., & Metzner, H. L. (1982). The association of social relationships and activities with mortality: Prospective evidence from the Tecumseh Community Health Study. *American Journal of Epidemiology, 116,* 123–140.

Hull, J. G., & Bond, C. F., Jr. (1986). Social and behavioral consequences of alcohol consumption. *Psychological Bulletin, 99,* 347–360.

Husaini, B. A., Neff, J. A., Newbrough, J. R., & Moore, M. C. (1982). The stress-buffering role of social support and personal confidence among the rural married. *Journal of Community Psychology, 10,* 409–426.

Jemmott, J. B., III, & Locke, S. E. (1984). Psychosocial factors, immunologic mediation, and human susceptibility to infectious diseases. *Psychological Bulletin, 95,* 78–108.

Kandel, D., Kessler, R. C., & Margulies, R. Z. (1978). Antecedents of adolescent initiation into stages of drug use. In D. B. Kandel (Ed.), *Longitudinal research on drug use* (pp. 73–99). New York: Wiley.

Kandel, D. B., & Lesser, G. S. (1972). *Youth in two worlds.* San Francisco: Jossey-Bass.

Kessler, R. C., & Essex, M. (1982). Marital status and depression: The role of coping resources. *Social Forces, 61,* 484–507.

Kessler, R., & McLeod, J. D. (1985). Social support and mental health in community samples. In S. Cohen and S. L. Syme (Eds.), *Social support and health* (pp. 219–240). Orlando, FL: Academic Press.

Kirscht, J. P. (1983). Preventive health behavior: A review of research and issues. *Health Psychology, 2,* 277–301.

Kobasa, S. C., Maddi, S. R., & Kahn, S. (1982). Hardiness and health: A prospective study. *Journal of Personality and Social Psychology, 42,* 168–177.

Langlie, J. K. (1977). Social networks, health beliefs, and health behavior. *Journal of Health and Social Behavior, 18,* 244–260.

LaRocco, J. M., House, J. S., & French, J. R. P. (1980). Social support, occupational stress, and health. *Journal of Health and Social Behavior, 21,* 202–218.

Larson, R. W. (1983). Adolescents' daily experience with family and friends: Contrasting opportunity systems. *Journal of Marriage and the Family, 45,* 739–750.

Larson, R., Csikszentmihalyi, M., & Freeman, M. (1984). Alcohol and marijuana use in adolescents' daily lives: A random sample of experiences. *International Journal of the Addictions, 19,* 367–381.

Lazarus, R. S., & Folkman, S. (1984). *Stress, coping, and adaptation.* New York: Springer.

Linn, J. G., & McGranahan, D. A. (1980). Personal disruptions, social integration, subjective well-being, and predisposition toward the use of counseling services. *American Journal of Community Psychology, 8,* 87–100.

McKinlay, J. B. (1973). Social networks, lay consultation, and help-seeking behavior. *Social Forces, 51,* 275–292.

Mermelstein, R., Cohen, S., Lichtenstein, E., Kamarck, T., & Baer, J. S. (1986). Social support and smoking cessation and maintenance. *Journal of Consulting and Clinical Psychology, 54,* 447–453.

Miller, P. M., & Ingham, J. G. (1979). Reflections on the life events to illness link with some preliminary findings. In I. G. Sarason & C. D. Spielberger (Eds.), *Stress and anxiety (Vol. 9*, pp. 313–339). New York: Hemisphere.

Okun, M. A., Stock, W. A., Haring, M. J., & Witter, R. A. (1984). The social activity–subjective wellbeing relation: A quantitative synthesis. *Research on Aging, 6*(1), 45–65.

Ostrove, N. M., & Baum, A. (1983). Factors influencing medical help-seeking. In A. Nadler, J. D. Fisher, & B. M. DePaulo (Eds.), *New directions in helping (Vol. 3): Applied perspectives on help-seeking and -receiving* (pp. 107–129). New York: Academic Press.

Patterson, G. R., & Dishion, T. J. (1986). The contribution of families and peers to delinquency. *Criminology, 23*(1), 63–79.

Paykel, E. S., Emms, E. M., Fletcher, J., & Rassaby, E. S. (1980). Life events and social support in puerperal depression. *British Journal of Psychology, 136,* 339–346.

Pearlin, L. I., Menaghan, E. G., Lieberman, M. A., & Mullan, J. T. (1981). The stress process. *Journal of Health and Social Behavior, 22,* 337–356.

Pennebaker, J. W., & Beall, S. (1986). Confronting a traumatic event: Toward an understanding of inhibition and disease. *Journal of Abnormal Psychology, 95,* 274–281.

Pennebaker, J. W., Hughes, C. F., & O'Heeron, R. C. (1987). The psychophysiology of confession: Linking inhibitory and psychosomatic processes. *Journal of Personality and Social Psychology, 52,* 781–793.

Pilisuk, M., Boylan, R., & Acredolo, C. (1987). Social support, life stress, and subsequent medical care utilization. *Health Psychology, 6,* 273–288.

Rehm, L. P. (1978). Mood, pleasant events, and unpleasant events. *Journal of Consulting and Clinical Psychology, 46,* 854–859.

Rook, K. S. (1984). The negative side of social interaction: Impact on psychological well-being. *Journal of Personality and Social Psychology, 46,* 1097–1108.

Ruberman, W., Weinblatt, E., Goldberg, J. D., & Chaudhary, B. S. (1984). Psychosocial influences on mortality after myocardial infarction. *New England Journal of Medicine, 311,* 552–559.

Sandler, I. N. (1980). Social support resources, stress and maladjustment of poor children. *American Journal of Community Psychology, 8,* 41–52.

Sarason, I. G., Sarason, B. R., & Shearin, E. N. (1986). Social support as an individual difference variable. *Journal of Personality and Social Psychology, 50,* 845–855.

Scheier, M. F., & Carver, C. S. (1985). Optimism, coping, and health: Assessment and implications of generalized outcome expectancies. *Health Psychology, 4,* 219–247.

Schoenbach, V. J., Kaplan, B. H., Fredman, L., & Kleinbaum, D. G. (1986). Social ties and mortality in Evans County, Georgia. *American Journal of Epidemiology, 123,* 577–591.

Seeman, M., Seeman, T. E., & Sayles, M. (1985). Social networks and health status: A longitudinal analysis. *Social Psychology Quarterly, 48,* 237–248.

Shiffman, S. (1985). Coping with temptations to smoke. In S. Shiffman & T. A. Wills (Eds.), *Coping and substance use* (pp. 223–242). Orlando, FL: Academic.

Stone, A. A. (1981). The association between perceptions of daily experiences and self- and spouse-related mood. *Journal of Research in Personality, 15,* 510–522.

Stone, A. A., Cox, D. S., Valdimarsdottir, H., Jandorf, L., & Neale, J. M. (1987). Evidence that secretory IgA antibody is associated with daily mood. *Journal of Personality and Social Psychology, 52,* 988–993.

Stone, A. A., & Neale, J. M. (1984a). The effects of severe daily events on mood. *Journal of Personality and Social Psychology, 46,* 892–906.

Stone, A. A., & Neale, J. M. (1984b). A new measure of daily coping. *Journal of Personality and Social Psychology, 46,* 392–406.

Taylor, S. E., Falke, R. L., Shoptaw, S. J., & Lichtman, R. R. (1986). Social support and the cancer patient. *Journal of Consulting and Clinical Psychology, 54,* 608–615.

Thoits, P. (1986). Social support as coping assistance. *Journal of Consulting and Clinical Psychology, 54,* 416–423.

Tucker, M. B. (1985). Coping and drug use among heroin-addicted women and men. In S. Shiffman & T. A. Wills (Eds.), *Coping and substance use* (pp. 147–170). Orlando: Academic Press.

Umberson, D. (1987). Family status and health behaviors: Social control as a dimension of social integration. *Journal of Health and Social Behavior, 28,* 306–319.

Vaillant, G. E. (1979). Natural history of male psychologic health: Effects of mental health on physical health. *New England Journal of Medicine, 301,* 1249–1254.

Wahler, R. G. (1980). The insular mother: Problems in parent-child treatment. *Journal of Applied Behavior Analysis, 13,* 207–219.

Wilcox, B. L., & Birkel, R. C. (1983). Social networks and the help-seeking process: A structural perspective. In A. Nadler, J. D. Fisher, & B. M. DePaulo (Eds.), *New directions in helping (Vol. 3): Applied perspectives on help-seeking and -receiving* (pp. 235–251). New York: Academic Press.

Wills, T. A. (1983). Social comparison in coping and help-seeking. In B. M. DePaulo, A. Nadler, & J. D. Fisher (Eds.), *New directions in helping (Vol. 2): Help-seeking* (pp. 109–141). New York: Academic Press.

Wills, T. A. (1985). Supportive functions of interpersonal relationships. In S. Cohen & S. L. Syme (Eds.), *Social support and health* (pp. 61–82). Orlando: Academic Press.

Wills, T. A. (1986). Stress and coping in early adolescence: Relationships to substance use in urban school samples. *Health Psychology, 5,* 503–529.

Wills, T. A. (1987). Help-seeking as a coping mechanism. In C. R. Snyder & C. Ford (Eds.), *Coping with negative life events: Clinical and social psychological perspectives* (pp. 19–50). New York: Plenum.

Wills, T. A. (1988). Coping and self-efficacy: Prospective analyses for adolescents in urban school samples. Submitted for publication.

Wills, T. A., Baker, E., & Botvin, G. J. (1989). Dimensions of assertiveness: Differential relationships to substance use in early adolescence. *Journal of Consulting and Clinical Psychology, 57,* 473–478.

Wills, T. A., & Shiffman, S. (1985). Coping and substance use: A conceptual framework: In S. Shiffman & T. A. Wills (Eds.), *Coping and substance use* (pp. 3–24). Orlando: Academic Press.

Wills, T. A., & Vaughan, R. (1989). Social support and smoking in early adolescence. *Journal of Behavioral Medicine, 12,* 321–339.

Wills, T. A., Weiss, R. L., & Patterson, G. R. (1974). A behavioral analysis of the determinants of marital satisfaction. *Journal of Consulting and Clinical Psychology, 42,* 802–811.

Wright, P. H., & Keple, T. W. (1981). Friends and parents of a sample of high school juniors: An exploratory study of relationship intensity and interpersonal rewards. *Journal of Marriage and the Family, 43,* 559–570.

# CHAPTER 6

# Communication and Negative Affect Regulation in the Family

**Kristin M. Lindahl**
**Howard J. Markman**
University of Denver

This chapter explores the interrelationships among marital communication, parent–child interactions, and children's psychological development, focusing on how negative affect regulation affects and is affected by these dimensions of family functioning. We define negative affect regulation as the processes and behaviors associated with responding to increased levels of negative emotions, primarily anger, hostility, and frustration, in a constructive manner. Whereas many researchers and theorists have been interested in affect regulation as an individual (and primarily internal) phenomenon, we are interested in the implications of affect regulation for marital and family interactions, and the exploration of how families establish external structures for dealing with negative feelings (e.g., establishing ground rules for discussing marital issues, such that one partner speaks while the other listens and then summarizes). In this interaction context, the differentiation between affect regulation and communication often becomes obscure, and the two concepts become difficult to disentangle. Although one way that dysfunctional negative affect regulation can be observed is in interpersonal communication, communication behaviors can also be considered a part of the process of affect regulation. For example, a communication behavior such as negative escalation can be a sign that negative affect is not being regulated. Other communication skills such as editing negative comments, or calling a "stop-action", are an integral part of the negative affect regulation process. Thus, communication behaviors can be used to regulate one's own and other family member's affect, as well as be signs or barometers of affect regulation processes. These two functions, however, are often easier to separate theoretically than in actual practice.

We hypothesize that the regulation of negative affect is a critical task for successful marital and parent–child relationships, which in turn are related to children's psychological development. We speculate that in distressed families, the presence of dysfunctional processes of affect regulation will be evidenced in communication patterns and in modes of emotional expression. Helping children learn to regulate their negative emotions requires sensitivity and responsiveness because, as Skinner points out in the opening chapter, the child's internal state needs to be inferred by the parent. We hypothesize that children of distressed as compared to satisfied couples are more likely to experience negative affect, and that their parents will experience trouble helping them become aware of and control negative affect. Without the ability to regulate their negative states, children who grow up in a context of marital distress are at risk for emotional and behavioral problems.

We begin with an integration of Skinner's opening chapter with our own thoughts about the interdependency of feelings and family relationships. This is followed by a brief discussion of the marital distress literature, and a review of the negative effects of marital distress on children. Here we also address the role of communication in general, and negative affect regulation in particular, in the development of marital turmoil. Next, we discuss the parent–child relationship as a potential pathway through which marital distress might affect children's psychological growth, and present evidence for parallel processes of negative affect regulation in the marital and parent–child relationships. Finally, we describe the importance of affect regulation as a critical developmental task and present directions for future research.

## Comments on B. F. Skinner's Chapter

Consistent with Skinner, we posit that, in the family, where each member's behavior is both a stimulus and a response to the behavior of others, the expression of feelings is the primary way that family members can tell each other how a behavior is affecting them. We read Skinner as saying that the expression of emotions or feelings is a way of communicating to another person about one's internal responses to stimuli. It is interesting to observe that, like most contemporary marriage and family theorists, Skinner targets the process of *communication* between family members as a central focus of theory and research. Given the reciprocal nature of family interaction, the expression of feelings (a behavior) serves as a stimulus for subsequent behavior. Thus, the following pathway is suggested: Person A behaves toward Person B; Person B has an internal response *and* an external response. Person B can communicate to Person A what the internal response is either directly through verbal behavior, such as the expression of feelings, or indirectly through nonverbal behavior, such as "acting out" the feelings. Person A responds to Person B's behavior, and so on.

Negative escalation results when, in the course of the interaction between Person A and Person B, A and B respond to each other in increasingly negative ways. In terms of the individual, we define negative affect regulation as the set of processes involved in being aware of one's internal emotional state, monitoring and controlling the expression and experience of negative affect, and being able to return oneself to a nonnegative emotional state. Several types of interrelated processes are involved in achieving affect regulation, including cognitions, communication behaviors, and the internalization of social display rules of emotions. This chapter focuses not on the internal processes themselves, but on the ramifications of these negative affect regulation processes for marital and parent–child interactions. Because it is vital for family members to know their impact on one another, and for family members to request changes in behavior from each other, a critical task for effective family functioning is the development of an effective communication system for emotional expression. In other words, we are interested in how the complex set of processes associated with understanding internal emotional responses and the monitoring and controlling of these responses is played out in family interactions.

In addition to exploring how dysfunctional negative affect regulation can be observed in family interactions, we also examine how dyads and triads within the family system may impose their own (external) regulatory mechanisms on their interactions in order to regulate negative affect effectively. For instance, when couples negotiate and agree upon rules such as only discussing problems at specified times, or setting up agendas to govern their problem discussions, they are using external structures to manage potential negative affect within the dyad. These conflict management strategies will consequently affect the level of conflict in the home, and this has implications for child development. Much of behavioral marital and family therapy and many prevention programs can be conceptualized as teaching "external" affect regulation skills. For example, in our prevention program for couples planning marriage, we teach couples how to argue constructively. As we describe below, evidence is building that family dysfunction can be conceptualized, at least in part, as involving problems in the expression (i.e., communication) of emotions in general, and negative emotions in particular. We show how communication behaviors can serve both as indicators of how well negative affect is being regulated and as facilitators of the negative affect regulation process. Before discussing why dysfunctional negative affect regulation is one of the primary signatures of marital distress, we address marital distress as a major social problem.

## Negative Effects of Marital Distress

Even though the divorce rate today is at its lowest point since 1975, couples marrying today still face a 50% chance of divorcing during their lifetime (National Center for Health Statistics, 1989). It is estimated that over 60% of divorces involve couples with one or more children and affect approximately one million children per year (Cherlin, 1981; Glick & Norton, 1976). In addition, divorce is often the result of many years of marital distress and conflict, and because not all discordant marriages dissolve, the statistics reflecting the number of children affected by divorce omit a significant number of children who are exposed to serious marital conflict.

   Much of the early clinical research that attempted to bridge the topic areas of marital functioning and child development focused on the adverse role of divorce in affecting early psychological development. Divorce has been found to be related to a variety of child adjustment and emotional problems (Hetherington, 1972; Hetherington, Cox, & Cox, 1978; Wallerstein & Blakeslee, 1989; Wallerstein & Kelly, 1979). The association between divorce and child behavioral and emotional problems has often been interpreted as proof that parental separation itself had a negative effect on children, regardless of the circumstances surrounding the separation (Bowlby, 1973). It was not until researchers began to differentiate between parental divorce, separation, and discord when studying children in high risk environments that they began to speculate that it was not the separation per se that was the critical factor, as much as it was the amount, intensity, and duration of the parental conflict that was related to child outcome (Emery, 1982; Markman & Jones-Leonard, 1985; O'Leary & Emery, 1982). Several lines of empirical work seem to support this conclusion.

Research findings have shown that children whose parents divorced but whose homes were conflict-free were less likely to have problems than children whose parents stayed together but experienced a great deal of conflict (Gibson, 1969; McCord, McCord, & Thurber, 1962; Nye, 1957; Power, Ash, Schoenberg, & Sorey, 1974) and that children whose parents divorce and continue to experience conflict after the divorce have more problems than children whose parents experience conflict-free divorces (Hetherington, Cox, & Cox, 1979; Jacobson, 1978; Westman, Cline, Swift, & Kramer, 1970). Finally, there is also data to suggest that many of the problems documented in children from a broken home can be seen before the children are actually separated from a parent (Lambert, Essen, & Head, 1977). In other words, the potentially damaging effects of parental divorce or separation seem to be ameliorated in families where there is less conflict between the parents, thus focusing attention on the distress, rather than the physical separation. In addition, some researchers have found support for the hypothesis that a good relationship with at least one parent can buffer some of the potentially negative effects associated with parental divorce (Hetherington, 1988). These results highlight marital distress, especially the presence of overt conflict and hostility, as one of the key factors influencing children's psychological development. We see below that handling conflict is a key factor in understanding marital distress.

## The Role of Communication in Marital Distress

In trying to understand how marital distress is related to children's adjustment, it is important to examine the characteristics of marital distress more closely. Consistent with Skinner's opening comments on the communicative value of emotions, marital research and theory agree that the quality of couples' communication is one of the most important determinants of current and future marital satisfaction (Markman & Notarius, 1987). Not surprisingly, couples experiencing marital distress have been found to show more negative communication behaviors toward each other than satisfied couples. For instance, they tend to display more negative affect, tend to show more conflict through put-downs, criticisms, and disagreements, and tend to be less responsive, supportive, and validating of each other (Birchler, Weiss, & Vincent, 1976; Gottman, 1979; Gottman, Markman, & Notarius, 1977).

From a longitudinal study of interpersonal relationships currently being conducted at the Denver Center for Marital and Family Studies, we have found negative communication behaviors assessed premaritally to be predictive of distress and divorce up to 5½ years later. Specifically, couples who later become distressed, compared to those who continue to be satisfied, demonstrate higher levels of negative affect reciprocity, higher levels of problem-solving inhibition and emotional invalidation, and higher levels of negative communication behaviors such as mind-reading (Markman, 1989). In addition to following couples' relationships over time, we are also interested in evaluating the effects of a premarital skills training program. The premarital intervention program teaches couples communication skills designed to help them handle conflict and disagreement, and to maintain and promote intimacy. We found that couples in the intervention group were more satisfied with their relationship, had higher rates of relationship stability, and showed significantly lower levels of negative communication (e.g., conflict, denial, negative affect) 4 years after the program, than couples in the control group (Markman, Floyd, Stanley, & Storaasli, 1988). Thus, teaching couples how to handle negative affect was associated with future marital success.

In summary, distressed marital relationships have been characterized by a predominance of negativity; negative affect, conflictual styles of communication, and poor listening skills. Consistent with Skinner's point about the role of emotional communication in the family, the results of marital interaction research show that dysfunctional expressions of emotions are at the heart of marital distress, that is, distressed spouses do not do a good job communicating the impact the other's behavior in a way that can be heard and understood. For example, stomping around the house, slamming doors, and being rude without explaining what is the source of the anger, certainly does not communicate the same message as, "When you come home late from work without calling me, I feel angry." Even the verbalization of one's anger by a statement such as, "I'm furious," without further elaboration, is limited in its effectiveness. An even more seriously dysfunctional pattern which is seen in abusive couples, is not even trying to verbalize one's internal state, and just acting them out through destructive means such as hitting the other person. Research documenting that communication deficits predict marital distress and that learning communication skills before marriage increases chances of successful marriage, provide further support for the hypothesis that communication deficits are one of the major causes of marital distress and divorce (Markman, 1984). We hypothesize that many of these communication deficits contribute to, and are symptoms of, poorly regulated negative affect; this hypothesis is discussed next.

## Regulating Negative Affect in the Marital Relationship

The above studies of marital communication focus attention on the salience of negative communication in discriminating between distressed and satisfied couples. Negative escalation cycles in particular, have been found to be one of the most effective discriminators between distressed and nondistressed spouses, and also one of the strongest premarital predictors of future marital distress (Gottman & Levenson, 1986; Julien, Markman, & Lindahl, 1989). Negative escalation is the process whereby one partner's expression of negative affect or negative behavior is reciprocated by negativity from the other partner. It seems that distressed couples are more likely to enter into, and to have more difficulties exiting out of, negative escalation cycles than satisfied couples (Gottman, Markman, & Notarius, 1977; Notarius, Benson, Sloane, Vanzetti, & Hornyak, 1989; Notarius, Markman, & Gottman, 1983). In addition, longitudinal research has shown that it is not the similarities and differences between partners that is important in predicting future divorce and marital distress, but *how* differences are handled (Markman, 1989). All couples inevitably are confronted with issues that need to be resolved, and it is in the process of handling differences or disagreements that couples are most likely to need ways of regulating, or controlling, negative emotions. Couples who are less effective at regulating their negative emotions will show symptoms of this in their marital and family communication patterns.

Distressed couples, because of their tendency to enter into escalating chains of negative behavior and to display more negativity toward each other in general, show evidence that they are less effective at regulating their negative affect. We consider these communication patterns to be symptoms of problems in negative affect regulation. As an illustration, consider the following absorbing string of negative behaviors. Husband: You never liked my mother; Wife: Uh, Uh (sarcastically); H: You never gave her a chance; W: Here we go again, you're picking on me; H: No, I'm not; W: Yes you are; and so on. In contrast to the above example, a satisfied couple would be more likely to respond to negative behaviors with neutral or positive behavior, rather than continuing to fuel the ensuing argument (Notarius, Markman, & Gottman, 1983). Several studies have shown that satisfied wives successfully *exit* out of the beginning stages of negative escalation cycles (Gottman, Notarius, & Markman, 1977; Notarius et al., 1989), suggesting that satisfied wives play an important role in marital affect regulation. Future research should explore this pattern in family interactions.

Distressed spouses' inability to control their own negative behaviors increases the difficulty of establishing an effective communication system for talking about emotional experiences (e.g., establishing an external source for regulating the affect in their interactions). A "stop-action" is an example of an externally created structure for helping the couple regulate their negative affect. Calling a "stop-action," by mutual agreement, forces a break in the conversation, and is one way of exiting out of a negatively escalating interaction (Gottman, Notarius, Gonso, & Markman, 1976). Other indicators that negative affect regulation is taking place include calmly discussing an emotional subject and talking about negative feelings in a constructive manner.

In summary, the hallmarks of marital distress such as conflictual communication, expression of negative affect, and the presence of negative escalation cycles, can be interpreted as partners' inability to control and edit their own behavior. This research specifically suggests that distressed couples are more emotionally reactive to their partners' expressions of negativity than satisfied couples. All of these behaviors are examples, or symptoms, of dysfunctional negative affect regulation.

*Gender Differences in Handling Negative Affect.* We conceptualize typical patterns of gender differences in distressed marriages as symptoms of problems in handling disagreements and the resulting negative affect. Data are converging from marital interaction studies and clinical experience that in distressed marriages, or in marriages at risk for distress, husbands tend to withdraw from conflict whereas wives tend to overreact emotionally (Markman & Kraft, 1989). In effect, a key signature of marital distress is a withdrawn, conflict-avoidant husband, and a wife who is desiring more intimacy and connection. For example, as noted by Gottman (1983), "in a sea of conflict, men sink, while women can swim" (p. 10). Patterns of husband withdrawal and wife engagement (or wife engagement and husband withdrawal) are reciprocally related and are at the heart of many negative escalation cycles for distressed couples. As unresolved disagreements fester and worsen over time, men and women attempt to cope, but use different styles: women try to establish intimacy and connection by expressing psychological pain, while men increasingly withdraw from conflict. These synergistic patterns fuel negative escalation cycles. Paradoxically, to the extent wives "turn up the volume" of their affective expression "to get their husbands to talk," the husbands' withdrawal may actually increase the chances of conflict.

To summarize at this point, we have shown that negative communication behaviors discriminate between distressed and satisfied couples, and that many of these behaviors, such as gender differences in withdrawal and reactivity, are symptoms of dysfunctional negative affect regulation. We hypothesize that distressed couples are less skillful at establishing effective communication systems for handling negative affect, and that without such a structure in place, distressed couples are less effective at monitoring and expressing their negative feelings.

In the next section we speculate that dysfunctional negative affect regulation may be a key mechanism in understanding how marital quality is related to child development. We hypothesize that parent–child interactions are a potential pathway through which dysfunctional affect regulation processes directly affect children, and help explain why children of distressed couples are at risk for behavioral and emotional problems. Thus, couples who have difficulty handling disagreements and the resulting negative emotions (e.g., anger, hostility, frustration) in their marriage are not only at risk for divorce and future marital distress (Markman, 1988), but their children are at risk for developing problems (Markman & Jones-Leonard, 1985). We will present preliminary evidence that distressed wives show similar patterns of engagement (overreactivity) with their children as they do with their husbands. We also suggest that, in the face of conflict, distressed husbands will show similar patterns of withdrawal (essentially an affect regulation strategy) with their children as they do with their wives. Thus, we are proposing that similar patterns exist in marital and parent–child interactions.

### Parent–Child Interaction as a Pathway

Numerous cross-sectional studies have documented small but reliable associations (e.g., $r$'s = .30–.40) between measures of marital quality (usually marital satisfaction) and measures of child functioning (usually child behavior problems), but few studies have examined potential pathways linking marital quality to child functioning (Emery, 1982). We are suggesting that the parent–child relationship, specifically how negative affect is regulated in parent–child interactions, is a potentially fruitful avenue to explore in trying to more fully explicate the marriage–child development connection. Although the parent–child relationship has only recently become a target of study, evidence is accumulating to suggest that this relationship is often disturbed in distressed homes (Markman & Jones-Leonard, 1985). Studies have shown that couples in less happy marriages are less likely to be sensitive to their children's needs (Goldberg & Easterbrooks, 1984); in addition, they tend to show less positive affect, approval, and affection toward their children (Easterbrooks, 1987). Engfer (1988) found that women who described their marriages as involving a great deal of conflict reported feelings of nervous exhaustion and angry impatience in their relationships with their children. Women in distressed marriages also tended to feel anxiously overprotective of their children and were judged to be significantly less sensitive with their children. In another study, Kerig (1987) found that mothers in dissatisfied marriages were more directive and less responsive with their children than were fathers. Thus, data are mounting to indicate that a distressed marriage is related to less sensitive and less "positive" parenting, whereas a satisfied marriage is associated with warm, engaged parenting, and that marital dysfunction is related to children's emotional development.

The above work goes beyond merely establishing a positive correlation between marital functioning and healthy parenting by lending support to the hypothesis that mothers in distressed marriages show similar patterns of overreactivity when dealing with their children as they do with their husbands. It will be recalled that mothers from distressed marriages were found to become excessively involved emotionally, to be more directive and intrusive, and to display more angry impatience with their children. These interactive behaviors can be compared with how distressed wives interact with their husbands. Our review of the marital interaction literature revealed that distressed wives were found to engage in negative escalation cycles and to overreact emotionally with their spouses. In other words, in terms of negative affect expression, the women from distressed marital relationships seemed to display similar communication behaviors with their spouses and with their children; these communication behaviors can be understood as reflecting poor affect regulation skills.

Data on father–child relationships are, unfortunately, more scarce, thus making comparisons with the husband's behavior in the marital relationship difficult. However, evidence from our research that links husbands' communication in marital interaction to children's emotional development provides some indirect evidence. Lindahl, Howes, and Markman (1988) examined the relationship between marital and parental functioning and toddler's empathy for parental distress. We found that husbands' negative communication behaviors observed in marital problem discussions were more predictive of children's empathic behavior than husbands' positive communication behaviors or wives' positive or negative communication. In particular, we found that the conflict, denial, and withdrawal that husbands expressed toward their wives were associated with fewer prosocial behaviors, more denial, and less emotional concern from the children when they witnessed one of their parents in distress. We interpret these results to suggest that, in some families, husbands and children show similar patterns of negative affect regulation. Although the above study did not directly investigate father–child interaction patterns, the results suggest that similarities exist between husbands' marital communication and children's response to parental distress (e.g., husbands' denial and withdrawal were related to children's denial and lack of emotional concern), thus providing indirect support for the premise that husbands display similar patterns of affect regulation with their spouses as with their children.

In line with the above findings, Howes, Markman, and Lindahl (1989) examined marital, parent–child, and triadic family interactions in families with a toddler-aged child and found that the family interaction pattern of triangulation was associated with less satisfying marriages. During problem discussions of marital issues, parents who were coded as high in negative and low in positive affect, were most likely to draw their toddler-age child into (i.e., triangulate) the marital discussion. The presence of high negative affect is an indicator of ineffective negative affect regulation. That couples who displayed higher levels of negative affect with each other were more likely to incorporate their children into the discussion suggests that the parents, unable to regulate the negative affect themselves, used their child to help them achieve this effect. When parents bring children into the marital discussion, the parent–child relationship may be distorted into a "parent-centered" mode of interaction. In this scenario, children may become concerned with how they can successfully regulate their parents' affect during conflict or disagreement. This study also found that triangulated children showed more negative feelings during a family play time, and were described by their parents as less securely attached and sociable; these observations may be early indicators of future problems for these children.

The above studies, although unable to establish a causal link between the parallel processes observed in the marital and parent–child relationships, do suggest several possibilities. We offer the hypothesis that it is the ability of the parents to regulate negative affect in their marriage that is related to marital quality and that is also related to the ability of the parents to regulate negative affect in their interactions with their children. How parents regulate negative affect in their interactions with their children is then related to the children's ability to regulate negative affect on their own and in their interactions with others. This has long-range implications. Patterns of negative affect regulation will be transmitted on to future generations as the children pass through adulthood and become spouses themselves, thus continuing the patterns they learned in their childhood. We do not mean to suggest that patterns or processes of negative affect regulation necessarily remain static throughout the lifespan. We hypothesize that dysfunctional patterns of affect regulation, like dysfunctional communication patterns, are difficult to modify, and that if they should stabilize over time, the dysfunctional patterns are likely to be passed on to future generations. The entrenchment of such maladaptive patterns may account, in part, for associations across generations of family violence and marital distress (Rosenbaum & O'Leary, 1981; Walker, 1979).

To summarize, we hypothesize that couples' ability to *handle or regulate negative affect* in their marriage (as seen in the ability to avoid negative escalation cycles and to handle conflict and disagreements constructively) is related to their children's ability to handle negative affect, which in turn is related to child functioning. We suggest that disturbances within the parent–child relationship, or more specifically, limitations placed on the parents' ability to regulate negative affect in the context of the parent–child relationship, is one pathway through which a distressed marriage can negatively influence a child's emotional growth. Sensitive parenting requires that parents be emotionally available to their children, a task that may be difficult for parents who feel drained by marital distress. In being emotionally available, parents must be able to regulate their own emotions so that they can be appropriately responsive, supportive, and attuned to their children's emotional state. Similarly, effective parenting also involves being able to deal with disagreements with children in a constructive manner. Parents who have difficulty regulating their own negative affect may be emotionally overreactive (often wives) or withdrawn (often husbands) with their children. This would handicap children's chances of learning how to regulate their negative affect in a healthy way. The developmental importance of children's affect regulation and its potential links to child functioning are discussed next.

## Affect Regulation as a Critical Developmental Task

The ability to regulate emotional expression and responses to emotionally charged experiences is often described as a critical developmental task. For example, developmental psychologists have studied behaviors believed to reflect processes of affect regulation, such as impulse control (Kopp, 1982), reflective versus impulsive style (Kagan, Rosman, Day, Albert, & Phillips, 1964), delay of gratification (Mischel & Underwood, 1974), and frustration tolerance (Van Leishout, 1975). Maccoby (1980) suggested that early childhood may be the most important period in terms of the development of emotional control and regulation. Young children are often consumed by strong emotional states that seem to overwhelm their minds and bodies. Infants, for instance, are frequently highly aroused; they turn red, cry vigorously, and thrash their arms and legs. In this state, babies seem single-minded as they show no interest in food, toys, or other events that might ordinarily capture their attention. They need to be soothed, generally by an adult caretaker, before they can resume regular activities. Through the second year of life children seem to lose their tempers or cry with little provocation. However, as children grow older, they learn to control and inhibit intense emotions, especially negative ones, and the frequency of emotional outbursts decreases (Maccoby, 1980). Developing internal structures to organize emotions, the growth of inhibitory controls, and the development of self-soothing mechanisms signal successful negative affect regulation.

To return to the primary purpose of this chapter, namely to expand upon the hypothesis that learning effective methods of regulating negative affect is a critical component of healthy marital and family functioning, the preceding review of affect regulation in young children also highlights the importance of negative affect regulation for psychological growth in general. We hypothesize that children who do not learn effective mechanisms for understanding, recognizing, and monitoring their negative affect early on, may later face additional difficulties in interpersonal relationships such as marriage.

## CONCLUSION

Many of the studies reviewed in this chapter are limited in terms of the information provided about the mechanisms linking marital distress and children's behavioral and emotional problems. They are handicapped by their reliance on global measures of marital quality and child functioning (few studies used interaction data) and by their lack of attention to potential pathways such as the parent–child relationship. Future research should increase use of interactional observations of both marital and parental interactions in order to capture the complexity of the interrelationships of the two family subsystems. With the advent of "second generation" cost-effective global observation systems, developed from the results of microanalytic systems, observational technology is now more readily available to researchers (Markman & Howes, 1989). Although this chapter offers a new way of interpreting empirical work on the interrelationships between marital, parental, and child functioning, there are many questions that remain. That there is covariance in patterns of handling negative affect in marital and parent–child relationships in distressed families is interesting, but nevertheless still begs the question of *why* the similarities exist.

It is a commonly accepted assumption that marriage and parenting are intertwined, and many researchers (e.g., Belsky, 1981; Easterbrooks & Goldberg, 1984; Engfer, 1988) have speculated about and attempted to study the relationship between marital and parental functioning. As a result, numerous theories have been proposed to account for the data linking the marital and parenting relationships. These theories include the following: (a) a dissatisfying marital relationship leaves parents too emotionally drained to be responsive to their children, (b) a dissatisfying marriage leads parents to seek comfort and nurturance from their children, (c) parents may compensate for a dissatisfying marriage by putting extra investment and energy into their relationships with their children, and (d) a satisfying marriage provides mutual support and emotional fulfillment, thus helping parents be emotionally available to their children (Engfer, 1988). Although each of the above hypotheses has some theoretical and empirical support, it is unclear at this point which of the above hypotheses, if any, make the most sense in explaining the parallel processes of affect regulation seen in marital and parental relationships. Although there is no existing research that directly addresses this question, the first hypothesis seems to fit best with the data on distressed families presented in this chapter. It takes patience and energy to be able to tolerate, understand, empathize with, and communicate about negative affect with children. It seems likely that a distressed marriage, which is emotionally draining, and in which the parents are unable to regulate and monitor their own negative affect, will leave the parents emotionally bankrupt and without resources to deal with similar issues of affect regulation with their child. However, this is speculative at this point. There is a pressing need for theory development fueled by research that provides information about how marriage, parenting, and child development are interrelated. Such research should extend and improve upon existing research by focusing on interpersonal interactions and by including fathers. We hope that this chapter has provided a preliminary framework to guide such efforts.

## REFERENCES

Belsky, J. (1981). Early human experience: A family perspective. *Developmental Psychology, 17,* 3–23.
Birchler, G. R., Weiss, R. L., & Vincent, J. P. (1975). Multimethod analysis of social reinforcement exchange between maritally distressed and nondistressed spouse and stranger dyads. *Journal of Personality and Social Psychology, 31,* 349–360.

Bowlby, J. (1973). *Attachment and loss: II. Separation.* New York: Basic Books.

Cherlin, A. J. (1981). *Marriage, divorce, and remarriage.* Cambridge, MA: Harvard University Press.

Easterbrooks, M. A. (1987, April). *Early family development: Longitudinal impact of marital quality.* Paper presented at the meeting of the Society for Research in Child Development, Baltimore, MD.

Easterbrooks, M. A., & Goldberg, W. A. (1984). Toddler development in the family: Impact of father involvement and parenting characteristics. *Child Development, 55,* 740–752.

Emery, R. E. (1982). Interparental conflict and the children of discord and divorce. *Psychological Bulletin, 92,* 310–330.

Engfer, A. (1988, January). *The interrelatedness of marriage and the mother–child relationship.* Paper presented at the International Conference on "Intrafamilial Relationships," Cambridge, Great Britain.

Gibson, H. B. (1969). Early delinquency in relation to broken homes. *Journal of Child Psychology and Psychiatry and Allied Disciplines, 10,* 195–204.

Glick, P. C., & Norton, A. J. (1976). Number, times, and duration of marriages and divorces in the United States. In *Current Population Reports,* Series P-20, No. 297, Bureau of the Census.

Goldberg, W. A., & Easterbrooks, M. A. (1984). The role of marital quality in toddler development. *Developmental Psychology, 20,* 504–514.

Gottman, J. M. (1979). *Empirical investigations of marriage.* New York: Academic Press.

Gottman, J. M. (1983). *The social psychophysiology of marriage.* Unpublished manuscript.

Gottman, J. M., & Levenson, R. W. (1986). Assessing the role of emotion in marriage. *Behavioral Assessment, 8,* 31–48.

Gottman, J. M., Markman, H. J., & Notarius, C. I. (1977). The topography of marital conflict: A sequential analysis of verbal and nonverbal behavior. *Journal of Marriage and the Family, 39,* 461–478.

Gottman, J. M., Notarius, C. I., Gonso, J., & Markman, H. J. (1976). *A couple's guide to communication.* Champaign, IL: Research Press.

Hetherington, E. M. (1972). Effects of father absence on personality development in adolescent daughters. *Developmental Psychology, 7,* 313–326.

Hetherington, E. M. (1988, October). *Stress and coping in divorce and remarriage.* Paper presented at the Conference of the American Association for Marriage and Family Therapy, New Orleans, LA.

Hetherington, E. M., Cox, M., & Cox, R. (1979). Family interaction and the social and cognitive development of children following divorce. In V. Vaughn & T. Brazelton (Eds.), *The family: Setting priorities.* New York: Science and Medicine.

Hetherington, E. M., Cox, M., & Cox, R. (1978). The aftermath of divorce. In J. H. Stephens & M. Mathews (Eds.), *Mother/Child Father/Child Relationships.* Washington, DC: National Association for the Education of Young Children.

Howes, P., Markman, H. J., & Lindahl, K. M. (1989). *Managing marital conflict in the family.* Manuscript in preparation.

Jacobson, D. S. (1978). The impact of marital separation/divorce on children: II. Interparental hostility and child adjustment. *Journal of Divorce, 2,* 3–20.

Julien, D., Markman, H. J., & Lindahl, K. M. (1989). A comparison of a global and a microanalytic coding system: Implications for future trends in studying interaction. *Behavioral Assessment, 11,* 81–100.

Kagan, J., Rosman, B. L., Day, D., Albert, J., & Phillips, W. (1964). Information processing in the child: Significance of analytic and reflective attitudes. *Psychological Monographs, 78.*

Kerig, P. K. (1987, April). *The family context: couple satisfaction, parenting style, and speech to young children.* Poster presented at the Biennial Meetings of the Society for Research in Child Development, Baltimore, MD.

Kopp, C. B. (1982). Antecedents of self-regulation: A developmental perspective. *Developmental Psychology, 18*, 199–214.

Lambert, L., Essen, J., & Head, J. (1977). Variations in behavior ratings of children who have been in care. *Journal of Child Psychology and Psychiatry and Allied Fields, 18*, 335–346.

Lindahl, K. M., Howes, P. W., & Markman, H. J. (1988, November). *Exploring links between marital communication, parent–child interactions, and the development of empathy.* Poster presented at the Meeting for the Association for Advancement of Behavior Therapy, New York, NY.

Maccoby, E. E. (1980). *Social development.* New York: Harcourt, Brace and Jovanovitch.

Markman, H. J. (1984). The longitudinal study of couples' interactions: Implications for cognitive/behavioral, social exchange, and social skills models of relationship development. In N. Jacobson & K. Hahlweg (Eds.,) *Marital interaction: Analysis and modification* (pp. 253–281). New York: Guilford Press.

Markman, H. J. (1988, September). The prevention of marital distress. Paper presented at the World Congress of Behavior Therapy, Edinborough, Scotland.

Markman, H. J. (1989). *Long term effects of premarital intervention.* Unpublished manuscript.

Markman, H. J., Floyd, F., Stanley, S., & Storaasli, R. (1988). The prevention of marital distress: A longitudinal investigation. *Journal of Consulting and Clinical Psychology, 56*, 210–217.

Markman, H. J., & Howes, P. W. (1989, April). Observational alternatives to global self-report measures in research on marital quality and child behavior. In E. Waters (Chair), *Advancing the study of marriage, parenting, and child development.* Symposium conducted at the Biennial Meetings of the Society for Research in Child Development, Kansas City, MO.

Markman, H. J., & Jones-Leonard, D. (1985). Marital discord and children at risk. In W. K. Frankenburg (Ed.), *Early interaction and psychopathology: Theories, methods, and findings* (pp. 59–77). New York: Plenum Press.

Markman, H. J., & Kraft, S. A. (1989). Men and women in marriage: Implications for treatment and prevention of marital distress. *The Behavior Therapist, 12*(3), 51–56.

Markman, H. J., & Notarius, C. (1987). Coding marital and family interaction: Current status. In T. Jacob (Ed.), *Family interaction and psychopathology: Theories, methods and findings* (pp. 329–390). New York: Plenum Publishing Co.

McCord, J., McCord, W., & Thurber, E. (1962). Some effects of paternal absence on male children. *Journal of Abnormal and Social Psychology, 64*, 361–369.

Mischel, W., & Underwood, B. (1974). Instrumental ideation in delay of gratification. *Child Development, 45*, 1083–1088.

National Center for Health Statistics. (1989). Births, marriages, divorces, and deaths for October, 1988. *Monthly Vital Statistics Report 37*, No. 10. DHHS Pub. No. (PHS) 89-1120. Public Health Service, Hyattsville, MD.

Notarius, C. I., Benson, P. R., Sloane, D., Vanzetti, N. A., & Hornyak, L. M. (1989). Exploring the interface between perception and behavior: An analysis of marital interaction in distressed and nondistressed couples. *Behavioral Assessment, 11*, 39–64.

Notarius, C. I., Markman, H. J., & Gottman, J. M. (1983). The Couples Interaction Scoring System: Clinical issues. In E. Filsinger (Ed.), *Marital measurement sourcebook* (pp. 117–136). Beverly Hills, CA: Sage.

Nye, F. I. (1957). Child adjustment in broken and unhappy broken homes. *Marriage and Family Living, 19*, 356–361.

O'Leary, K. D., & Emery, R. E. (1982). Marital discord and child behavior problems. In

M. D. Levine & P. Satz (Eds.), *Middle Childhood: Developmental variation and dysfunction* (pp. 345–364). New York: Academic Press.

Power, M. J., Ash, M., Schoenberg, E., & Storey, E. C. (1974). Delinquency and the family. *British Journal of Social Work, 4,* 17–38.

Rosenbaum, A., & O'Leary, D. (1981). Marital violence: Characteristics of abusive couples. *Journal of Consulting and Clinical Psychology, 49,* 63–71.

Van Leishout, C. F. M. (1975). Young children's reactions to barriers placed by their mothers. *Child Development, 46,* 879–886.

Walker, L. (1979). *The battered woman.* New York: Harper & Row.

Wallerstein, J., & Blakeslee, S. (1989). *Second Chances.* New York: Ticknor & Fields.

Wallerstein, J., & Kelly, J. (1979). Children and divorce. A review. *Social Work, 24,* 468–475.

Westman, J. D., Cline, D. W., Swift, W. J., & Kramer, D. A. (1970). The role of child psychiatry in divorce. *Archives of General Psychiatry, 23,* 416–420.

# CHAPTER 7

# Toward a Behavioral Conceptualization of Adult Intimacy: Implications for Marital Therapy

**Alan E. Fruzzetti**
**Neil S. Jacobson**
University of Washington

$R$are is the couple entering marital therapy who describe their difficulties in behaviorally specific terms. More typical are husbands and wives who report no longer "feeling close" and describe themselves as having "lost intimacy," or as having "grown apart." With careful assessment, the problems described by the spouses may often be conceptualized as: reinforcement erosion or deprivation, where formerly pleasing behaviors have lost their potency or the rate of their performance has diminished; a deficit in communication skills, problem-solving skills, or a situation where existent skills are not employed; or a pattern of interaction that maintains or increases distance between the spouses.

It is the job of therapy in such cases either to restore the power of partners' rewarding behaviors and exchanges or to help the couple to engage in new behaviors that are more rewarding. It may also be important to help couples learn clearer and more direct methods of communication and to solve problems in a mutually beneficial and respectful way. Furthermore, couples may engage in one or more problematic patterns of interaction that have developed over time. Such couples may need to examine what current contingencies in their relationship, if any, maintain these patterns, and attempt to alter them. Alternatively, negative interaction patterns may be the result of formerly important, but no longer salient relationship rules. In these cases it may be necessary to help couples contact current contingencies in order to render negative patterns less powerful.

The preceding paragraph clearly (if briefly) describes the current Behavioral Marital Therapy (BMT) approach (Jacobson & Holtz-worth-Munroe, 1986; Jacobson & Margolin, 1979; Schmaling, Fruzzetti, & Jacobson, 1989), which has proven effective in remediating marital problems (Hahlweg & Markman, 1988; Jacobson, Follette, Revensdorf, Baucom, Hahlweg, & Margolin, 1984), especially in improving communication and problem-solving skills (Hahlweg, Revensdorf, & Schindler, 1984). However, BMT is not always effective: A significant proportion of couples still report marital difficulties even after therapy (Baucom & Hoffman, 1986; Jacobson et al., 1984). Thus, it is important to continue to reconceptualize dysfunctional dyadic interactions and seek new interventions designed to remediate these problems.

Of course, some couples' problems may not be those of reinforcement deprivation/erosion, communication difficulties, and/or an inability to solve problems, at least not in their simplest form. What distressed spouses describe as having "lost intimacy" may in fact reflect specific behavioral interactions associated with a diminution of emotional closeness.

One specific pattern of interaction associated with reduced intimacy that has been described by both clinicians and researchers is the "demand/withdraw" pattern (Gottman & Levinson, 1986; Jacobson & Margolin, 1979; Napier, 1978; Wile, 1981), where one spouse's demand for increased time together and emotional closeness is at odds with the other's concomitant withdrawal. This pattern is common, clearly related to relationship satisfaction (Christensen, 1988), and may even discriminate premarital couples who stay together from those that do not (Fruzzetti & Jacobson, 1988).

Because certain patterns of interaction in couples clearly affect the well-being of relationships, it seems likely that such interaction patterns may also (at least indirectly) affect the emotional health of individual partners. There is ample evidence that marital relationships influence psychopathology and that individual psychological distress influences marital functioning (Biglan, Hops, Sherman, Friedman, Arthur, & Osteen, 1985; Brown & Harris, 1975; Coleman & Miller, 1975; Crowther, 1985; Jacobson, Holtzworth-Munroe, & Schmaling, 1989; Waring & Patton, 1984), but the mechanisms of influence have not been well established.

Skinner (chapter 1) notes that in order for therapy to be effective changes must be made and reinforcing consequences must follow. BMT therapists have typically focused on overt behaviors such as behavioral exchanges between spouses, communication and problem-solving training, et cetera. But private behaviors such as physiological states of arousal (feelings, e.g., love, intimacy) play an important role in couple interactions and relationship satisfaction. These states of physiological arousal may be very pleasant or quite painful, and may be important determinants (discriminitive stimuli or consequences) of couple interactions. Although we may not be able to observe publicly many states of arousal, we may be able to employ what we know about physiological arousal in a behavioral analysis of couple interactions. Thus, including private levels of emotional arousal as behavior in dyadic interactions may help explicate interaction patterns some couples demonstrate.

We attempt in this chapter to develop one account of emotional arousal in the context of dyadic interactions in a marital relationship, how such arousal may facilitate development and maintenance of the "demand/withdraw" interaction pattern in some distressed couples, and the consequent influence on partners' level of intimacy and expression of affect in couple interactions. To help make this account more complete, we also consider the possible role of positive affect and its effect on dyadic interactions. Finally, we discuss some of the clinical implications of this emergent behavioral model of intimacy.

## DYADIC INTERACTIONS AND THE ROLE OF AFFECT AND AROUSAL

In a comprehensive review of the research examining affect in couples, Schaap (1984) noted that one finding, at least, is consistent across studies: maritally distressed couples display more negative and less positive affect than maritally nondistressed couples across a wide range of interactions (emotional expression, problem-solving, etc.). Yet, marital distress is not simply a concomitant of negative affective expression. Rather, Gottman and Krokoff (1989) found that conflict engagement (including expression of negative affect, e.g., anger) is predictive of longer term *increases* in marital satisfaction at a 3-year follow-up (although couples were not necessarily happy at follow-up). They found that *withdrawal* from interaction, especially by the husband, was predictive of decreased marital satisfaction at the 3-year follow-up.

One way to account for the seemingly contradictory finding that negative affective expression (e.g., anger) is associated with short-term relationship dissatisfaction but longer-term positive changes in satisfaction is to consider the range of possible aversive consequences of negative affective expression: Negative emotional arousal at a low, moderate, or sporadic level may not be as aversive *physiologically* as it is at high or chronic levels where it has been found to be unpleasant and aversive (Gottman & Levinson, 1986; Levinson & Gottman, 1983). Expressions of anger and dissatisfaction toward a spouse in tolerable doses may allow, or even facilitate, subsequent conflict resolution; regular withdrawal from interactions in conflict situations might be a result of acute and/or persistent negative arousal, and precludes conflict resolution.

Thus, including physiological arousal that is associated with expressions of negative emotion as a variable of interest may help explain why negative affective expression predicts short-term dissatisfaction but longer-term improvement in marital satisfaction. Perhaps engagement in conflict situations for some couples does not raise physiological arousal levels to a sufficiently aversive level to result in disengagement or withdrawal. That is, some couples may engage in conflict (including negative affective expression) until resolution, while others disengage at a much earlier point, precluding successful resolution and its consequences.

Not only is skill in communication and problem-solving essential for conflict resolution, but often couples must engage in resolution-focused tasks for sustained periods of time. Although difficult in the short-term, conflict engagement leading to resolution may result in improved relationship satisfaction over time because couples have the opportunity to understand each other and respond in new ways. This explanation is consistent with Gottman and Krokoff (1989).

Thus, a couple's ability to endure short-term negative affective expression may be integral to long-term relationship satisfaction. The level of physiological arousal that partners reach in conflict situations may determine, at least in part, how long conflict engagement continues, hence the likelihood of successful resolution. Higher levels of negative physiological arousal would not likely be tolerable for as long as lower levels, and would more often lead to early withdrawal from conflict. Couples in which one or both spouses achieve aversive levels of arousal in conflict situations may then be less likely to develop a pattern or habit of conflict resolution.

Of course, there may be many reasons why some individuals achieve more arousal or less arousal under the same apparent circumstances. There may be individual differences in physiological arousal mechanisms, and/or physiological parameters of arousal that are simply the result of genetic variation. There may also be historical variables or prior determinants that have shaped current arousal responses, such as interactions with parents, siblings, or friends, or in other intimate relationships, that act alone or interact with basic physiological arousal mechanisms. With the possible exception of drug interventions (which are problematic at best, and beyond the scope of this chapter), changing the learned behavioral responses to situations is the only direct mechanism to alter destructive dyadic interactions and their associated levels of arousal.

Gottman and Levinson (1986) found that dissatisfied couples show greater reciprocity of negative affect and that their interactions display more structure and predictability than those of nondistressed couples. Thus it seems that among distressed couples a small negative interaction, once started, is more likely to continue unabated in a negative, unresolved way, whereas nondistressed couples seem more likely to break this punishing cycle of interaction and achieve conflict resolution.

Couples who express negative affect at a tolerable level of arousal may reap benefits: They may be reinforced for such engagement by solving problems and hence develop "relational efficacy" (Notarius & Vanzetti, 1983). Not only will the learned experience of successful engagement in conflict situations facilitate further engagement in problem/conflict situations (with increased chances of successful outcomes), but successful engagement will feed back to reduce the aversive level of arousal partners experience when presented with a conflict/anger exchange situation in the future. What individuals may report as "confidence" that conflict engagement will lead to resolution may result in part from a diminution of negative arousal that facilitates repeated, successful resolution of conflict.

Figure 7.1 displays the components of this emerging model, one that considers both the behavioral interaction and the level of emotional arousal (positive or negative) reached by each partner. The conflict or problem situation is a discriminative stimulus for an initial level of arousal. This initial physiological arousal has been conditioned through prior learning (in problem or conflict situations with the partner and others). When arousal levels are not excessive, engagement in problem or conflict resolution is more likely, with the probability of successful resolution in turn increased. This success reinforces engagement in a conflict or problem situation in the future.

Through the repeated successful process of problem/conflict engagement and resolution, physiological arousal in conflict situations is likely to be maintained at low or moderate levels over time. Problem situations become, through successful engagement, discriminative stimuli not for heightened arousal and reciprocated expressions of ever more negative affect, but for tempered arousal. This results in an increased probability that positive affect will be infused into the conflict situation to supplant negative arousal. This would further reinforce engagement in conflict resolution tasks when the situation arises, supplanting conflict avoidance or disengagement. The in-

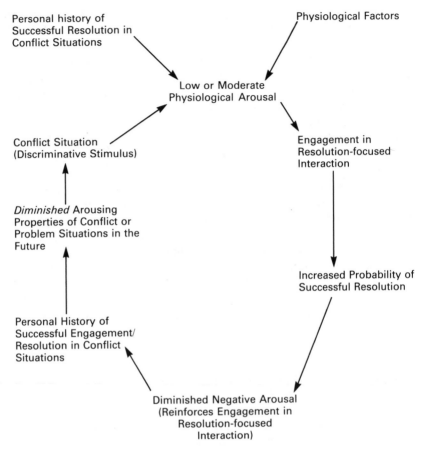

FIG. 7.1.    De-escalating Arousal–Interaction–Feedback Cycle Leading to Resolution

creased likelihood that positive affect will be displayed further reduces the opportunity and reinforcement for conflict escalation.

This proposed arousal–interaction–feedback cycle may be considered a de-escalating cycle because of the diminished negative arousal that is likely to occur through repeated, successful conflict engagement. This model may suggest clues as to why, for many couples, traditional BMT efforts such as increasing emotional expressiveness through communication training, increasing behavior exchanges, and problem-solving skills training are quite effective. If a pattern of conflict escalation is not already entrenched, these BMT techniques likely reduce negative arousal, facilitate success and mastery experiences, and provide couples with skills to engage in a more positive interaction cycle. For such couples traditional BMT interventions disrupt and redirect the negative cycle.

The first step in any redirection of this negative cycle is the creation of a therapeutic environment in which couple behaviors temporarily come under control of the therapist. That is, the therapist makes rules that help reduce arousal: He or she allows each spouse an opportunity to speak and be heard, reinforces partner listening through modeling and direct skill training, interrupts negative behaviors that are part of the conflict-escalating cycle, and generally helps spouses to identify and carry out behaviors that reward modulated engagement. Partners then typically are able, in the therapy session, to suspend their anger with spouses in favor of attempts at conflict resolution. Over time, the therapist helps them extend gains made in therapy to their interactions at home so that each spouse's behavior gradually becomes maintained through reinforcement by the other spouse in their own environment, rather than by the therapist in the session. In addition, improvements in communication and problem-solving skills help the couple avoid old situations which previously served as discriminative stimuli for quick arousal-escalation. These improvements also make conflict engagement more efficient and focused (hence, of shorter duration), thereby maximizing the likelihood of resolution and its arousal-diminishing feedback effects.

In contrast to the de-escalating arousal–interaction–feedback cycle fostered in BMT, many couples may exhibit an escalating cycle of conflict engagement, aversive arousal, and eventual withdrawal without conflict resolution. With couples who display an established and entrenched destructive cycle such as this, even occasional success experienced in therapy sessions may not be sufficient to diminish painful negative emotional arousal. In contrast to less entrenched distressed couples, these distressed couples may be locked in an aversive, punishing cycle where painful emotional arousal is increased through consistent, reciprocal negative interactions that do not solve problems. Without successful remediation or reward on any consistent basis, the only results of attempted conflict engagement are *increased* physiological arousal, which may be even more aversive (especially without concomitant relationship benefits, e.g., a problem solved), and earlier disengagement in future conflict situations. Heightened negative arousal feeds back to reduce the likelihood of successful conflict/problem engagement and resolution, leading instead to withdrawal without resolution.

In this escalating cycle, depicted in Fig. 7.2, engagement in dyadic interactions is punished by subsequent aversive physiological arousal, and ultimately results in earlier withdrawal from conflictual interac-

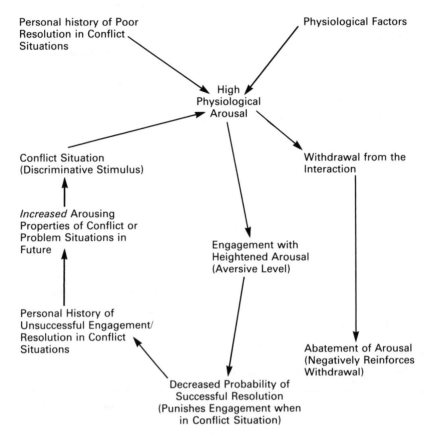

FIG. 7.2.  Escalating Arousal–Interaction–Feedback Cycle Leading to
Withdrawal From Interaction Without Resolution

tions or avoidance of such situations. In these cases, withdrawal and/
or avoidance is reinforced as unpleasant arousal abates. This negative
reinforcement paradigm is analogous to the coercive family interaction
pattern described by Patterson (1982).

Sometimes, there may be conflict resolution without immediate
reduction in negative emotional arousal (because of the infrequency
of successful resolution). Without the timely abatement of intense,
negative emotional arousal, this outcome still punishes conflict-en-
gagement and increases the likelihood of future early withdrawal from
conflict.

An apparent exception to this scenario is couples who repeatedly
fight destructively for a long time and then "make up" somewhat
later (perhaps their only "intimate" time)—after their arousal has

diminished. In these cases the subsequent experience of intimacy and positive affect reinforces their destructive fights.

Why would some individuals/couples manifest an escalating arousal–interaction–feedback cycle and others a de-escalating one? First, a given level of physiological arousal may not be equally aversive to everyone. Thus, some people may be more sensitive to negative emotional arousal than others, which makes it more likely they would engage in the escalating pattern. Second, beyond a certain level of arousal the likelihood of conflict/problem resolution may diminish: Disengagement follows because repeated engagement in this pattern is punished, while withdrawal is reinforced by reduced negative arousal. Most couples will agree that it is difficult to solve even simple problems if they are very upset. Some couples, perhaps due to a lack of problem-solving skills or the intensity of their problems, may learn patterns of avoidance and withdrawal rather than engagement and resolution.

Finally, physiological predisposition and learned patterns of engagement may interact. Those for whom arousal is less aversive may be more likely to engage in problem-solving long enough to enjoy more reinforcing consequences, that is, more successful resolutions, which feed back to decrease the negative stimulus properties of a conflict situation. For people who experience even low levels of emotional arousal as aversive, engagement in resolution-focused tasks in emotionally evocative situations may be short-lived, rarely allowing the natural reinforcers of conflict- or problem-resolution and the concomitant decreased negative arousal to follow from engagement in these interactions. Instead, heightened and/or chronic arousal persists and feeds back, creating an ever more aversive stimulus situation whenever conflicts or problems arise.

Of course, the escalating and de-escalating interaction cycles described above are extreme examples of behavior that lie on a continuum. Most couples exhibit some range of arousal and engagement, depending on the particular conflict situation, individual variables (e.g., level of interest, alertness, hunger, goals, etc.), and other situational variables (the presence of a third party, time of day, etc.). Moreover, within a couple the spouses may vary considerably in the amount of positive versus negative affect generated by a conflict situation, perhaps leading to "sub-patterns" driven by the differing desires and thresholds of either partner.

In the next section we describe one particular interaction pattern around issues of intimacy and independence that poses difficulty for couples and marital therapists alike. We then explore how the arousal–interaction–feedback model may help to understand the pattern, as well as have implications for remediation.

## DEMAND/WITHDRAW INTERACTIONS AND INTIMACY

Although some couples exhibit no consistent pattern of engagement/ disengagement in conflict situations, it is common, as noted earlier, to find couples in which there is an engagement *differential:* one partner tends to withdraw in conflict situations whereas the other tends to engage. This type of interaction may occur only in circumscribed conflict situations (e.g., the more one spouse nags the other to perform some task, the less likely the other is to do it), or may be part of a more general relationship theme.

Several noted clinician/researchers have described this pattern, with varying emphases. For example, Napier (1978) focused on the rejecting component of withdrawal, whereas Jacobson and Margolin (1979) conceptualized the pattern as one of different optimal levels of intimacy. Wile (1981) described in this pattern three components: anger, self-criticism, and a sense of incompatibility.

The demand/withdraw pattern exemplifies the escalating arousal–interaction–feedback cycle presented earlier. Of particular interest to us are situations in which demanding and withdrawing do not necessarily revolve around performance of a specific task or set of specific conflicts, but rather around the process of relating itself, of closeness and intimacy. Christensen (1988) demonstrated that the demand/withdraw pattern is closely associated with differences in desired intimacy in married couples, and Fruzzetti and Jacobson (1988, 1989) found similar results among premarital couples.

Intimacy has been described by Wynne and Wynne (1986) as a "subjective relational experience in which the core components are trusting self-disclosure to which the response is communicated empathy" (p. 384). Waring (1988) contended that intimacy has four components: "The behavioral aspect of intimacy is predictability; the emotional aspect is a feeling of closeness; the cognitive aspect is understanding through self-disclosure; and the attitudinal aspect is commitment" (p. 38).

Although we do not dispute at all the above definitions, we prefer to specify intimacy further as a class of specific couple interactions that occur in the context of a close relationship and facilitate that relationship's continued or increased closeness. Thus, behavioral intimacy is an interaction that typically follows a specific pattern and is self-revealing and/or relationship-focused in its content. In an intimate interaction one partner does or says something either self-revealing or relationship-focused. This behavior is readily discriminated (e.g., it is not misinterpreted as an attack, the salience of the behavior is not missed, etc.) by the partner, who responds in a positive, understanding, and/or self-revealing way her- or himself. This in turn results in continued reciprocated positive, empathic, and/or self-revealing responses.

This description of intimacy includes interactions in which both partners demonstrate positive affect concerning their relationship or each other as well as interactions in which one partner reveals his or her feelings (e.g., joy, sadness, or even anger) and is heard and supported in these feelings by her or his partner. In the context of a close relationship, intimacy is an interaction that increases understanding and vulnerability between partners and is accompanied by positive emotional arousal. Interactions that do not include increased partner understanding or that end with one partner punishing the other's self-revelations or vulnerability do not constitute intimacy.

Thus, intimacy is an ongoing *process,* one that is dynamic and has no goal beyond the positive emotional experience that accompanies the interaction; it is not an end-point itself. Conversely, non-intimate responding is that which ignores, withdraws from, or punishes the other's behaviors that were designed to increase closeness; instead, partners move toward greater independence. Intimate behavior results in increased closeness, understanding, agreement in interpretation or explanation, and commonality, that sense of agreed-upon "connectedness" toward which many couples want to work in therapy.

Self-disclosure likely facilitates reciprocated self-disclosure. In these situations, one partner expresses vulnerability first, which both describes his or her affective state, beliefs, and so forth, and entreats the other to support and reciprocate. Supportive behaviors and reciprocated vulnerability likely continue this interaction and lead to further intimacy. Intimacy is thus manifested in *sequences* of behaviors. Predictability may be quite important, for in order to trust and allow oneself to be vulnerable, one must be confident that the outcome will be positive.

It is important to note that preferred levels of intimacy vary greatly. The preferences for optimal levels of intimacy likely range from social isolation to nearly complete enmeshment. Most importantly for couples therapy, individual partners sometimes find divergent levels of closeness desirable.

The demand/withdraw interaction pattern often characterizes couples in which one partner seeks greater closeness, more shared experiences, and greater interpersonal intensity, whereas the other partner does not. One partner, seeking greater intimacy, is more solicitous, wants more time together, and perhaps demands that the other respond to his or her concerns. The other partner finds his or her optimal level of closeness surpassed, and seeks distance. This withdrawal increases the distance between the partners, which makes the first spouse more eager, more demanding, and more intense in his or her determination for closeness. The increased intensity drives the second spouse to further withdrawal, which intensifies the cycle.

This escalating pattern of demanding and withdrawing may be further illuminated by considering how it might fit into the escalating arousal–interaction–feedback cycle explicated earlier: If the "closeness threshold" of one member of the couple is surpassed, that person may become negatively aroused when faced with a situation in which he or she feels pressure to reciprocate closeness. At some point beyond the intimacy "comfort range," this partner will likely balk at further engagement in the cycle, and will withdraw from whatever interaction is taking place. For this partner, the other's quest for intimacy may create a conflict situation (see Fig. 7.2), although it may not be defined by either spouse as a conflict over desired level of intimacy. If the other partner is still *below* the level of closeness he or she considers optimal, that person will continue to engage the withdrawing partner because he or she wants further closeness, not more distance. Thus, the partners may be locked in a battle to which there is no obvious alternative to the conflictual engagement/disengagement cycle. Perhaps neither partner recognizes the pattern or each other's opposite needs and desires. As each tries harder to meet her or his individual needs, successful resolution grows ever-further away. Just as a child's thumb-cuffs tighten as each hand is pulled, pushing harder for one's own needs is exactly the way to maintain, not resolve, the demand/withdraw cycle of interactions.

## GENDER ROLES

In couples where the struggle over intimacy is manifested in a demand/withdraw pattern, the wife is usually in the demanding role, while the withdrawing spouse is typically the husband (Christensen, 1988; Jacobson, 1989). These differences probably reflect discrepant learning histories and gender roles (Jacobson, 1989).

It also has been suggested that differences in roles between genders may be associated with physiological differences between men and women that are consistent with the arousal–interaction–feedback model. Gottman and Levinson (1986) suggested that there may be gender differences in autonomic nervous system arousal that affect dyadic interactions. That is, men may show a higher physiological stress response, respond more quickly, but recover more slowly than women. The model we have proposed supports the observed preponderance of withdrawing males as opposed to withdrawing females when these physiological findings are considered. That is, men would enter the escalating cycle with higher negative arousal, perhaps establishing their threshold for disengagement at a lower level than that of women.

It is important to note that any observed physiological arousal differences between husbands and wives does not necessarily imply that they are biologically determined. It may be that boys and girls/men and women learn quite different mechanisms for addressing and diminishing aversive arousal in certain interpersonal situations: males may be more often reinforced for having a "stiff upper lip" and being emotionally self-reliant, whereas females may be more often reinforced for expressiveness and relying on others. Jacobson (1989) articulated the inherent power differential present in relationships where the husband is empowered through his avoidance of intimacy vis-à-vis the wife's expressed desire for more closeness. Thus, not only might a husband's withdrawal be reinforced negatively with the abatement of aversive arousal, but withdrawal may be positively reinforced with increased relationship power and control.

## IMPLICATIONS FOR MARITAL THERAPY

The arousal–interaction–feedback model for couple interactions described earlier may add a conceptual framework to help explain why certain strategies and interventions are useful when treating couples who demonstrate particular interaction problems, especially the demand/withdraw pattern. Furthermore, this model may have implications for additional clinical strategies to employ when working with difficult couples to help break destructive interaction cycles.

First, behavioral marital therapists should pay close attention both to any conflict themes the couple may have and to any pattern of conflict engagement/disengagement that they demonstrate. There may be a number of cues available that indicate an escalating arousal–interaction–feedback cycle. For example, exploring the steps involved in a recent argument might be very instructive in helping to define any emergent destructive interaction pattern. In fact, what may be even more helpful is in-session enactment of the problem or conflict situation. This may be accomplished either by asking the couple to continue a discussion/argument begun recently or just "letting the couple go" should conflict emerge spontaneously in the therapy session, while carefully monitoring the level of affect and arousal each spouse experiences and expresses.

Although many therapists seek to interrupt and reduce in-session conflict, enactment of conflict allows the identification and monitoring of affective arousal during conflict, as well as the exploration of subjective feelings and thoughts about the process. We call this technique *troubleshooting* (Jacobson & Holtzworth-Munroe, 1986; Schmaling, Fruzzetti, & Jacobson, 1989), but it is not very different from techniques employed from different theoretical perspectives (Greenberg & Johnson, 1986; Wile, 1981).

If de-escalation occurs naturally, the therapist can help point out the process and the natural reward of engagement: successful resolution. On the other hand, if conflict escalates and is reciprocated, the therapist can interrupt the interaction and help each partner focus on her or his level of physiological arousal (perhaps with special emphasis on the husband's arousal, since it may be more indicative of outcome), as well as what he or she is thinking and feeling about the escalation process at each step. This process of controlled self-disclosure and affective expression (positive or negative) may be an important rehearsal of successful conflict engagement leading to resolution. The therapist may work with the couple to develop mutually agreed-upon rules for such conflict situations, maximizing the chance that spouses will self-disclose and respond in facilitative and empathic ways, leading to positive resolution and change.

It is important to find out what typically happens to end the destructive engagement. Does one partner withdraw while the other continues to try to engage him/her? Do they both fight until exhausted? And what happens next? Do they distance themselves from each other? For how long? Under what circumstances do they re-engage? A full exploration of the whole interaction process is essential to identify the variables controlling the interaction (antecedents and consequences).

There may be certain topics that serve as discriminative stimuli for heightened negative arousal and conflict escalation. In one couple, for example, whenever the topic of finances arose the husband straightened up in his chair, clenched his teeth, and tightly gripped the arms of his chair. With other couples the "triggers" may be in-laws, work schedules, household tasks, or other issues. Although it seems unlikely that a couple would engage in a destructive pattern only when dealing with certain issues and not with others, accurate assessment of the parameters of the escalation situations is important. Perhaps not just one topic, but some constellation of topics in particular situations, leads to conflict escalation.

Alternatively, for some couples an escalating conflict pattern may be initiated in virtually any relationship-focused situation. For such couples, almost any interaction that may alter the distance between partners arouses intense, negative affect for one or both partners.

It was noted earlier that withdrawal from interaction (especially by the husband) predicts diminishing marital satisfaction over time (Gottman & Krokoff, 1989); withdrawal also precludes resolution. Thus, it is particularly important to assess for withdrawal from interactions and work to obviate this withdrawal. However, if withdrawal is viewed as a means to curtail increasing negative emotional arousal, and resolution of conflict is unlikely in states of acute or chronic arousal, clearly some other means to achieve arousal reduction must be found before withdrawal can be eliminated from the couple's pattern of interaction. Some alternative behaviors must be found that have more rewarding consequences, rather than simply trying to force the withdrawing partner to engage his or her partner immediately and intensively.

There are two ways in which a BMT therapist can influence this process: (a) help the partners to identify early cues of escalation before arousal reaches aversive levels; and (b) increase the range of possible responses to each successive step in the escalating cycle.

While assessing the sequence of events in the escalating process, either or both partners may discover certain "early warning signs" that conflict will likely reach a destructive level. Some of these cues may be easy for either spouse to self-observe, or observe in the other (looking away from the partner, raised voice, pacing, deep sighs, sweating, fidgeting, etc.). Other cues may be more internal ones that only the individual him-or herself can observe reliably (racing heart, heat flush, anger, heightened anxiety, fear, etc.).

The therapist should help spouses, perhaps over a period of time and several escalating situations, to identify a whole *sequence* of cues and then self-monitor them, determining many different opportunities for either partner to break out of the escalation mode.

The next step, of course, is to help both partners generate *alternative* behaviors from those in the destructive sequence. This might be accomplished simply by asking each partner at crucial times: "What could you do differently this time to help prevent things from getting worse?" It may be quite useful to have spouses write down a whole range of possible alternative responses that would not continue escalation of the conflict (or heighten conflict arousal).

Time should then be devoted to corrected reenactment of conflicts in-session: the therapist can offer supportive encouragement when positive alternatives have been employed and can gently cajole couples to try even more new behaviors. As with other BMT approaches, the therapist and couple should work together to develop useful between-session tasks to complement in-session efforts.

The therapist can also help the couple to self-identify emergent interaction patterns and how each spouse can influence the other's behavior in the sequence *positively or negatively*. This helps to reduce partner-blaming because each person recognizes options in his or her own behavior that facilitate de-escalation and conflict resolution.

It may be particularly helpful for couples to have a conversation about their interaction (whether conflict escalated or successfully de-escalated) soon afterward. This helps them to continue to monitor and understand their negative (hopefully by now more positive) pattern of interaction, to identify more cues, and to generate more alternative positive behaviors. Regular monitoring and "fine-tuning" may help couples engage in interaction patterns with more positive affect and lower negative arousal, enabling the couple to employ more straightforward or traditional BMT skills such as problem solving. (Their inability to employ BMT problem-solving techniques successfully is a useful clue for high-arousal escalating conflict patterns.) In addition, simply conversing about their interactions may have other consequences, if conducted in a positive and reciprocal manner: Relationship-focused discussion often leads to increased intimacy through the self-disclosure and vulnerability inherent in these situations.

Thus, considering the influence that aversive levels of emotional arousal may have on engagement in and/or withdrawal from a conflict situation may help to understand many entrenched, negative interaction patterns found in distressed couples. This model may further inform an assessment strategy designed to discern levels of arousal in conflict situations, patterns of withdrawal, or partners' differing intimacy thresholds. The idea that reducing arousal to tolerable levels might facilitate successful conflict resolution, which in turn reduces future arousal in similar conflict situations, may have specific treatment implications for unusual presenting problems or interaction patterns.

Moreover, the positive emotional arousal levels felt after successful, non-escalating resolution of a conflict situation may be quite pleasant for spouses. In contrast to the acute and chronic negative arousal that might have been typical when seeking marital therapy, such couples may label the experience they have after successful, joint engagement in tasks as "feeling closer," "more intimate," or "connected" with each other.

When a difference is desired intimacy is the theme around which a demand/withdraw pattern revolves, intervention may be even more difficult. A careful explication of the pattern to the couple may help to explain the futility of their respective efforts: For the partner who wants greater intimacy, moving closer results in further distance instead. For the withdrawing partner, attempting to assert independence leads to conflicts in which the other partner demands more closeness.

Understanding the paradox of their interaction pattern (that seeking greater closeness results in greater distance, and vice versa) may attenuate the intensity of their efforts, and lead to rapprochement. It may help spouses view conflict about intimacy not as premeditated, but rather as a natural product of differing needs for intimacy. It may be more palatable (and accurate) to view demanding and withdrawing behavior around issues of intimacy and independence as a natural process, one that has ties to levels of physiological arousal and influences their ability to engage and/or disengage each other.

The therapist may directly assign tasks she or he believes would require compromise by both spouses, especially if there is a range of intimacy that might overlap both partners' "comfort zones." Interestingly, the very process of trying to work out a shared level of intimacy requires considerable vulnerability for both partners. Thus, exercises both within and outside therapy sessions help provide shared experiences that often increase feelings of intimacy. The therapist should therefore exercise caution to avoid levels of arousal in intimacy interactions that would likely result in a return to old, negative patterns and disengagement. Rather, with sufficient self-disclosure and risk-taking by the spouses in situations controlled by the therapist, and careful efforts to foster new patterns of interaction dependent on new, modulated responses, generalization to other situations can proceed. New contingencies can take over.

## CONCLUSION

In a way, examining couple interaction patterns is really no newer than Bandura's (1969) ideas about reciprocal influence: one's own behavior is not the sole determinant of subsequent events or behaviors. Rather, behavior occurs in a context of social interaction. Yet, trying to identify problematic behavioral sequences couples have without any structure to guide the effort may be quite difficult.

We have attempted in this chapter to provide a structure for identifying, focusing upon, and resolving escalating conflict interactions common among distressed couples. By including physiological arousal in a behavioral framework of these interactions, we have tried to explain the development of such destructive couple interactions, account for the success of commonly used intervention strategies, and to suggest new remediation techniques.

Finally, it is important to note that B.F. Skinner's analysis of feelings (chapter 1) has informed the emerging model described in this chapter: it is up to the behavior analyst (in the person of a marital therapist) to determine the patterns of interaction that maintain conditions of negative arousal, which in turn maintain destructive interactions. We might add that marital therapists may be able to help partners alter their levels of arousal in conflict situations by engaging in new behaviors (informed by a careful behavioral analysis) long before the physiologists can fully explain this phenomenon.

## REFERENCES

Bandura, A. (1969). *Principles of behavior modification.* New York: Holt, Rinehart and Winston.

Baucom, D. H., & Hoffman, J. A. (1986). The effectiveness of marital therapy: Current status and application to the clinical setting. In N. S. Jacobson and A. S. Gurman (Eds.), *Clinical handbook of marital therapy* (pp. 597–620). New York: Guilford.

Biglan, A., Hops, H., Sherman, L., Friedman, L. S., Arthur, J., & Osteen, V. (1985). Problem-solving interactions of depressed women and their husbands. *Behavior Therapy, 16,* 431–451.

Brown, G. W., & Harris, T. O. (1975). *Social origins of depression: A study of psychiatric disorder in women.* New York: Free Press.

Christensen, A. (1988). Dysfunctional interaction patterns in couples. In P. Noller & M. A. Fitzpatrick (Eds.), *Perspectives on marital interaction* (pp. 31–52). Clevedon, England: Multilingual Matters Ltd.

Coleman, R. E., & Miller, A. G. (1975). The relationship between depression and marital maladjustment in a clinical population: a multitrait–multimethod study. *Journal of Consulting and Clinical Psychology, 43,* 647–651.

Crowther, J. H. (1985). The relationship between depression and marital maladjustment: A descriptive study. *Journal of Nervous and Mental Disease, 173,* 227–231.

Fruzzetti, A. E., & Jacobson, N. S. (1988, November). *Factors affecting the dissolution of intimate (dating) relationships.* Paper presented at the 22nd Annual Convention of the Association for Advancement of Behavior Therapy, New York.

Fruzzetti, A. E., & Jacobson, N. S. (1989). *Predicting depressed mood following relationship dissolution: A more naturalistic test of the Hopelessness Theory of Depression.* Unpublished manuscript.

Gottman, J. M., & Krokoff, L. (1989). Marital interaction and marital satisfaction: A longitudinal view. *Journal of Consulting and Clinical Psychology, 57,* 47–52.

Gottman, J. M., & Levinson, R. W. (1986). Assessing the role of emotion in marriage. *Behavioral Assessment, 8,* 31–48.

Greenberg, L. S., & Johnson, S. M. (1986). Emotionally focused couples therapy. In N. S. Jacobson & A. S. Gurman (Eds.), *Clinical handbook of marital therapy* (pp. 253–276). New York: Guilford.

Hahlweg, K., & Markman, H. J. (1988). The effectiveness of behavioral marital therapy: Empirical status of behavioral techniques in preventing and alleviating marital distress. *Journal of Consulting and Clinical Psychology, 56,* 440–447.

Hahlweg, K., Revensdorf, D., & Schindler, L. (1984). Effects of behavioral marital therapy on couples' communication and problem-solving skills. *Journal of Consulting and Clinical Psychology, 52,* 553–566.

Jacobson, N. S. (1989). The politics of intimacy. *The Behavior Therapist, 12,* 29–32.

Jacobson, N. S., Follette, W. C., Revensdorf, D., Baucom, D. H., Hahlweg, K., &

Margolin, G. (1984). Variability in outcome and clinical significance of behavioral marital therapy: a reanalysis of outcome data. *Journal of Consulting and Clinical Psychology, 52,* 497–504.

Jacobson, N. S., & Holtzworth-Munroe A. (1986). Marital therapy: A social learning–cognitive perspective. In N. S. Jacobson & A. S. Gurman (Eds.), *Clinical handbook of marital therapy* (pp. 29–70). New York: Guilford.

Jacobson, N. S., Holtzworth-Munroe, A., & Schmaling, K. B. (1989). Marital therapy and spouse involvement in the treatment of depression, agoraphobia, and alcoholism. *Journal of Consulting and Clinical Psychology, 57,* 5–10.

Jacobson, N. S., & Margolin, G. (1979). *Marital therapy: Strategies based on social learning and behavior exchange principles.* New York: Brunner/Mazel.

Levinson, R. W., & Gottman, J. M. (1983). Marital interaction: Physiological linkage and affective exchange. *Journal of Personality and Social Psychology, 45,* 587–597.

Napier, A. Y. (1978). The rejection-intrusion pattern: A central family dynamic. *Journal of Marriage and Family Counseling, 4,* 5–12.

Notarius, C. I., & Vanzetti, N. A. (1983). The marital agendas protocol. In E. Filsinger (Ed.), *Marriage and family assessment.* Beverly Hills, CA: Sage.

Patterson, G. R. (1982). *Coercive family process.* Eugene, OR: Castalia Publishing.

Schaap, C. (1984). A comparison of the interaction of distressed and nondistressed married couples in a laboratory situation: literature survey, methodological issues, and an empirical investigation. In K. Hahlweg & N. S. Jacobson (Eds.), *Marital interaction: Analysis and modification* (pp. 133–158). New York: Guilford.

Schmaling, K. B., Fruzzetti, A. E., & Jacobson, N. S. (1989). Marital problems. In K. Hawton, P. Salkovskis, D. Clark, & J. Kirk (Eds.), *Cognitive-behavioural approaches to adult psychiatric disorders: A practical guide.* Oxford: Oxford University Press.

Waring, E. M. (1988). *Enhancing marital intimacy through facilitating cognitive self-disclosure.* New York: Brunner/Mazel.

Waring, E. M., & Patton, D. (1984). Marital intimacy and depression. *British Journal of Psychiatry, 145,* 641–644.

Wile, D. B. (1981). *Couples therapy: A nontraditional approach.* New York: Wiley.

Wynne, L. C., & Wynne, A. R. (1986). The quest for intimacy. *Journal of Marital and Family Therapy, 12,* 383–394.

# CHAPTER 8

# Emotional Change Processes in Couples Therapy

**Leslie S. Greenberg**
York University
**Susan M. Johnson**
University of Ottawa

Evidence that feelings are independent conscious experiences accompanied by specific physiological and expressive patterns is abundant (Leventhal & Tomarken, 1986). Feeling is that which is sensed: external stimulus or internal tension, pain, emotion, or intent. Feelings in specific, and consciousness in general, should be the preeminent concern of psychology. Physiological activity without felt experience is not psychological. The psychological study of emotion cannot exclude feelings.

Based on a constructive theory of emotional processing (Leventhal 1979, 1982), we assert that emotion is a conscious experience (Greenberg & Johnson, 1988; Greenberg & Safran, 1987; Johnson & Greenberg, 1987) that emerges from a tacit synthesis of subsidiary information. As Leventhal (1979) and Lang (1983) have suggested, emotion is constituted from different types and levels of information that are integrated preattentively (Broadbent, 1977), emerging into awareness as a holistic emotional experience. An emotion is a synthesis of expressive motor and autonomic responses, schematic emotional memories, and conceptual processing. Emotion is an omnipresent readout of the automatic parallel processing of experience.

### The Experience of Emotions

Although Skinner (chapter 1) assumes that knowledge of one's own emotional state is learned, in our view people have innate knowledge about their own and others' emotions. When given photographs of primary emotional expressions, people around the world can reliably name the emotion (Ekman, Friesen, & Ellsworth, 1982a, 1982b). Children can reliably discriminate between emotions (Russel & Ridgeway, 1983).

Primary emotions such as anger, sadness, fear, joy, disgust, and surprise are easily identified (Ekman & Friesen, 1975). They are not vague, subjective, covert states for which labels must be learned. Complexity in labelling emerges with complex emotion blends and the integration of cognition and emotion into feelings.

The concepts of prototypes and fuzzy sets inform the study of people's knowledge about emotions (Horowitz, French, & Anderson, 1982; Rosch, 1978). From a prototype perspective (Shaver, Schwartz, Kirson, & O'Connor, 1987), the categories of love, joy, anger, sadness, fear, and surprise suffice for everyday distinctions among emotions. Except for love, these categories match the basic facial emotional expression and overlap with criteria of biological primacy (Ekman et al., 1982a; Izard, 1977). The more subtle feeling terms (of which there are hundreds) are useful for finer distinctions of emotion blends and emotion/cognition integrations.

The finer terms might be called feelings and the basic terms, emotions. Both are conscious experiences. The basic emotions represent innate, universal aspects of human experience available to consciousness. The feeling terms represent individually learned, cultural/social/cognitive/emotional syntheses. Feelings must have a sensory/motor/bodily component. Thus, sadness, the basic emotion, may combine with other aspects of experience to produce feelings of hurt, sorrow, anguish, hopelessness, regret, loneliness, insecurity, or sympathy. Feelings such as bitterness, hate, scorn, spite, annoyance, irritation, contempt, resentment, dislike, and revenge differ from one another but all include basic anger. Although the word "feeling" is traditionally used to describe purely sensory bodily experience (such as touch), we use the word feeling to refer to all the fine differentiations of human affective experience. Feelings are dependent on learning and are idiosyncratic. Emotions are innate and universal. Anger is the universal primary response to violation or restraint. Sadness is the universal primary response to loss. Culture and learning, however, determine whether and when we feel pride, jealousy, or envy.

We use the term affect for the biological responses to stimulation that involve no reflective evaluation. Thus, one may experience an affective reaction before being consciously aware of the nature of the stimulus or the reason for one's response. We distinguish between affect (the visceral and vascular reaction), emotion (the conscious experience and the basic state), and feeling (the differentiated felt meaning of an experience).

Moreover, we distinguish among emotions, because the origins and processes of each basic emotion merit recognition. Those who lump anger and joy, fear and sadness, into one category, confuse as much as they clarify. This is especially true in psychotherapy. Each basic emotion serves a unique therapeutic function and requires a unique therapeutic posture.

Consider how the basic emotions differ in intensity. Intensified anger may become dysfunctional rage, whereas intensified sadness may become healthy grief. Intense fear becomes panic; intense joy, ecstasy. In therapy, continual low-grade anger or sadness is best intensified and brought into awareness to clarify individual experience and interpersonal interaction. Yet low-grade happiness is neither problematic nor a desirable target of therapeutic exploration.

Consider how unique each basic emotion is. Love, for example, differs from emotions with recognizable facial expressions. Love is also unique in its attachment and comforting effects. Equally unique are the reparative and succor-evoking functions of grief, the empowering, territorial, and destructive functions of anger, the self-preservative functions of fear, the self-protective gustatory function of disgust, and the orienting function of surprise.

We need to focus on each emotion's unique function in self-regulation and in social interaction. We need to learn more about when it is therapeutic to evoke, dampen, bypass, or intensify an emotion. Improved measurement of emotional expression is needed. However, inadequate scientific technology for discrimination among emotions should not be taken as an indication that people do not know the difference between their own emotions. People know how they feel even if behavioral scientists can't yet assess this knowledge.

### The Expression of Emotions

When using emotion for therapeutic change, it is necessary to differentiate between three classes of emotional expression (Greenberg & Safran, 1984b, 1987, 1989): a biologically based category of primary emotions, and two culturally based categories of secondary and instrumental emotions. The experience and expression of primary emotions conveys biologically adaptive information that aids in problem solving, unified action, and constructive relationship definition.

Secondary emotional reactions often take the form of defensive, coping strategies that obstruct therapeutic change. In couples' therapy, expression of secondary emotions is often the couple's problem. These secondary emotions have been cited by behavioral (Stuart, 1980) and cognitive-behavioral therapists as apt targets for extinction. Secondary emotions such as anger or bitterness toward the spouse are readily available to consciousness and often motivate couples to seek therapy. Exploration or intensification of these emotions is undesirable and even harmful. Using clinical judgment, the therapist must distinguish between secondary and primary emotional reactions (Greenberg & Safran, 1987). The therapist must explore anger if it is a primary response to being violated, and bypass it if it is a secondary reaction to hurt or fear.

In the third category, instrumental emotions serve an interpersonal function and are called roles or manipulative feelings by transactionally oriented therapists (Berne, 1961). Examples include expressions of helplessness aimed at securing sympathy, and expressions of anger and hurt aimed at avoiding responsibility. Instrumental emotions are easy to interrupt or divert, because clients can easily notice and control them. Instrumental emotions are not founded in primary emotional experience. Transactional therapists encourage clients to understand how they benefit from instrumental emotions in order to become less manipulative.

Primary emotions are rarely in awareness when the client begins therapy. They are acknowledged, disavowed, or ignored. "Getting in touch" with primary emotions encourages therapeutic change. Awareness of primary emotions results from meaningful, cognitive synthesis of sensorimotor and perceptual information. Primary emotions have an undeniable authenticity. They involve and move the client through bodily sensations, images, and evocative language. Primary emotions are inherent in the stable interaction patterns of distressed couples. Awareness of primary emotions is a first step in the creation of new perceptions, responses, and interaction patterns. This approach to restructuring intimate relationships forms the basis of Emotionally Focused Marital Therapy (EFT) (Greenberg & Johnson, 1988).

In EFT, a therapist works to access a client's primary emotional experience (e.g., anger) underlying secondary or instrumental responses (e.g., indignant helplessness) that manipulate the client's partner (e.g., via guilt). To use primary emotions as an agent of change, the EFT therapist explores and probes for primary affect. When encountered, this affect has a deeply involving, newly discovered quality. Thus, EFT therapists often help clients recognize a fear of abandonment or a need for love which underlies secondary, instrumental, anger and blame. This recognition can produce both intra-and interpersonal change. EFT therapists must identify different classes of emotional experience and adjust their interventions accordingly. This complex identification, guided by clients' nonverbal expressions, culminates in exploration of adaptive emotional responses. The therapist enables exploration by evoking emotional experience, helping clients engage fully in the experience, and using the experience to promote problem solving. This approach is radically different from therapies that teach clients to label physiological sensations or to rationally restructure their experiences through insight.

## The Impact of Emotions

*Emotion Motivates.*  Our thesis is that recognition of basic emotions enhances individual motivation and interpersonal communication. Emotions are partial causes of action in adults. Action results from emotion and from higher cognitive processes that establish goals and action plans. The probability of any given action is determined by emotion and cognition, not by unevaluated, unfelt stimuli. A stimulus has reinforcing properties only if it is experienced as emotionally rewarding or punishing or evaluated along the same dimensions. For us (unlike Skinner), emotional and cognitive responses mediate the influence of every external and internal stimulus. It is the increase of a pleasant internal feeling or thought that cues and reinforces behavior, rather than the presentation of an external antecedent and consequence.

Stimulus–response pairings of significance in human functioning are mediated by affect and cognition in a complex information structure or schema. In human functioning, it is the internal affective experience of a particular stimulus that is reinforcing. We are born with a set of innate affect-evoking stimulus patterns. It is the cognitive evaluation or appraisal of the stimulus that is conditioned rather than the behavior (Levey & Martin, 1983). On tasting spoiled fish, it is the evaluation "this tastes bad" that is conditioned. This evaluation controls future rejection of similar fish. In this manner, powerful links between cognition and affect are formed, in which evaluations are associated with biologically based affective experience. These appraisals lead to a variety of behaviors, depending on the situation. Thus, a person might eat spoiled fish to be polite or to survive a famine. Ultimately, the meaning of all aspects of a situation determines action.

*Emotion Gives Meaning.*  Our view of emotion emphasizes the fundamental role of experience in the construction and organization of reality (Greenberg & Johnson, 1986a, 1986b; 1986c; Greenberg & Safran, 1981, 1984b; Safran & Greenberg, 1986). Emotional experience is independent of logical or conscious conceptual processes. The experience of sadness or anger is more similar to "apprehension" or to "seeing" than to reasoning or problem solving. Emotional experience is "pre-reflective" and immediate. It is a constructive synthesis of incoming information. It orients the individual to the world and strongly influences self-and world-views. It informs the individual about his or her current internal states in reaction to external events. It provides the individual with comprehensive feedback about the present moment. Awareness of emotional experience provides the individual with information crucial to basic need gratification, to survival, and to effective problem solving.

Leventhal's (1979) perceptual-motor processing model of emotion involves three automatic mechanisms. These are: an expressive motor system, a schematic or emotional memory, and a conceptual system that stores rules and beliefs about emotional experiences. Expressive motor responses are elaborations or responses biologically innate in the neonate. Schemas are current representations of stored reactions to past situations. Schemas guide attention and perception in current information gathering. The conceptual system involves conscious and volitional analysis, evaluation, and storage of concrete experience. Experienced emotion is a pre-attentive synthesis of expressive motor information, implicit emotional schemas, and conceptual cognition. These components are all aspects of a person's current information processing, many of which are out of awareness and all of which are continually being integrated to form some final conscious emotional experience. In sum, emotion is interwoven with thought. It disposes to action, it is dependent on meaning, and it cannot be completely controlled by external stimuli.

*Emotion Communicates.*    Emotions serve an adaptive communicative function in social interaction (Buck, 1984; Greenberg & Safran, 1984b, Izard, 1977; Izard, Kagan, & Zajonc, 1980; Plutchik & Kellerman, 1980). Infants have innate emotional responses to specific stimulus configurations which alert caregivers. The infant shows fear at looming shadows and spider-like forms, joy at human facial configurations, and anger at restriction. Contact/comfort (Harlow & Harlow, 1969) is a primary human need as evidenced by infants' failure to thrive when human contact is insufficient (Bowlby, 1969). Infants' innate attempts to maintain optimal contact include clinging, anxiety with strangers, and distress at separation from caretakers. Evidence is emerging of an in-wired timing for different emotions. Distress and smiling appear in the first months, followed by anger and fear after 4 and 8 months (Izard, 1979), respectively.

Our argument concerning the role of emotion in therapy in general (Greenberg & Safran, 1984b, 1987) and in couples' therapy in particular (Greenberg & Johnson, 1986b, 1988), centers on emotions' adaptive role in human relationships. Emotions are omnipresent, amplifying the effect of motives on behavior, orienting individuals toward and away from objects in the physical environment, connecting individuals with people in the social environment. Emotions are rapid, direct responses to situations. In combination with higher-level processing, they organize individuals for action. Individuals who ignore their emotions are deprived of a large, relevant fund of information.

## The Social Expression of Emotional Experiences

The significance of communication in marriage and family therapy was initially highlighted in *Pragmatics of Human Communication* (Watzlawick, Beavin, & Jackson, 1967). Much of human communication involves exchanges of signals about participants' emotional states. The process of relating to other people involves the continuous sending and receiving of emotional signals. In marital therapy, the therapist must receive the emotional signals partners send to each other.

The notion of emotional expression as a biologically based signal system was first suggested by Darwin (1872). In *The Expression of Emotions in Man and Animals,* Darwin argued that facial expressions and other displays have adaptive value in social animals. These expressions, which publicize the individual's unobservable inner state, improve the prediction of individual behavior and promote more cooperation and less conflict between individuals. Reliance upon emotional expression for social coordination required the evolutionary development of sending and receiving mechanisms permitting emotion expression and identification (Buck, 1984).

The facial expression of emotion is known to be cross-culturally consistent (Ekman, 1982) and generally has priority over verbal expression when the two are inconsistent (Mehrabian, 1972). Thus, the facial expression of emotion is a powerful regulator of social interaction. For example, facial expression of aggressive emotions communicates the intent of attack and can intimidate a weak enemy into flight. Similarly, facial expression of fear signals the need for help.

Voice quality also conveys emotions in a manner that influences others. Vocal characteristics communicate dominance, submission, and sympathy. Anger, sadness, indifference, and joy are easily recognized just from vocal cues.

Nonverbal emotional expression is of great importance in marital therapy. Emotional expression is spontaneous rather than intentional and analogic rather than symbolic (Buck, 1984). Emotional expression is an outward sign of an internal state, and this nonverbal expression is not usually under the individual's volitional control. It is, therefore, influential in partners' reading of each others' intentions, particularly when they lack trust and need valid cues. The experience of emotion and its expression are interdependent such that the individual's emotional experience is conveyed to others through emotional expression and simultaneously influenced by that expression.

Communication is a complex interactional process heavily influenced by the reciprocal expression of nonverbal cues. Intimacy, for example, is controlled by reciprocal nonverbal signals including eye gaze, body lean, and spatial placement, which convey match or mismatch between individuals' expectations and desire for involvement. Nonverbal signals also compensate and offset the behavior of the partner when expectations and preferences are violated (Argyle, 1969). The emotional conversation between partners at the gestural level is an extremely important aspect of marital communication and therapy. If the therapist is to change the conversation between people in a marriage it is essential that the emotional communication be restructured.

We thus construe affect as a primary signalling system in interpersonal interaction. Emotion in humans serves a communicative function from birth. Infants are equipped with set of adaptive expressive patterns long before their capacities for exclusively-human cognitive operations are developed. From birth, infants, through certain organized behavior patterns, communicate their needs, wants, and distress. Their ability to communicate through the facial musculature is highly developed and serves as a nonverbal system of affective communication. This affective behavior is not a release but a form of communication that is either understood or misunderstood by the parent.

Affective expression, therefore, is a form of communication crucial for human interaction (Buck, 1984). For example, vulnerability tends to "disarm" while anger creates "distance." Expression of fear and vulnerability, besides evoking compassion, also communicates analogically that "this is not an attack" and often represents a major change in position from blaming or withdrawing. Similarly, expressions of sadness and pain communicate a need for support, while newly recognized anger and resentment help define differences, delineate individual boundaries in the relationship, and represent major changes in position in an interaction.

Levels of closeness–distance and dominance–submission, two critical dimensions of couple interaction (Greenberg & Johnson, 1988), can be modified via affective expression. Expression of fear or sadness tends to evoke protection and compassion in the other and can result in closeness. Anger or disgust produces clear personal and interactional boundaries, greater independence, appropriate separateness, and recognition by the other of one's rights.

In the therapy session, the emergence of emotions as *currently "lived"* and as a *change* provides useful new information to the partners. Information results directly from analogic communication and indirectly from the comparison between current and past emotional expression. In EFT, we avoid the oft-repeated litany of resentments and sadness. Instead, we seek previously unexpressed resentment and buried sadness.

Finally, communication forms and maintains each partner's self-organization, feeling states, and interactional stances. All three are interdependent field events that draw upon internal and external information (Greenberg & Johnson, 1988). Thus, a wife with a vulnerable self-organization characteristically sends different messages than does a wife with a confident self-organization. At the same time, a husband with an accepting, interested communication stance can change his vulnerable wife's self-organization as he receives her message.

## Emotion in Close Relationships

Close relationships are the best context for investigating and understanding adult human emotional experience in general and emotional processes affecting marriage in particular. The marital relationship, as the primary adult emotional bond, is an area in which feelings and their communication play a powerful role. Because so much is at stake in marriage, feelings are evoked between partners as in no other relationship. The marital relationship provides the opportunity for interdependence, the chance to have one's feelings and needs respected, and the opportunity to be the most important person to a significant other. This type of relationship between adults can promote trust, intimacy, disclosure, and the expression of intense feelings. Couples' therapy affords a unique opportunity to observe and study human affective experience and expression in the context of people's most significant affectional relationships. In close relationships, authentic emotions such as anger and sadness are most clearly expressed and emotional states such as vulnerability and love are most powerfully experienced. It is in close relationships that feelings are most influential to well-being.

Marriage is the home of most people's emotional life. Subtle changes in experience and expression of a large range of emotions related to intimacy and identity are continuous in marriage. These changes provide partners and the discriminating observer with a continuous readout of the current emotional state of each partner and of the relationship. When something goes wrong in the relationship, it is usually a change in the individual's emotional experience and expression that first indicates the problem. Emotions, as complex syntheses of all that is experienced, are the most accurate indicators of an individual's current state. Feelings, less susceptible to conscious control than thoughts, are often the best clue to what goes on within and between people.

Within our conceptualization of emotion, love is a form of attachment. Attachment theory has been elaborated by ethologists such as Bowlby (1969). From this perspective, adult sexual love is part of the innate, adaptive need for belonging and security. Human love is an emotional bond encompassing attachment behaviors, including secure behavior in the presence of the other and distressed behavior upon separation. Unlike a conceptualization of love as an economic exchange of reinforcements (Stuart, 1980), this view allows for the persistence of attachment in the face of repeated punishment.

Partners' different preferences for separateness versus connectedness is a core issue in marital conflict, and facilitation of accessibility and responsiveness (Ainsworth, 1973) is the core agenda of marital therapy. Until recently, the attachment literature has focused upon the infant–parent bond. Now this framework is increasingly applied to adult relationships (Hazen & Shaver, 1987). As much as children, adults crave easy access to attachment figures (such as marital partners), particularly in times of stress. They derive comfort and anxiety reduction from their partners. Their distress and anxiety increase when partners are inaccessible. If the affectional bond is threatened, protest behaviors such as clinging, crying, and anger coercion become more frequent and extreme. In distressed marriages, where constant disagreement or distance threaten the relationship, protests are common. When protests succeed, stress is alleviated. When protests fail, withdrawal and despair ensue.

We view attachment behaviors from the vantage point of information processing. If a set goal of proximity to an attachment figure is not maintained, then attachment behaviors will be initiated to create that proximity. Affect is the organizing force for such attachment behaviors. A more detailed discussion of the bonding and exchange paradigm of love and its implication for marital therapy may be found elsewhere (Johnson, 1986).

## Emotion in Couples Therapy

Cognitive and behavioral analyses of couples' interaction that omit emotional processes provide less than satisfying accounts of psychotherapeutic change (Jacobson & Margolin, 1979; Stuart, 1980). However, the combination of affective, cognitive, and behavioral processes adequately account for therapeutic change. The experience and expression of emotion is central to change via EFT's systemic-experiential marital therapy. Emotional expression promotes change as a means of communication and as a self-organizer and motivator of action.

*Interpersonal Change.* Although expressions of love and intimacy can be inherently reparative in intimate relationships, these expressions are more often the result of an affectively oriented couples' therapy than the means of therapy. The primary emotions expressed most often in affective therapy are fear and vulnerability, sadness and pain, anger and resentment. Major change can be brought about by reframing a negative interactional cycle in terms of the unexpressed aspect of the person's feelings and restructuring the interaction based on the need or motivation amplified by the emotional experience. A "pursue–distance" interaction can be reframed in terms of the pursuer's underlying caring or fear of isolation and the distancer's fear or unexpressed resentment. The reframe is much more likely to be experienced as valid when these previously unacknowledged feelings are experienced and expressed during therapy. The deeper the experience and expression of these feelings, the stronger the reframe and the change in the meaning of the interaction. The new expressions are themselves changed in the interactional sequence, promoting further change in interaction. Thus, evoked loneliness intensifies the need for connection and motivates more affiliative behavior. Evoking anger in the previously passive partner amplifies the need for autonomy and motivates more self-defining actions.

*Intrapersonal Change.* Affectively laden self-schemas tend to override other cues and dominate the formation of meaning. As such, they play an important role in three individual change processes (Greenberg & Safran, 1984a, 1987) pivotal to successful couples' therapy. One process involves recognition of unacknowledged basic emotions and application of this new information to problem solving. A second process involves restructuring of emotional schemata representing self, other, and situation. A third process involves modification of core cognitions that emerge for therapeutic consideration only when the client is in the aroused affective state.

Affective change occurs in each partner during successful couples' therapy. Access to primary emotions, previously omitted from partners' organization of their experience, contributes to improved self-definition and communication. In emotional restructuring, affectively charged emotional schema are aroused in order to make them amenable to change. Using a computer analogy, the underlying response program needs to be run in order to assess where the problem lies and to have the program links available for change. As Lang (1983) pointed out, the more the stimulus configuration matches the internal structure or schema, the more likely the whole structure will be evoked and once evoked will govern experience. The expression of the emotional experience embedded in its network of associations is necessary before the experience can be restructured. Thus, fear of intrusion or self-disgust needs to be evoked in order to be changed. Restructuring is achieved by allowing certain incomplete expressions to run their course and by admitting new information to the scheme, thereby altering its organization.

Inspection of episodes involving the evocation of emotion in therapy (Greenberg & Safran, 1987) reveals two change mechanisms. One is a combination of relief and recovery after the completed expression of an emotion, such as grief or anger. A second is the cognitive reorganization resulting from the expression.

Affect leads to therapeutic change in yet another way. Arousal of currently experienced emotions can provide access to state-dependent cognitions (Blaney, 1986; Bower, 1981). Core cognitions or cognitive-affective sequences involving meanings learned in particular affective states are much more accessible when that state is revived. Accessing these "hot cognitions" (Greenberg & Safran, 1987) can shed more light on couples' arguments than cool, rational, post hoc discussion. When couples recreate and relive emotions in therapy, they bring to light cognitions (e.g., "No one will ever be there for me.") that govern behavior in a way that permits inspection, clarification, and modification of interaction.

### Research on EFT

*Outcome research.* Three studies have evaluated manual-guided EFT, an approach that focuses on affective change processes. The first study (Johnson & Greenberg, 1985a) compared the relative effectiveness of EFT with cognitive-behavioral problem-solving and communication training (PS). This study randomly assigned 45 moderately distressed couples to EFT or PS or a wait-list control group. Eight sessions of each treatment were implemented by six experienced therapists committed to one of the two active treatments. Adherence to treatment manuals was monitored and maintained with a high degree of consistency. The perceived quality of the therapeutic alliance was also measured and was found to be equivalent across treatment groups.

Both treatment groups made significant gains over untreated controls on measures of goal attainment, marital adjustment, intimacy levels, and target complaint reduction. In addition, EFT had more impact than PS at the end of treatment and at follow-up on marital adjustment measured by the Dyadic Adjustment Scale (DAS) (Spanier, 1976), on intellectual intimacy measured by the PAIR (Schaefer & Olson, 1981), and on target complaints.

This study is one of the first controlled comparative studies of an experiential and behavioral treatment for marital distress and indeed one of the few controlled outcome studies of a more "intrapsychically" oriented (as opposed to behaviorally oriented) marital therapy. The EFT approach has thus been shown to have a positive effect on the couple's ability to achieve goals and change specific complaints as well as on variables such as marital satisfaction that were more directly addressed by the treatment interventions and are viewed by marital partners as being highly related to positive emotions (Broderick, 1981).

The second outcome study (Johnson & Greenberg, 1985b) involved a within-subject design in which control subjects placed on the waiting list in the first study were treated and postwait, posttreatment, and follow-up outcomes were assessed. The therapists in this study were novice marital therapists who received 12 hours of training in EFT plus ongoing weekly supervision. No significant changes on dependent measures (the same as in the first study) were found at the end of the 3 month postwait period. This finding of no change after waiting adds to evidence that marital distress is not a phenomenon prone to spontaneous remission.

After an 8-week long EFT treatment, the couples changed on all the outcome measures. The results were generally consistent with the previous study. However, the effect size (.94) was smaller. The most likely explanation for the smaller effect size is the inexperience of the therapists. Nevertheless, EFT was delineated with sufficient specificity that it could be successfully taught to novices.

In the third outcome study (Greenberg & Goldman, 1985), EFT was compared with an interactional systemic (IS) treatment that involved the use of a team behind a mirror suggesting tasks to restructure the interaction and sending paradoxical messages to reframe and prescribe the negative interaction cycle. In this study, 42 couples were randomly assigned to EFT, IS, or a wait-list control. Eligibility criteria for this study selected couples with low DAS scores in order to test the hypothesis that an interactional systemic approach would be superior to EFT for more distressed couples. The couples in this study (mean DAS score of 84) were, as a result, more distressed than the couples in the first two studies (mean DAS score of 92).

In this study, ten sessions of each treatment were implemented by seven experienced therapists committed to the approach they were using. After treatment, compared to the wait-list condition, both treatments significantly improved the quality of the marital relationship. Outcome measures included marital adjustment, goal attainment, target complaints, and conflict resolution. Contrary to our expectations, no interaction between level of distress and type of treatment emerged. The proportion of couples with improved marital adjustment (as measured by the Dyadic Adjustment Scale, Spanier, 1976) according to the stringent criteria suggested by Jacobson, Follette, and Elwood (1984), was 71%, or 10 of the 16 couples.

*Process Research.*   Ignorance of the processes leading to therapeutic improvement makes psychotherapy indistinguishable from home remedies for the common cold. Explaining how change takes place in psychotherapy by describing process pathways to outcome is the preeminent goal of psychotherapy research (Greenberg, 1986).

Our hypothesis about the process of change in EFT is that accessing underlying emotions will change partners' self-perceptions and interaction patterns. To test this hypothesis we have conducted a number of studies (Greenberg & Johnson, 1988).

One study (Johnson & Greenberg, 1988) compared the peak sessions of the two most improved and the two least improved couples who had received emotionally focused therapy. The peak sessions of the most improved couples showed deeper experiencing (Klein, Mathieu-Coughlin, & Kiesler, 1986) and more affiliation (Benjamin, 1974). The second study (Alden, 1989) selected peak and poor sessions of a sample of 11 couples using therapists' and couples' reports. A 20-minute conflict resolution episode from each session was rated for depth of experience (Klein et al., 1986) and for degree of affiliative and autonomous behavior (Benjamin, 1974). Peak sessions showed significantly greater depth of experience and more affiliative and autonomous behavior.

## CONCLUSION

In this chapter, we have addressed a number of the original points made by Dr. Skinner and we have elaborated on our view of emotional change processes in couples' therapy. In our view, emotions are not vague, covert, intangible states. The concept of prototypes helps when considering the categorization of basic emotions and more complex feelings. Specific emotions evoke specific action tendencies and play specific roles in orienting the individual to the environment. The affective consequences of action are the essence of reinforcement.

Emotion may best be viewed from an information processing perspective as a construction of elements of experience that determine the significance of environmental cues and the likelihood of particular responses. It is important to differentiate emotion as presented in couples' therapy into primary, secondary, and instrumental responses in order to tailor intervention to suit clients' individual needs.

From our perspective, primary emotion is innate and adaptive resulting in a predisposition toward particular types of thought and action. It is a powerful tool for therapeutic change both as a source of motivation and as the basis of communication and relationship definition. Our view of emotion can be translated into a specific set of change processes in marital therapy. As to the general question of how what is felt can be changed, we suggest that emotion can be recognized, reprocessed, resynthesized, or restructured, leading to change in the individual's orientation to the world. In the context of intimate attachments, we view emotions as primary motivating factors and as the very building blocks of such attachments. In the maintenance and breaking of such attachments, the strongest emotions arise and our intimate engagement with others is decided.

## REFERENCES

Ainsworth, M. (1973). The development of infant motor attachment. In B. Caldwell & H. Ricciuti (Eds.), *Review of child development research, Vol. 3* (pp. 779–795). Chicago: University of Chicago Press.

Alden, L. (1989). Peak and poor sessions of couples therapy. Unpublished master's thesis. University of British Columbia, Vancouver.

Argyle, M. (1969). *Social interaction.* New York: Atherton Press.

Benjamin, L. S. (1974). Structural analysis of social behavior, *Psychological Review, 81,* 392–425.

Berne, E. (1961). *Transactional analysis in psychotherapy.* New York: Ballantine.

Blaney, P. H. (1986). Affect and memory: A review. *Psychological Bulletin, 99,* 229–246.

Bower, G. H. (1981). Mood and memory. *American Psychologist, 31,* 129–148.

Bowlby, J. (1969). *Attachment and loss, (Vol. III): Loss, sadness and depression.* London: Hogarth.

Broadbent, D. (1977). The hidden preattentive process. *American Psychologist, 32,* 109–118.

Broderick, C. (1981). A method for deviation of areas for assessment in marital relationships. *The American Journal of Family Therapy, 9,* 25–34.

Buck, R. (1984). *The communication of emotion.* New York: Guilford Press.

Darwin, C. (1872). *The expression of emotion in men and animals.* New York: Philosophical Library.

Ekman, P. (1982). Methods of measuring facial action. In K. R. Scherer & P. Ekman (Eds.), *Handbook of methods in nonbehavioral research* (pp. 45–90). Cambridge, England: Cambridge University Press.

Ekman, P., & Friesen, W. V. (1975). *Unmasking the face.* Englewood Cliffs, NJ: Prentice-Hall.

Ekman, P., Friesen, W. V., & Ellsworth, P. C. (1982a). What are the similarities and differences in facial behavior across cultures? In P. Ekman (Ed.), *Emotion in the human face* (2nd ed., pp. 128–143). Cambridge: Cambridge University Press.

Ekman, P., Friesen, W. V., & Ellsworth, P. C. (1982b). What emotion categories or dimensions can observers judge from facial behavior? In P. Ekman (Ed.), *Emotion in the human face* (2nd ed., pp. 39–55). Cambridge: Cambridge University Press.

Greenberg, L. (1986). Change process research. *Journal of Consulting and Clinical Psychology, 54,* 4–9.

Greenberg, L., & Goldman, A. (1985). *Interactional systemic treatment manual.* Unpublished manuscript, University of British Columbia, Vancouver, B.C.

Greenberg, L., & Johnson, S. (1986a). Emotionally focused couples therapy: An affective systemic approach. In N. S. Jacobson & A. S. Gurman, (Eds.), *Handbook of Clinical and Marital Therapy* (pp. 253–276). New York: Guilford Press.

Greenberg, L., & Johnson, S. (1986b). Affect in marital therapy. *Journal of Marital and Family Therapy, 12,* 1–10.

Greenberg, L., & Johnson, S. (1986c). When to evoke emotion and why. *The Journal of Marital and Family Therapy, 12,* 19–24.

Greenberg, L., & Johnson, S. (1988). *Emotionally focused therapy for couples.* New York: Guilford Press.

Greenberg, L., & Safran, J. (1981). Encoding and cognitive therapy: Changing what clients attend to. *Psychotherapy Theory, Research and Practice, 18,* 163–169.

Greenberg, L., & Safran, J. (1984a). Hot cognition: Emotion coming in from the cold. A reply to Rachman and Mahoney. *Cognitive Therapy and Research, 8,* 591–598.

Greenberg, L., & Safran, J. (1984b). Integrating affect and cognition: A perepective on the process of therapeutic change. *Cognitive Therapy and Research, 3,* 559–578.

Greenberg, L., & Safran, J. (1987). *Emotion in psychotherapy: Affect and cognition in the process of change.* New York: Guilford Press.

Greenberg, L., & Safran, J. (1989). Emotion in Psychotherapy, *American Psychologist, 44,* 19–29.

Harlow, M., & Harlow, M. (1969). Effects of various mother–infant relationships on rhesus monkey behaviors. In B. M. Foss (Ed.), *Determinants of infant behavior, Vol. 4.* London: Methuen.

Hazan, C., & Shaver, P. (1987). Romantic love conceptualized as an attachment process. *Journal of Personality and Social Psychology, 52,* 511–524.

Horowitz, L. M., French, R., & Anderson, C. A. (1982). The prototype of a lonely person. In L. A. Peplau & D. Perlman (Eds.), *Loneliness: A sourcebook of current theory, research and therapy.* (pp. 183–205). New York: Wiley-Interscience.

Izard, C. E. (Ed.). (1977). *Human emotions.* New York: Plenum Press.

Izard, C. E. (Ed.). (1979). *Emotion in personality and psychopathology,* New York: Plenum.

Izard, C. E., Kagan, J., & Zajonc, R. B. (Eds.). (1980). *Emotion, cognition & behavior.* New York: Cambridge University Press.

Jacobson, N. S., Follette, W. C., & Elwood, R. W. (1984). Outcome research in behavioral marital therapy: A methodological and conceptual reappraisal. In K. Hahlweg & N. S. Jacobson (Eds.), *Marital interaction: Analysis and Modification,* (pp. 113–129). New York: Guilford.

Jacobson, N., & Margolin, G. (1979). *Marital therapy: Strategies based on social learning and behavior exchange principles.* New York: Bruner/Mazel.

Johnson, S. (1986). Bonds or Bargains: Relationship paradigms and their significance for marital therapy. *Journal of Marital and Family Therapy, 12,* 259–267.

Johnson, S., & Greenberg, L. (1985a). The differential effects of experiential and problem-solving interventions in resolving marital conflict. *Journal of Consulting and Clinical Psychology, 53,* 175–184.

Johnson, S., & Greenberg, L. (1985b). Emotionally focused marital therapy: An outcome study. *Journal of Marital and Family Therapy, 11,* 313–317.

Johnson, S., & Greenberg, L. (1987). Emotionally focused marital therapy: An overview. *Psychotherapy, 24,* 552–560.

Johnson, S., & Greenberg, L. (1988). Relating process to outcome in marital therapy. *Journal of Marriage and Family Therapy, 14,* 175–184.

Klein, M. H., Mathieu, I., Coughlin, P. L., & Kiesler, D. J. (1986). The Experiencing Scales. In L. Greenberg & W. Pinsof (Eds.), *The therapeutic process: A research handbook* (pp. 21–72). New York: Guilford Press.

Lang, P. J. (1983). Cognition in emotion: Concept and action. In C. E. Izard, J. Kagan, & R. B. Zajonc (Eds.), *Emotion, cognition and behavior* (pp. 192–226). New York: Cambridge University Press.

Leventhal, H. (1979). A perceptual–motor processing model of emotion. In P. Pliner, K. Blankstein, & I. M. Spigel (Eds.), *Perception of emotion in self and others. (Vol. 5)* (pp. 1–46). New York: Plenum Press.

Leventhal, H. (1982). The integration of emotion and cognition: A view from the perceptual–motor theory of emotion. In M. S. Clarke & S. T. Fiske (Eds.), *Affect and cognition: The 17th Annual Carnegie Symposium of Cognition* (pp. 121–156). Hillsdale, NJ: Lawrence Erlbaum Associates.

Leventhal, H., & Tomarken, A. (1986). Emotion: Today's problems. *Annual Review of Psychology, 37,* 565–610.

Levey, A., & Martin, I. (1983). Cognitions, evaluations and conditioning: Rules of sequence and rules of consequence. *Advances in Behavior Research and Therapy, 4,* 181–195.

Mehrabian, A. (1972). *Nonverbal communication.* Chicago: Aldine-Atherton.

Plutchik, R., & Kellerman, H. (Eds.). (1980). *Emotion: Theory, research and experience. Vol. 1. Theories of emotion.* New York: Academic Press.

Rosch, E. (1978). Principles of categorization. In E. Rosch & B. B. Lloyd (Eds.), *Cognition and categorization,* (pp. 27–48). Hillsdale, NJ: Lawrence Erlbaum Associates.

Russel, J. A., & Ridgeway, D. (1983). Dimensions underlying children's emotion concepts. *Developmental Psychology, 19,* 795–804.

Safran, J. D., & Greenberg, L. S. (1986). Hot cognition and psychotherapy process: An information processing/ecological approach. In P. Kendall (Ed.), *Advances in cognitive-behavioral research and therapy. (Vol. 5)* (pp. 144–178). New York: Academic.

Schaefer, M. T., & Olson, D. H. (1981). Assessing Intimacy: The pair inventory. *Journal of Marital and Family Therapy, 1,* 47–60.

Shaver, P., Schwartz, J., Kirson, D., & O'Connor, C. (1987). Emotion Knowledge: Further exploration of a prototype approach. *Journal of Personality and Social Psychology, 52,* 1061 – 1086.

Spanier, G. (1976). Measuring dyadic adjustment. *Journal of Marriage and the Family, 38,* 15–28.

Stuart, R. B. (1980). *Helping couples change: A social learning approach to marital therapy.* New York: Guilford Press.

Watzlawick, P., Beavin, J. H., & Jackson, D. D. (1967). *Pragmatic of human communication: A study of interactional patterns, pathologies and paradoxes.* New York: W. W. Norton.

# CHAPTER 9

# Contextual Effects in Mother–Child Interaction: Beyond an Operant Analysis

**Jean E. Dumas**
University of Western Ontario

$B$ehavioral researchers and therapists commonly acknowledge, as this volume illustrates well, that the emotional and physical health of family members is influenced not only by the discrete stimuli that individuals exchange with each other in the course of their interactions, but also by the broader socioemotional context of which the family is a part. However, the assessment of contextual effects in behavioral analysis is a fairly recent development, and the use of the results of such assessments to modify dysfunctional family interaction when appropriate has hardly begun.

This chapter argues that this state of affairs stems to a considerable extent from the fact that the operant model to which most behavioral researchers and therapists subscribe is ill-suited to assess and modify contextual effects. To support this argument, I discuss briefly the major thrust of this model and review empirical data that point to its limitations when applied to contextual studies. Particular emphasis is put on studies that have sought to evaluate the role that positive and adverse socioemotional variables characteristic of the context in which a family functions play on mother–child interactions. On the basis of this review, I suggest that behavioral research with families may benefit from a conceptual and methodological expansion. At the conceptual level, an analysis of processes that may account for the impact of contextual factors on families points beyond the mechanisms of discriminative and reinforcing control that play a central role in traditional operant assessment. At the methodological level, new procedures for assessment and intervention are being sought that adequately reflect the complexity of any contextual assessment. I discuss these issues and conclude that behavioral research with families ought to take on the challenge of complexity that contextual effects represent while insisting that such effects be studied with the rigor that is characteristic of sound work in this area.

## SKINNER'S OPERANT MODEL

"Operant psychology started with a meal," as Collier, Hirsch, and Kanarek (1977, p. 28) reminded us in their discussion and critique of Skinner's operant model. Although Skinner began his studies of animal behavior by focusing on eating in free-feeding situations, he rapidly made access to food contingent upon an arbitrary response, the operant (e.g., lever pressing). This response was brought under control of more or less complex stimuli by relying upon a physiological mechanism (deprivation) to generate, shape, and maintain it. And so the well-known three-term contingency of operant psychology was born. "The simplest contingencies involve at least three terms—stimulus, response, and reinforcer—and at least one other variable (the deprivation associated with the reinforcer) is implied" (Skinner, 1966, p. xii).

The operant model represents a psychological application of the classical experimental model of the physical sciences. Like its parent, it is reductionistic, mechanistic, and isolationist in nature. It seeks to reduce complex phenomena to their basic "building blocks." In his search for the fundamental psychological atom, Skinner elected to focus initially on the reflex as the functional unit of behavior (Skinner, 1935), a unit that could relatively easily and reliably be brought under stimulus control and that displayed obvious machine-like properties. More importantly, in his later work on schedules of reinforcement, Skinner (1953) showed that, under controlled experimental conditions, complex behaviors could be constructed on the basis of such functional units; complexity could be accounted for in terms of machine-like interactions among simple or fundamental components of behavior. The emphasis on controlled experimental conditions is of central importance here. Skinner demonstrated his ability to predict and control increasingly complex behaviors in situations in which animals were *always* isolated from their natural surroundings and limited in the number of behavioral alternatives available to them. His reliance on the classical experimental paradigm was obviously intended to maximize accurate prediction and control. It provided a reliable means of controlling for the influence of variables judged to be "extraneous" or "irrelevant" to the problem under study by the experimenter and, thus, of discovering the fundamental principles or laws that governed behavior.

Although the analytical procedure just described has played a fundamental role in the advancement of most if not all sciences since the 16th century (Randall, 1976), its applicability in psychology relies on the unspoken assumption that the principles that govern an animal's behavior in an experimental situation characterized by deprivation and isolation do not differ fundamentally from those that govern it in the natural habitat. This is not to say that Skinner considers knowledge of the animal's evolutionary history, genetic makeup, or current environmental conditions irrelevant to the analysis of behavior; rather, he assumes that such knowledge does not play a fundamental role in the understanding of the procedures that govern the acquisition, maintenance, or modification of behavior (Collier et al., 1977). However, as these authors and others (e.g., Balsam & Tomie, 1985) have shown, the stimuli that govern and the principles that appear to account for an animal's behavior in its natural habitat often differ from those typically observed in restrictive conditions in which the animal is limited to pressing a lever or pecking a key. If this is correct, the "other variable" that Skinner says is implied in the three-term contingency model (see previous quote) must be made explicit. It should be obvious that the animal's behavior depends not only on the stimulus arrangements that characterize a specific experiment but also on its context: a deprived animal will perform differently from a satiated one. There is no doubt that the experimental method has had considerable success in identifying and describing important principles of behavioral organization. However, it has not demonstrated that these principles were context-free. Consequently, when they are applied to the assessment of complex phenomena such as family interaction, care must be taken to insure that they reflect rather than disregard the context in which the behavior of interest is displayed. Typically, the classical experimental approach is ill-suited for such a task:

> "The systematic experimental method separates the variables controlling behavior from the fabric in which they are embedded, and this destroys the pattern of correlations between variables as it exists in natural situations . . . If we wish to generalize the results of behavioral research to the context in which the behavior normally occurs, we must not destroy the pattern of correlations that exists in such contexts" (Petrinovich, 1979, p. 375).

This quotation raises a fundamental question that, since its inception, has dominated behavioral analysis in general, and its application to children and families in particular: what should our unit of analysis be?

## WHICH UNIT OF ANALYSIS?

The major emphasis of any behavioral analysis is on prediction and control. Behavior can be accounted for and modified to the extent that one can demonstrate stimulus control over its occurrence (Baer, Wolf, & Risley, 1968; Skinner, 1938). For decades this emphasis has influenced the choice of a unit of analysis in assessment and treatment. Typically, in order to demonstrate stimulus control, researchers and therapists have focused on molecular rather than molar segments of behavior and have sought control in stimuli that can be observed in close spatial and temporal proximity to such segments. It is obviously easier to measure and manipulate "hitting" than "aggression" and to seek its functional control in stimuli that immediately precede it than in environmental circumstances that have long ceased to exist.

When it is successful, this focus on relatively discrete segments of behavior has the advantage of being a more reliable assessment tool than more traditional approaches (e.g., traditional medical diagnosis) and of offering practical suggestions of immediate relevance to therapeutic change (Wahler & Dumas, 1987a). However, as noted earlier and discussed in several reviews and theoretical papers (Balsam, 1985; Morris, 1982; Reese, 1982; Scarr, 1985; Willems, 1974), a focus on the assessment and modification of narrowly defined contingencies may fail to address those environmental circumstances of which a behavioral target is a function. It would appear that this is particularly true of studies of family functioning (Griest & Wells, 1983; Patterson & Reid, 1984; Wahler & Dumas, 1987a; Wahler & Fox, 1981a; Wahler & Graves, 1983). For example, a functional analysis of the pattern of interactions between a child referred for noncompliant, aggressive behavior and her mother may indicate that her aversive response class appears to be maintained by maternal failure to enforce rules and instructions and reward instances of cooperative and compliant behavior. On the basis of such an assessment, a successful intervention could rely on teaching mother to modify her behavior accordingly. There is no doubt that this approach will prove valid in many cases. In some, however, it may be too narrow because it fails to take into account the context in which the dyad's interactional problems occur. This mother's failure to interact with her child in an appropriate manner

nctionally related to her own pattern of social support
or be a part of a broader response class that may be
ional and involve other responses (e.g., emotional
ssion) besides inappropriate childrearing skills. In
cteristics that extend beyond the immediate setting
tial role in moderating the behavioral contingencies
nd modify, while the discrete behaviors which make
ncies may themselves be part of complex response
classe                ies are illustrated in a brief review of contextual
effects in i.          studies.

## CONTEXTUAL EFFECTS IN FAMILY STUDIES

### The Context as a Moderator

The behavioral predilection to describe and account for behavior on
the basis of its immediate antecedents and consequences has, often
implicitly, limited the definition of the environment to the immediate
setting in which the behavior of interest is most commonly exhibited.
This has restricted the number of independent variables generally
investigated in functional analyses. This is not to say that behavioral
researchers and therapists who work with families have remained
unaware of the influence of the socioemotional context on the contingencies they analyze. Rather, they have been reluctant to recognize
that events occurring outside the immediate setting in which a child
or family is assessed can *control* these contingencies, even though they
are removed from them in both space and time.

There is growing evidence (e.g., Dumas, 1986; George & Main,
1979; Griest & Wells, 1983; Hetherington, Cox, & Cox, 1978; Patterson & Reid, 1984; Wahler, 1980; Wahler & Graves, 1983) to support
the commonsense notion that a parent's behavior toward a child and
vice versa can be influenced by events that do not involve both interactants. Assessment and treatment outcome studies that have investigated the relation between mother– child interactions and maternal
emotional distress, marital conflict, or social isolation support this
point.

*Assessment Studies.*   There is considerable behavioral evidence to support the existence of an association between child behavior problems
and maternal self-reports of depression or general emotional distress
(Brody & Forehand, 1986; Christensen, Phillips, Glasgow, & Johnson,
1983; Forehand, Wells, & Griest, 1980; Forehand, Wells, McMahon,

Griest, & Rogers, 1982; Griest, Forehand, Wells, & McMahon, 1980; Griest, Wells, & Forehand, 1979; Mash & Johnston, 1983; Patterson, 1976; Rickard, Forehand, Wells, Griest, & McMahon, 1981). Besides discriminating between referred and non-referred families, several studies show that emotional distress also predicts maternal perception of their children. Christensen and colleagues (1983), Forehand and colleagues (1982), and Griest and colleagues (1979) found that a standardized measure of personal distress was a better predictor of maternal evaluations of child behaviors in clinic samples than were the actual behaviors on which these evaluations were supposedly based. Griest and colleagues (1980) further demonstrated that scores on the same measure were not related to the evaluations of mothers who were managing their children adequately. Brody and Forehand (1986) confirmed and extended these results in a comparison of four groups of mother–child dyads with high maternal distress/high child noncompliance, high maternal distress/low child noncompliance, low maternal distress/high child noncompliance, and low maternal distress/low child noncompliance. Results showed a significant interaction effect: Children in the first group were perceived to be more maladjusted than their counterparts in the other three groups, who did not differ from each other.

Turning to marital discord, it has often been shown that separation and divorce are more common in referred than in nonreferred families (Love & Kaswan, 1974), and intact families who seek help for child behavior problems commonly present high levels of marital strife, whether this is assessed by measures of self-reported marital satisfaction (Johnson & Lobitz, 1974; Oltmanns, Broderick, & O'Leary, 1977) or open marital conflict (Porter & O'Leary, 1980; Rutter, Yule, Quinton, Rowlands, Yale, & Berger, 1974). For example, Rutter and colleagues found that ratings of marital adjustment in families with clinically disturbed children were significantly worse than in comparison families. Specifically, these ratings, which were split on two dimensions, one reflecting discord, tension, and hostility, the other apathy and indifference, showed that child deviance was most closely associated with the first dimension. The role played by open conflict in this area is emphasized in studies that observed couples with children in laboratory situations requiring interpersonal negotiation or likely to lead to some degree of discord (Leighton, Stollak, & Ferguson, 1971; Love & Kaswan, 1974).

Finally, a dysfunctional mother–child relationship may, to some extent, reflect the adverse nature of the social context in which one or both of them function (Dumas & Wahler, 1985; Griest & Wells, 1983; Wahler, 1980; Wahler & Graves, 1983). Specifically, the dynamic nature of this context was highlighted in a study of 14 mothers who experienced severe management problems with their children and reported high levels of aversive interactions with adults in their environment (Dumas, 1986). This study compared base rate and conditional probabilities of mother and child behaviors between baseline home observations preceded by maternal self-reports of positive community contacts and comparable observations preceded by self-reports of aversive community contacts. Although the probabilities of child behavior did not differ under the two contact conditions, mothers were more likely to act in an aversive manner toward their children when they had experienced a large proportion of aversive contacts with adults prior to an observation than when they had not. More importantly, conditional probabilities indicated that this response tendency applied irrespective of child behavior antecedent. In other words, under observation conditions preceded by high levels of aversive contacts, both aversive and nonaversive child behaviors acted as if they were discriminative for aversive maternal responding. This suggests that, in some cases at least, daily changes in mother–child interactions may be related to changes in the socioemotional context in which one or both interactants function, as well as to the discrete stimuli they exchange. A similar conclusion comes from treatment outcome studies.

*Treatment Outcome Studies.* In keeping with the assessment results reported by his group, Forehand and his colleagues (1980) reported a reduction in emotional distress among mothers who completed a parent training program designed to increase parenting skills. This reduction was accompanied by improvements in child behavior, maternal childrearing skills, and maternal perceptions of their children. Similarly, Griest and colleagues (1982) found that to supplement parent training with treatment for maternal depression led to a reduction in the latter and an improvement in treatment outcome, and Patterson (1980) found that the elevated depression scores of mothers of aggressive children decreased after parent training.

Not surprisingly, evidence indicates that marital discord frequently undermines behavior therapy with children and families (Kent & O'Leary, 1976; Patterson, Cobb, & Ray, 1973; Reisinger, Frangia, & Hoffman, 1976). For example, Reisinger and colleagues reported that mothers who experienced no marital difficulties, in contrast with mothers who did, were better able to apply behavioral management techniques at home following a clinic intervention. It should be noted that contradictory results have been reported by Oltmanns and colleagues (1977). The significance of this is unclear, however, as the authors used parental reports of child behavior change as their only outcome measure. The results might have been different if a behavioral measure of outcome had also been used.

Finally, the socioemotional and socioeconomic conditions in which families function have also been related to treatment outcome. For example, Dumas and Wahler (1983) reported two identical studies of 67 families who had taken part in a standardized parent training program. Prior to treatment, scores on several measures of socioeconomic disadvantage and social isolation or "insularity" were obtained for each family. These measures formed the basis of two indices of material and social stress. Treatment effectiveness was assessed at a 1-year follow-up on the basis of behavioral home observations. In each study, results indicated a steady increase in the probability of treatment failure in the presence of disadvantage, isolation, or both. A discriminant analysis model including the two indices as predictor variables accounted for 49% of the variance in outcome and classified over 80% of the families correctly. In a separate study of a different parent training program, Dumas (1984) confirmed and extended these results. Specifically, a child's chance of benefiting from treatment in this program depended less upon his/her own characteristics than upon the extent to which his/her family had additional problems. Treatment outcome was significantly related to variables such as maternal psychopathology, marital violence, maternal education, and income, but not to the child's age, sex, birth history, or intellectual functioning.

Comparable results can be found in Wahler (1980) and Wahler and Dumas (1987b). These last two studies suggest that the association between socioeconomic adversity and treatment outcome may be functional rather than merely correlational. Both studies assessed treatment effectiveness through home observations before and during treatment and at a 1-year follow-up. In each, mothers showed significant improvements in their childrearing skills from baseline to treatment. However, in all families, these skills returned to their baseline level at follow-up.

In another, apparently conflicting, study Baum and Forehand (1981) reported 1- to 4.5-year maintenance of treatment gains in a sample of families who had participated in another standardized program. Although direct comparisons between studies are not possible, it should be noted that only one of the 34 families studied by Baum and Forehand was described as receiving welfare. In contrast, all families studied by Wahler (1980) and Wahler and Dumas (1987b) subsisted on extremely low incomes and presented multiple problems in addition to their children's behavioral difficulties. To illustrate, Wahler and Dumas worked with six families whose incomes averaged

$5,400 per year. All of them were coerced into treatment by social service agencies following abuse/neglect charges brought against the parents. Only two mothers were married and one had completed high school. Children ranged in age from 4 to 12. Their referral problems included noncompliance, property destruction, and stealing (six children), physical assault (five children—with problems ranging in severity from fist fights and use of dangerous objects to sexual molestation and killing one person), and drug use (two children). Their mothers described themselves as experiencing frequent depression and anger and reported chronic verbal threats and arguments with extended family members, spouse or boyfriend, social service agents, and neighbors (six mothers), physical violence by spouse or boyfriend (five mothers), and significant health problems (four mothers—including Lupus, cancer, and heart dysfunctions). The fact that these highly disadvantaged mothers did demonstrate significant behavior changes in the course of intervention but a return to baseline at follow-up suggests that their behavior may have been under the control of powerful contextual contingencies that intervention could only override temporarily. If this is correct, it may be more profitable to consider a parent's behavior toward a child as the product of multiple sources of influence that can act in unison rather than of discrete contingencies that parent and child exchange in brief spatial and temporal proximity. The same conclusion is supported by studies of response class phenomena.

## Contextual Effects and Response Classes

The behavioral focus on the immediate antecedents and consequences of behavior has resulted in some reluctance to recognize that, although they are often advantageously described in molecular terms and isolated for the purpose of intervention, the contingencies we study and seek to modify are usually part of complex repertoires of responses. These repertoires or response classes themselves define and provide a broader context than has traditionally been relied upon and within which we may be able to describe and account for interactional complexity. Specifically, they may be essential to describe the complex behavioral phenomena often of interest to researchers and therapists (e.g., syndromes, generalization, cross-situational consistency) and could also prove beneficial to the management of behavioral dysfunctions (Kazdin, 1982; Voeltz & Evans, 1982; Wahler & Fox, 1981b).

The concept of response class or response covariation is not new to behavior analysis with children and families (e.g., Budd, Green, & Baer, 1976; Herbert et al., 1973; Nordquist, 1971; Sajwaj, Twardosz,

& Burke, 1972; Wahler, 1975), but it has rarely been used to describe interactional phenomena or bring about behavior change. It refers to the observation that two or more behaviors are associated and that, therefore, a change in one of them reliably affects the others. Although the concept is readily understood when one refers to responses that, on the face of it, can be considered to represent the same construct (e.g., affectionate behavior may include discrete behaviors such as smiling, holding, caressing, etc.), it should not be so limited (Kazdin, 1982; Parrish, Cataldo, Kolko, Neef, & Egel, 1986). The concept requires only that changes in one behavior be reliably associated with changes in one or more other behaviors in the same individual, irrespective of the conceptual or topographical relation between them.

Reviews of the response class literature (Kazdin, 1982; Voeltz & Evans, 1982) indicate that a deliberate change in one behavior can affect other behaviors in the same person that were not manipulated directly. For example, successful reductions in disruptive, noncompliant behavior in children who presented additional behavioral problems resulted in beneficial reductions in nontargeted behaviors such as stuttering (Wahler, Sperling, Thomas, Teeter, & Luper, 1970), bedwetting (Nordquist, 1971), physical aggression (Jackson & Calhoun, 1977; Russo, Cataldo, & Cushing, 1981), and inappropriate activities (Parrish et al., 1986). The nature of response class phenomena remains poorly understood, however, as changes in nontargeted behaviors may not always be positive or significant (Breiner & Forehand, 1981). Family studies that reported positive response covariations were typically not set up to make use of the phenomenon as a behavior change procedure. In what may be the only study of its kind with children, however, Wahler and Fox (1980) relied specifically on the existence of an observed inverse covariation between child oppositional behavior and solitary toy play in an attempt to bring about such change. They were able to reduce the oppositional behavior of four referred boys at home by teaching mothers to reinforce them for increasingly longer periods of solitary play, rather than by targeting their disruptive behavior directly.

It is clear that applied work on response class effects has only begun. However, the results just reviewed suggest that studies in this area may prove useful to broaden our traditional assessment and treatment methods and may offer an empirical means of determining which behaviors to teach as alternatives to replace those we want to eliminate (Kazdin, 1982; Parrish et al., 1986; Russo et al., 1981; Wahler & Fox, 1980). Beyond these applications, response class phenomena are likely to be of major theoretical relevance. Specifically, I believe that response covariations not only describe the complex organizational properties of a person's behavioral repertoire but also exercise as much of a controlling influence on that person's behavior as the immediate environmental events that precede and follow it. For example, a mother who becomes party to an aversive exchange with a boyfriend or social worker may display a class of aversive responses both within *and* outside the setting that gave rise to this class. She may later be observed to reject her child's positive request for help, a response which could reflect not only the immediate stimuli provided by the child but also this broader aversive context. If this is correct, response class phenomena may enable us to account for more variance in this dyadic interchange than would those immediate stimuli alone. Similarly, these phenomena may help to account for the absence of therapeutic effects reported in some studies or for the failure of such effects to generalize to other settings or to be maintained at follow-up. New contingencies imposed as part of an intervention may be unable to modify specific responses because they are part of complex classes controlled by more powerful, "natural" contingencies, or may only modify them in one situation or temporarily.

The literature summarized in this section supports the conclusion that the contextual characteristics of the immediate environment in which a family functions are related to the personal adjustment of individual family members, mothers and children in particular. Although it is tempting to conclude that contextual variables exercise a causal impact on personal adjustment, it should be emphasized that the bulk of available evidence is correlational rather than functional in nature. This reflects for the most part the fact that quasi-experimental manipulations of contextual variables are almost impossible to set up, and analogue studies of direct relevance are difficult to devise. Having said that, I would contend that applied studies that have sought a semblance of manipulation of contextual factors support the notion that such factors exercise a functional impact on family interactions and are not merely correlated with them because of the joint effect of unknown third variables.

For example, dysfunctional mothers behaved differently toward their children in the course of home observations on "good days" than on "bad days" (Dumas, 1986). Similarly, mothers who participated in a parent training program demonstrated significant therapeutic gains from baseline to treatment but lost these gains at follow-up (Wahler, 1980; Wahler & Dumas, 1987b). Finally, children who showed improvements in targeted behaviors as a function of intervention evidenced reliable changes in nontargeted covariate responses (Parrish et al., 1986). Despite these findings, this argument is tenuous. Assuming that it is correct, it requires that we shift our attention from product to process variables and ask what mechanisms may account for the impact of contextual factors on family functioning.

## IN SEARCH OF PROCESS

In an attempt to account for the influence of contextual variables on family functioning, Wahler and Dumas (1984) proposed that emphasis be placed on the behavioral *and* attentional demands that are put on parents, especially mothers. In this perspective, effective parenting requires more than management skills. It requires also that parents be able to track the influence that their children's behavior, the behavior of other social agents, and the daily occurrences of nonsocial events has on their own actions, and that they be able to appraise the manner in which these variables are related. In other words, this approach assumes that dysfunctional parents may present both management and attentional skill deficits. Consequently, training in child management may not be sufficient to insure long-term change in parent–child interactions because, even with adequate skills, they may fail to monitor accurately the many environmental events that repeatedly "set them up" to act toward their children in way likely to maintain their deviance. There are two classes of events of interest here: the immediate discriminative stimuli provided by the child and, further removed in space and time, the many stimulus–response contingencies that involve the parent in interaction with the child, with other members of the environment, or with nonsocial events. Like others, I refer to the former class as stimulus events and to the latter as setting events (Bijou & Baer, 1961; Kantor, 1959; Wahler & Fox, 1981a). The concept of setting event is thus useful as a descriptive term to refer to a variety of contextual factors that are known or presumed to impinge on parenting. The many adverse events that are associated with dysfunctional family interactions and that were reviewed above are commonly discussed in the literature under the general label of stress.

### Stress and Performance

Considerable evidence from laboratory and field studies indicates that exposure to stressful setting events can lead to performance deficits in a variety of perceptual, cognitive, and behavioral tasks. Reviews of the literature (Averill, 1973; Cohen, 1980) show that these effects of stress are pervasive and highly reliable. They have been obtained with a wide variety of stressors applied to different populations in a variety of settings. Of particular relevance here is the finding that these effects are most likely to occur with stressors that induce high attentional demands or are unpredictable and/or uncontrollable.

It has been known for some time that stressful events are typically accompanied by a narrowing of attention (Baddeley, 1972; Callaway & Dembo, 1958; Easterbrook, 1959; Kahneman, 1973). Subjects who are asked to complete more than one task under stress will tend to focus on one and ignore the other(s). More precisely, experimentally induced stress has been found to reduce the efficiency with which subjects detect stimuli in their immediate environment, in part because it restricts the breadth of stimuli attended to (Broadbent, 1971; Hockey, 1973; Teichner, 1968). Typically, subjects focus on those stimuli or events they consider central in a given situation at the expense of peripheral ones (Hockey, 1970; Bacon, 1974). For example, Weltman, Smith, and Egstrom (1971) reported that inexperienced subjects exposed to a simulated dive in a pressure chamber showed increases in physiological and psychological measures of arousal. These were associated with a decrease in attention to peripheral but not central stimuli in a visual detection task.

Such perceptual decrements are commonly accompanied by both cognitive and behavioral deficits. At the cognitive level, restrictions in a subject's breadth of attention under stress are usually coupled with a reduction in the process of reexamination and verification generally observed under normal conditions (Broadbent, 1971; Hockey, 1973). These deficits have been found to be associated with major limitations in problem-solving ability. Typically, subjects fail to perceive the full range of alternatives available to them in solving a problem. As they engage in what has been described as oversimplified and stereotyped thinking, they often have difficulty discriminating between alternatives entailing success in solving that problem, usually misjudging the expected outcomes and overlooking the long-term consequences of their decisions (Janis, 1982; Mandler, 1982).

At the overt behavioral level, it would appear that responding under stress may also be viewed as disorganized and stereotypic. Although behavior under normal circumstances is highly flexible and depends to a large extent upon the behavior exhibited by others and the demands imposed by the social situation and the physical environment, behavior under stress is more limited in its topography and more aversive in nature. Studies of panic behavior (Schultz, 1964) speak to this issue, as do studies of the aftereffects of stress on social behavior. As examples of the latter, laboratory exposure to unpredictable and uncontrollable stressors has been found to be associated with a decrease in helping behavior (Cohen & Spacapan, 1978; Sherrod & Downs, 1974) and an increase in aggression (Donnerstein & Wilson, 1976) in tests conducted following exposure.

## Stress and Parenting

The experimental and human factors literature just reviewed has not, to my knowledge, been related to the parenting issues discussed earlier. However, it seems reasonable to assume that there may be parallels between a subject's skilled performance under conditions of experimentally induced stress and a parent's pattern of child interactions under conditions of stressful contextual effects such as emotional and socioeconomic difficulties. In fact, laboratory (Passman & Mulhern, 1977; Vasta & Copitch, 1981; Zussman, 1980) and field (Azar, Robinson, Hekimian, & Twentyman, 1984; Mash, Johnston, & Kovitz, 1983; Reid, Taplin, & Lorber, 1981) studies of parental behavior under stress have described effects similar to the ones just summarized. Vasta and Copitch (1981) attempted to create a laboratory analogue of child abuse by placing undergraduate students in a teaching situation with a child learner whose performance deteriorated in spite of the teacher's efforts. Participants were found to increase the intensity with which they punished the child's performance despite the fact that punishment provided no control over the latter's responses.

In another analogue study, Passman and Mulhern (1977) placed mothers in a similar teaching situation with their children. Each child's performance was again independent of maternal responses. In addition to the previous study, however, mothers had to monitor their children's performance while simultaneously attending to increasing situational demands that were directly related to their children's behavior (child interruptions) or independent of it. These demands were clearly specified in one condition but left unclear in another. Results showed that maternal punishment was a function of the children's frequency of interruptions and the level of certainty of the competing task the mothers had to attend to. More frequent interruptions and unpredictable task requirements were associated with more intense punishment than less frequent interruptions and clearly specified task demands. Comparable findings were also reported by Zussman (1980).

These results are supported by a naturalistic study of mother–child interactions in abusive and nonabusive dyads (Mash et al., 1983). The dyads were observed in an unstructured play and a structured task situation. Although the children's behavior did not differ between samples, abusive mothers attempted to exercise considerably more control over them than necessary, but only in the more stressful task situation when specific demands for performance were placed on both members of the dyads. As anticipated, these mothers reported higher levels of stress associated with childrearing and perceived their children as having significantly more behavioral problems than the nonabused children. In keeping with these results, Azar and colleagues' (1984) and Reid and colleagues' (1981) comparison of abusive and nonabusive mothers showed that the former exhibited poorer problem-solving skills. Specifically, they generated fewer solutions to common childbearing difficulties and tended to be less able to elaborate on the solutions they provided than their nonabusive counterparts.

## Stress, Marital Interaction, and Depression

Finally, and not surprisingly, there is considerable evidence that adverse contextual variables are associated with marital difficulties and depression in adults in general, and parents in particular (Belle, 1982; Brown & Harris, 1978; Coyne, Kahn, & Gotlib, 1987; Ilfeld, 1982). Of immediate interest here is not so much the fact that such associations have reliably been found, but rather that attentional deficits commonly accompany them. Evidence indicates that depressed persons tend to focus a significantly larger proportion of negative and neutral attention to themselves than do nondepressed persons (Ingram, Lumry, Cruet, & Sieber, 1987; Pyszczynski & Greenberg, 1985). Ingram (1984) speculated that this tendency is associated with a narrowing of the breadth of attention in depressed individuals, who may be limited in their ability to shift attention in response to changing situational demands. It is interesting to speculate that this narrow breadth of attention may interfere with a depressed person's problem-solving ability. Evidence suggests that depressed individuals show difficulties in their ability to solve interpersonal and social problems effectively (e.g., Gotlib & Asarnow, 1979). This deficit has been investigated extensively by Nezu and his colleagues (Nezu, 1985; Nezu, Nezu, Saraydarian, Kalmar, & Ronan, 1986; Nezu & Ronan, 1985). Their studies confirm the existence of this deficit. Specifically, they show that depressed individuals are limited in their ability to generate alternative solutions and make decisions when presented with real-life problems. In addition, Nezu (1986) showed that a problem-solving oriented therapy may be an effective means of helping depressed individuals. In keeping with this evidence, studies of maritally dysfunctional couples have repeatedly pointed to their limited problem-solving ability (e.g., Vincent, Weiss, & Birchler, 1975; Weiss, 1978) and often relied on teaching effective problem-solving as a therapeutic tool (Beach

& O'Leary, 1986; Jacobson, 1977). The Beach and O'Leary study, although preliminary, is particularly relevant in the contextual framework developed here, as it demonstrated that behavioral marital therapy that included training in effective problem-solving resulted in significant reductions in marital discord and depression in women who were clinically depressed and presented marital problems.

Taken together, the studies reviewed in this section support the conclusion that effective parents need more than specific management skills (as taught in traditional behavioral parent training) to fulfill their childrearing responsibilities. They must also be able to attend to the environmental conditions that call upon the use of these skills, an ability that appears to be negatively affected by stress. Although it is clear that the impact of environmental stressors is multifaceted, it would appear that they influence performance in families by narrowing the range of stimuli or cues to which a parent is able to attend and respond at any one time. If this is correct, it should not be surprising that stress is associated with inaccurate descriptions of the child's and others' behavior at the verbal level, and with indiscriminate and aversive responding toward the child and others at the overt behavioral level. The literature on contextual effects certainly supports these two outcomes.

The contextual analysis developed here has implications for both assessment and intervention, to which I turn briefly before closing.

## IMPLICATIONS

In his opening chapter to this volume, Skinner discusses the place of feelings in the analysis of behavior and concludes that what remains for students of the role of family variables in the regulation of emotions and health are "the contingencies of reinforcement under which things come to be seen and the verbal contingencies under which they come to be described". In other words, what remains according to Skinner is the operant model. Allow me to disagree.

The contextual effects that I have reviewed in this chapter and the proposed attentional processes that may account for their impact on family functioning describe, I believe, a behavioral control process that differs from operant control as it is traditionally interpreted in at least two ways. They demonstrate first that behavior can be controlled both by discrete, observable events *and* by relations between or among these events. In other words, relations between events can exercise a stimulus function. This is essential in an analysis of contextual effects, as it provides a means of understanding how events that are separated in space and time can influence each other, without having to rely on hypothetical cognitive or motivational constructs.

Second, contextual effects reflect a behavioral control process in which the responses we wish to assess and change do not all function as operants, and the stimuli eliciting these responses are not always discriminative. To be considered an operant, a response must be controlled by its consequences. To be considered discriminative, a stimulus must elicit a different (higher or lower) response rate when it is present than when it is absent, reflecting a history of differential reinforcement (or punishment) in its presence as compared with its absence (see Michael, 1982). However, contextual effects indicate that a stimulus need not always be associated with reinforcement or punishment to influence a response. (Reinforcement may be a sufficient cause for a stimulus and a response to become associated, but it is not a necessary cause to all such associations.) Environmental conditions can influence parent–child interchanges without necessarily acting as discriminative stimuli for such interchanges. As mentioned earlier, a mother who has an aversive exchange with a boyfriend or social worker may display a class of aversive responses both within *and* outside the setting that gave rise to this class. She may later be observed to reject her child's positive request for help, a response which could reflect not only the immediate stimuli provided by the child but also this broader aversive context. It would be difficult to see how a discriminative relation (as defined above) could have become established between this mother's interpersonal difficulties with adults and her later aversive behavior toward her child. These conclusions have implications for both assessment and intervention with children and families.

*Assessment.* In a brief history of the experimental analysis of behavior, Skinner (1980) emphasized the need to study not only stimulus–response–reinforcer contingencies but also the conditions that change the relations between these terms. These conditions, which he referred to as "third variables", are the contextual effects I have discussed. To study them will require a broadening of our unit of analysis in both space and time. We have until now relied almost exclusively on a simple, linear model that seeks to demonstrate behavior control by manipulating a small number of variables. These variables are studied on a background in which as many other variables as possible are held constant. We know, however, that behavior takes place on the background of "other" variables to which they are functionally related. These variables change continually as they influence and are influenced by the behavior on which we focus. Consequently, our functional analyses will need to include both the immediate contingencies we wish to modify and at least some of the contextual variables known or suspected to impinge upon them. In other words, instead of attempting to hold background variables constant (a practice that severely limits generalizability and is usually unfeasible in applied settings), I suggest that we seek to assess the impact of as many freely interacting factors as we can practically and economically investigate (Bronfenbrenner, 1977; Petrinovich, 1979). If social isolation or depression can affect the moment-by-moment interchanges between a mother and her child, an assessment of the nature of the relations among these variables will be necessary, even though some may find the subjective nature of such variables unappealing (see Wolf, 1978). This assessment will, in all likelihood, involve different levels of analysis and different methodologies. Events such as mother– child interchanges that are of figural interest (typically, but not necessarily the referral problems) may need to be assessed at a molecular level (e.g., via direct observation procedures), while background variables such as isolation and depression may be adequately measured at a more molar or global level (e.g., via standardized rating scales or self-report measures) (Wahler & Fox, 1981a).


*Intervention.* An assessment-in-situation approach would broaden our traditional unit of analysis by allowing us to investigate the immediate variables that control behavior without separating them from the context in which they are embedded. In all likelihood, it would also broaden our unit of intervention. Although concurrent or successive interventions to modify more than one behavior, often in two or more settings, are common, care should be taken to base such intervention on functional analyses of immediate and contextual effects. Relying on response-class phenomena may be beneficial here. For example, an intervention aimed at modifying a girl's pattern of solitary, withdrawn behavior may be most effective if it focused not only on the discrete responses that make up this pattern but also on their intercorrelations and sought to modify those responses that are most closely related as units. This intervention might be further enhanced by investigating contextual factors likely to be functionally related to the child's maladaptive behavior (e.g., marital discord). Attempts could then be made to treat the child and her family through different treatment modalities (e.g., social skills training and behavioral marital therapy) or to treat her by focusing exclusively on her parents.

## CONCLUSION

Two points should be emphasized before closing. The first one is obvious but worth repeating: A contextual approach should not be embarked upon at the expense of proper experimental design and methodology. Although they are likely to be more complex than the contingencies we have generally focused on until now, the assessment and modification of contextual variables must not sacrifice the precision that has proved to be one of the major assets of the behavioral approach. We do not have to choose between experimental rigor that ignores known contextual effects and thus lacks generalizability, and applied relevance that addresses these effects but in a methodologically inadequate manner and thus lacks credibility. The approach advocated here states only that if background variables are known to affect the maladaptive contingencies that we wish to change, these variables or some members of the response classes they represent must be assessed and, if feasible, modified. But any assessment and intervention must obviously be valid and reliable.

The second point may not be as obvious but is certainly as important: Theoretical developments must keep pace with changes in assessment and intervention. Although we understand intuitively that contextual variables can have a powerful impact on human behavior as it frames it in a web of complexity, our theoretical understanding of contextual processes lags far behind. The operant model has proved to be a useful guide but new models are needed to understand the processes of family interaction. We have relied until now almost exclusively on a conceptual model we borrowed from the physical sciences and have sought to account for complex behavior in terms of simple elements (e.g., stimuli and responses) that are interrelated in an associationist fashion. This model has been found to be too limiting for physics (Bohr, 1958; Heisenberg, 1963) and may also be too limiting for psychology. Contextual phenomena in general, and response co-variations in particular suggest, as do the attentional findings discussed above, that behavior may be organized into dynamic units or classes that extend over time and across situations. Because of such organization, a change in one member of a unit is likely to affect the unit as a whole. Thus, for example, an environmental stressor may affect an individual's perception, cognition, and behavior, even though the event itself may be "perceptual" or "behavioral" in nature. It may be time for us to develop new models that will seek to do justice to the complexity of human behavior. I believe that the concept of attention provides a useful lead for those of us interested in such development. However, it is only one lead and others will have to be followed also.

## ACKNOWLEDGMENT

Preparation of this chapter was supported by grants from the William T. Grant Foundation and the Social Sciences and Humanities Research Council of Canada.

## REFERENCES

Averill, J. R. (1973). Personal control over aversive stimuli and its relationship to stress. *Psychological Bulletin, 80*, 286–303.
Azar, S. T., Robinson, D. R., Hekimian, E., & Twentyman, C. T. (1984). Unrealistic expectations and problem solving ability in maltreating and comparison mothers. *Journal of Consulting and Clinical Psychology, 52*, 687–691.
Bacon, S. J. (1974). Arousal and the range of cue utilization. *Journal of Experimental Psychology, 102*, 81–87.
Baddeley, A. D. (1972). Selective attention and performance in dangerous environments. *British Journal of Psychology, 63*, 537–546.
Baer, D. M., Wolf, M. M., & Risley, T. R. (1968). Some current dimensions of applied behavior analysis. *Journal of Applied Behavior Analysis, 1*, 91–97.
Balsam, P. D. (1985). The function of context in learning and performance. In P. D. Balsam & A. Tomie (Eds.), *Context and learning* (pp. 1–21). Hillsdale, NJ: Lawrence Erlbaum Associates.
Balsam, P. D., & Tomie, A. (Eds.). (1985). *Context and learning.* Hillsdale, NJ: Lawrence Erlbaum Associates.
Baum, C. G., & Forehand, R. (1981). Long term follow-up assessment of parent training by use of multiple outcome measures. *Behavior Therapy, 12*, 643–652.
Beach, S. R., & O'Leary, K. D. (1986). The treatment of depression occurring in the context of marital discord. *Behavior Therapy, 17*, 43–49.
Belle, D. (1982). The stress of caring: Women as providers of social support. In L. Goldberger & S. Breznitz (Eds.), *Handbook of stress. Theoretical and clinical aspects* (pp. 496–505). New York: The Free Press.
Bijou, S. W., & Baer, D. M. (1961). *Child development I: A systematic and empirical theory.* Englewood Cliffs, NJ: Prentice-Hall.
Breiner, J., & Forehand, R. (1981). An assessment of the effects of parent training on clinic-referred children's social behavior. *Behavioral Assessment, 3*, 31–42.
Bohr, N. (1958). *Atomic physics and human knowledge.* New York: Wiley.
Broadbent, D. E. (1971). *Decision and stress.* New York: Academic Press.
Brody, G. H., & Forehand, R. (1986). Maternal perceptions of child maladjustment as a function of the combined influence of child behavior and maternal depression. *Journal of Consulting and Clinical Psychology, 54*, 237–240.
Bronfenbrenner, U. (1977). Toward an experimental ecology of human development. *American Psychologist, 32*, 513–531.

Brown, G. W., & Harris, T. (1978). *Social origins of depression. A study of psychiatric disorder in women.* New York: The Free Press.

Budd, K. S., Green, D. R., & Baer, D.M. (1976). An analysis of multiple misplaced parental social contingencies. *Journal of Applied Behavior Analysis, 9,* 459–470.

Callaway, E., & Dembo, D. (1958). Narrowed attention: A psychological phenomenon that accompanies a certain physiological change. *AMA Archives of Neurology and Psychiatry, 79,* 74–90.

Christensen, A., Phillips, S., Glasgow, R. E., & Johnson, S. M. (1983). Parental character-istics and interactional dysfunction in families with child behavior problems: A preliminary investigation. *Journal of Abnormal Child Psychology, 11,* 153–166.

Cohen, S. (1980). Aftereffects of stress on human performance and social behavior: A review of research and theory. *Psychological Bulletin, 88,* 82–108.

Cohen, S., & Spacapan, S. (1978). The aftereffects of stress: An attentional interpreta-tion. *Environmental Psychology and Nonverbal Behavior, 3,* 43–57.

Collier, G., Hirsch, E., & Kanarek, R. (1977). The operant revisited. In W. K. Honig & J. E. R. Staddon (Eds.), *Handbook of operant behavior* (pp. 28–52). Englewood Cliffs, NJ: Prenctice-Hall.

Coyne, J. C., Kahn, J., & Gotlib, I. H. (1987). Depression. In T. Jacob (Ed.), *Family interaction and psychopathology. Theories, methods, and findings* (pp. 509–533). New York: Plenum.

Donnerstein, E., & Wilson, D. W. (1976). Effects of noise and perceived control on ongoing and subsequent aggressive behavior. *Journal of Personality and Social Psychol-ogy, 34,* 774–781.

Dumas, J. E. (1984). Child, adult-interactional, and socioeconomic setting events as predictors of parent training outcome. *Education and Treatment of Children, 7,* 351–364.

Dumas, J. E. (1986). Indirect influence of maternal social contacts on mother–child interactions: A setting event analysis. *Journal of Abnormal Child Psychology, 14,* 205–216.

Dumas, J. E., & Wahler, R. G. (1983). Predictors of treatment outcome in parent training: Mother insularity and socioeconomic disadvantage. *Behavioral Assessment, 5,* 301–313.

Dumas, J. E., & Wahler, R. G. (1985). Indiscriminate mothering as a contextual factor in aggressive–oppositional child behavior: "Damned if you do, damned if you don't." *Journal of Abnormal Child Psychology, 13,* 1–17.

Easterbrook, J. A. (1959). The effect of emotion on cue utilization and the organization of behavior. *Psychological Review, 66,* 183–201.

Forehand, R., Wells, K. C., & Griest, D. L. (1980). An examination of the social validity of a parent training program. *Behavior Therapy, 11,* 488–502.

Forehand, R., Wells, K. C., McMahon, R. J., Griest, D., & Rogers, T. (1982). Maternal perception of maladjustment in clinic-referred children: An extension of earlier research. *Journal of Behavioral Assessment, 4,* 145–151.

George, C., & Main, M. (1979). Social interactions of young abused children: Approach, avoidance, and aggression. *Child Development, 50,* 306–318.

Gotlib, I. H., & Asarnow, R. F. (1979). Interpersonal and impersonal problem-solving skills in mildly and clinically depressed university students. *Journal of Consulting and Clinical Psychology, 47,* 86–95.

Griest, D. L., Forehand, R., Rogers, T., Breiner, J., Furey, W., & Williams, C. A. (1982). Effects of parent enhancement therapy on the treatment outcome and generalization of a parent training program. *Behavior Research and Therapy, 20,* 429–436.

Griest, D. L., Forehand, R., Wells, K. C., & McMahon, R. J. (1980). An examination of differences between nonclinic and behavior-problem clinic-referred children and their mothers. *Journal of Abnormal Psychology, 89,* 497–500.

Griest, D. L., & Wells, K. D. (1983). Behavior family therapy with conduct disorders in children. *Behavior Therapy, 14,* 37–53.

Griest, D. L., Wells, K. C., & Forehand, R. (1979). An examination of predictors of maternal perceptions of maladjustment in clinic-referred children. *Journal of Abnormal Psychology, 88,* 277–281.

Heisenberg, W. (1963). *Physics and philosophy.* London: Allen & Unwin.

Herbert, E., Pinkston, E., Hayden, M., Sajwaj, T., Pinkston, S., Cordua, G., & Jackson, C. (1973). Adverse effects of differential parental attention. *Journal of Applied Behavior Analysis, 6,* 15–30.

Hetherington, E. M., Cox, M., & Cox, R. (1978). The aftermath of divorce. In J. H. Stevens & M. Mathews (Eds.), *Mother– child father–child relations* (pp. 149–176). Washington, DC: National Association for the Education of Young Children.

Hockey, G. R. J. (1970). Effect of loud noise on attentional selectivity. *Quarterly Journal of Experimental Psychology, 22,* 28–36.

Hockey, G. R. J. (1973). Changes in information selection patterns in multiscore monitoring as a function of induced arousal shifts. *Journal of Experimental Psychology, 101,* 35–42.

Ilfeld, F. W. (1982). Marital stressors, coping styles, and symptoms of depression. In L. Goldberger & S. Breznitz (Eds.), *Handbook of stress. Theoretical and clinical aspects* (pp. 482–495). New York: The Free Press.

Ingram, R. E. (1984). Toward an information-processing analysis of depression. *Cognitive Therapy and Research, 8,* 443–478.

Ingram, R. E., Lumry, A. E., Cruet, D., & Sieber, W. (1987). Attentional processes in depressive disorders. *Cognitive Therapy and Research, 11,* 351–360.

Jackson, J. L., & Calhoun, K. S. (1977). Effects of two variable-ratio schedules of time-out: Changes in target and nontarget behaviors. *Journal of Behavior Therapy and Experimental Psychiatry, 8,* 195–199.

Jacobson, N. S. (1977). Problem solving and contingency contracting in the treatment of marital discord. *Journal of Consulting and Clinical Psychology, 45,* 92–100.

Janis, I. L. (1982). Decision-making under stress. In L. Goldberger & S. Breznitz (Eds.), *Handbook of stress. Theoretical and clinical aspects* (pp. 69–87). New York: The Free Press.

Johnson, S. M., & Lovitz, G. K. (1974). The personal and marital adjustment of parents as related to observed child deviance and parenting behaviors. *Journal of Abnormal Child Psychology, 2,* 193–207.

Kahneman, D. (1973). *Attention and effort.* Englewood Cliffs, NJ: Prentice-Hall.

Kantor, J. R. (1959). *Interbehavioral psychology.* Granville, OH: Principia Press.

Kazdin, A. E. (1982). Symptom substitution, generalization, and response covariation: Implications for psychotherapy outcome. *Psychological Bulletin, 91,* 349–365.

Kent, R. N., & O'Leary, K. D. (1976). A controlled evaluation of behavior modification with conduct problem children. *Journal of Consulting and Clinical Psychology, 44,* 586–596.

Leighton, L. A., Stollak, G. E., & Ferguson, L. (1971). Patterns of communication in normal and clinical families. *Journal of Consulting and Clinical Psychology, 36,* 252–256.

Love, L. R., & Kaswan, J. W. (1974). *Troubled children: Their families, schools, and treatments.* New York: Wiley.

Mandler, G. (1982). Stress and thought processes. In L. Goldberger & S. Breznitz (Eds.), *Handbook of stress. Theoretical and clinical aspects* (pp. 88–104). New York: The Free Press.

Mash, E. J., & Johnston, C. (1983). Sibling interactions of hyperactive and normal children and their relationship to reports of maternal stress and self-esteem. *Journal of Clinical Child Psychology, 12,* 91–99.

Mash, E. J., Johnston, C., & Kovitz, K. (1983). A comparison of the mother–child interactions of physically abused and nonabused children during play and task situations. *Journal of Clinical Child Psychology, 12,* 337–346.

Michael, J. L. (1982). Distinguishing between discriminative and motivational functions of stimuli. *Journal of the Experimental Analysis of Behavior, 37,* 149–155.

Morris, E. K. (1982). Some relationships between interbehavioral psychology and radical behaviorism. *Behaviorism, 10,* 187–216.

Nezu, A. M. (1985). Differences in psychological distress between effective and ineffective problem solvers. *Journal of Counseling Psychology, 32,* 135–138.

Nezu, A. M. (1986). Cognitive appraisal of problem solving effectiveness: Relation to depression and depressive symptoms. *Journal of Clinical Psychology, 42,* 42–48.

Nezu, A. M., Nezu, C. M., Saraydarian, L., Kalmar, K., & Ronan, G. F. (1986). Social problem solving as a moderating variable between negative life stress and depressive symptoms. *Cognitive Therapy and Research, 10,* 489–498.

Nezu, A. M., & Ronan, G. F. (1985). Life stress, current problems, problem solving, and depressive symptoms: An integrative model. *Journal of Consulting and Clinical Psychology, 53,* 693–697.

Nordquist, V. M. (1971). The modification of a child's enuresis: Some response–response relationships. *Journal of Applied Behavior Analysis, 4,* 241–247.

Oltmanns, T. F., Broderick, J. E., & O'Leary, K. D. (1977). Marital adjustment and the efficacy of behavior therapy with children. *Journal of Consulting and Clinical Psychology, 45,* 724–729.

Parrish, J. M., Cataldo, M. F., Kolko, D. J., Neef, N. A., & Egel, A. L. (1986). Experimental analysis of response covariation among compliant and inappropriate behaviors. *Journal of Applied Behavior Analysis, 19,* 241–254.

Passman, R. H., & Mulhern, R. K. (1977). Maternal punitiveness as affected by situational stress: An experimental analogue of child abuse. *Journal of Abnormal Psychology, 86,* 565–569.

Patterson, G. R. (1976). The aggressive child: Victim and architect of a coercive system. In E. J. Mash, L. A. Hamerlynck, & L. C. Handy (Eds.), *Behavior modification and families. 1. Theory and research* (pp. 267–316). New York: Brunner/Mazel.

Patterson, G. R. (1980). Mothers: The unacknowledged victims. *Monographs of the Society for Research in Child Development, 45,* (5, Serial No. 186).

Patterson, G. R., Cobb, J. A., & Ray, R. S. (1973). A social engineering technology for retraining the families of aggressive boys. In H. E. Adams & I. P. Unikel (Eds.), *Issues and trends in behavior therapy* (pp. 139–210). Springfield, IL: Charles C. Thomas.

Patterson, G. R., & Reid, J. B. (1984). Social interactional process within the family: The study of the moment-by-moment family interactions in which human social development is embedded. *Journal of Applied Developmental Psychology, 5,* 237–262.

Petrinovich, L. (1979). Probabilistic functionalism. A conception of research method. *American Psychologist, 34,* 373–390.

Porter, S., & O'Leary, K. D. (1980). Types of marital discord and child behavior problems. *Journal of Abnormal Child Psychology, 8,* 287–295.

Pyszczynski, T., & Greenberg, J. (1985). Depression and preference for self-focusing stimuli after success and failure. *Journal of Personality and Social Psychology, 49,* 1066–1075.

Randall, J. H. (1976). *The making of the modern mind. A survey of the intellectual background of the present age.* New York: Columbia University Press.

Reese, H. W. (1982). Behavior analyses and life-span developmental psychology. *Developmental Review, 2,* 150–161.

Reid, J. B., Taplin, P. S., & Lorber, R. (1981). A social interactional approach to the treatment of abusive families. In R. Stuard (Ed.), *Violent behavior: Social learning approaches to prediction, management, and treatment* (pp. 83–101). New York: Brunner/ Mazel.

Reisinger, J. J., Frangia, G. W., & Hoffman, E. H. (1976). Toddler management training: Generalization and marital status. *Journal of Behavior Therapy and Experimental Psychiatry, 7,* 335–340.

Rickard, K. M., Forehand, R., Wells, K. C., Griest, D. L., & McMahon, R. J. (1981). A comparison of mothers of clinic-referred deviant, clinic-referred nondeviant, and nonclinic children. *Behavior Research and Therapy, 19,* 201–205.

Russo, D. C., Cataldo, M. F., & Cushing, P. J. (1981). Compliance training and behavioral covariation in the treatment of multiple behavior problems. *Journal of Applied Behavior Analysis, 14,* 209–222.

Rutter, M., Yule, B., Quinton, D., Rowlands, O., Yule, W., & Berger, M. (1974). Attainment and adjustment in two geographical areas: III. Some factors accounting for area differences. *British Journal of Psychiatry, 125,* 520–533.

Sajwaj, T., Twardosz, S., & Burke, M. (1972). Side effects of extinction procedures in a remedial preschool. *Journal of Applied Behavior Analysis, 5,* 163–175.

Scarr, S. (1985). Constructing psychology. Making facts and fables for our times. *American Psychologist, 40,* 499–512.

Schultz, O. P. (Ed.). (1964). *Panic and behavior: Discussion and readings.* New York: Random House.

Sherrod, D. R., & Downs, R. (1974). Environmental determinants of altruism: The effects of stimulus overload and perceived control on helping. *Journal of Experimental Social Psychology, 10,* 468–479.

Skinner, B. F. (1935). The generic nature of the concepts of stimulus and response. *Journal of General Psychology, 12,* 40–65.

Skinner, B. F. (1938). *The behavior of organisms: An experimental analysis.* New York: Appleton-Century-Crofts.

Skinner, B. F. (1953). *Science and human behavior.* New York: Macmillan.

Skinner, B. F. (1966). Preface to the seventh printing of *The behavior of organisms. An experimental analysis.* New York: Appleton-Century-Crofts.

Skinner, B. F. (1980). The experimental analysis of operant behavior: A history. In R. W. Rieber & K. Salzinger (Eds.), *Psychology: Theoretical-historical perspectives* (pp. 191–202). New York: Academic Press.

Teichner, W. H. (1968). Interaction of behavioral and physiological stress reactions. *Psychological Review, 75,* 271–291.

Vasta, R., & Copitch, P. (1981). Simulating conditions of child abuse in the laboratory. *Child Development, 52,* 164–170.

Vincent, J. P., Weiss, R. L., & Birchler, G. R. (1975). Dyadic problem-solving behavior as a function of marital distress and spousal vs. stranger interaction. *Behavior Therapy, 6,* 475–487.

Voeltz, L. M., & Evans, I. M. (1982). The assessment of behavioral interrelationships in child behavior therapy. *Behavioral Assessment, 4,* 131–165.

Wahler, R. G. (1975). Some structural aspects of deviant child behavior. *Journal of Applied Behavior Analysis, 8,* 27–42.

Wahler, R. G. (1980). The insular mother: Her problems in parent–child treatment. *Journal of Applied Behavior Analysis, 13,* 207–219.

Wahler, R. G., & Dumas, J. E. (1984). Changing the observational coding styles of insular and noninsular mothers: A step toward maintenance of parent training effects. In R. F. Dangel & R. A. Polster (Eds.), *Parent training: Foundations of research and practices* (pp. 379–416). New York: Guilford Press.

Wahler, R. G., & Dumas, J. E. (1987a). Family factors in childhood psychopathology. A coercion-neglect model. In T. Jacob (Ed.), *Family interaction and psychopathology. Theories, methods, and findings* (pp. 581–627). New York: Plenum.

Wahler, R. G., & Dumas, J. E. (1987b). Stimulus class determinants of mother–child coercive interchanges in multi-distressed families: Assessment and intervention. In J. D. Burchard & S. N. Burchard (Eds.), *Prevention of delinquent behavior* (pp. 190–219). Newbury Park, CA: Sage.

Wahler, R. G., & Fox, J. J. (1980). Solitary toy play and time out: A family treatment package for children with aggressive and oppositional behavior. *Journal of Applied Behavior Analysis, 13*, 23–39.

Wahler, R. G., & Fox, J. J. (1981a). Setting events in applied behavior analysis: Toward a conceptual and methodological expansion. *Journal of Applied Behavior Analysis, 14*, 327–338.

Wahler, R. G., & Fox, J. J. (1981b). Response structure in deviant child–parent relationships: Implications for family therapy. In D. J. Bernstein (Ed.), *Nebraska Symposium on Motivation, Vol. 29* (pp. 1–46). Lincoln, NE: University of Nebraska Press.

Wahler, R. G., & Graves, M. G. (1983). Setting events in social networks: Ally or enemy in child behavior therapy? *Behavior Therapy, 14*, 19–36.

Wahler, R. G., Sperling, K., Thomas, M., Teeter, N., & Luper, H. (1970). The modification of childhood stuttering: Some response–response relationships. *Journal of Experimental Child Psychology, 9*, 411–428.

Weiss, R. L. (1978). The conceptualization of marriage from a behavioral perspective. In T. J. Paolino & B. S. McCrady (Eds.), *Marriage and marital therapy* (pp. 165–239). New York: Brunner/Mazel.

Weltman, G., Smith, J. E., & Egstrom, G. H. (1971). Perceptual narrowing during stimulated pressure-chamber exposure. *Human Factors, 13*, 99–107.

Willems, E. P. (1974). Behavioral technology and behavioral ecology. *Journal of Applied Behavior Analysis, 7*, 151–166.

Wolf, M. M. (1978). Social validity: The case for subjective measurement or how applied behavior analysis is finding its heart. *Journal of Applied Behavior Analysis, 11*, 203–214.

Zussman, J. U. (1980). Situational determinants of parental behavior: Effects of competing cognitive activity. *Child Development, 51*, 792–800.

# CHAPTER 10

# Influences of Parental Mood on Parent Behavior

**Ernest N. Jouriles**
University of Houston
**K. Daniel O'Leary**
State University of New York at Stony Brook

Skinner argued in chapter 1 that emotions do not cause behavior and that there is no acceptable science of feeling. This position on the role of emotion in understanding and predicting behavior is similar to Skinner's familiar stance on cognition (Skinner, 1953, 1974). The burgeoning empirical literature on the influences of cognitive processes on behavior (see Bandura, 1986, for a review) indicates that Skinner's stance on cognition was erroneous. Similarly, a growing body of literature on the effects of mood on behavior suggests that Skinner's position regarding emotion is also mistaken. In this chapter we review theory and empirical data on the influences of parental mood on parent behavior. We believe that a comprehensive understanding of parent–child interaction patterns necessitates an examination of the roles of parental mood.

Parental mood is frequently implicated as an important determinant of parent behavior. Theoretical models of parenting (e.g., Belsky, 1984; Patterson, 1982) often highlight the importance of parental mood and mood disorders, particularly depression, in influencing parent–child interaction patterns. Depressed parental moods have been consistently associated with child problems (see Beardslee, Bemporad, Keller, & Klerman, 1983; Forehand, McCombs, & Brody, 1987; Orvaschel, 1983, for reviews), and one hypothesis frequently offered to explain this relationship is the influence of depression on parent behavior. It is also interesting to note that many parents report that their moods influence the way they parent. For example, a colleague of ours, Linda Pfiffner, asked 65 mothers of toddler-aged children who participated in studies on family interaction (Jouriles, Pfiffner, & O'Leary, 1988; Pfiffner & O'Leary, 1987): "How often do you think that the kind of punishment you give your child depends on your mood?" Nine percent of the mothers indicated that their mood influenced their punishments "most of the time," 15% of the mothers claimed that their mood "often" influenced their punishments, 51% of the mothers stated that their punishments "sometimes" or "once in a while" depended upon their mood, and 25% of the mothers indicated that their mood "hardly ever" influenced their punishments.

In spite of converging opinions regarding the effects of mood on parenting, empirical work on this topic is sparse, with the bulk of the available data focusing on correlates of parental depression. At this point, little knowledge exists regarding the behaviors potentially influenced by mood or the mechanisms by which mood might alter parent behavior. In this chapter, we review several theories on how mood might affect cognitive processes, and we consider how these effects may influence parent behavior. Next, we consider mood's role as an operant and its influence on parenting from this perspective. Then we provide a brief review of the available empirical literature assessing the relationship between parental mood and observations of parent behavior. We conclude the chapter with a presentation of experimental data assessing the influence of parental mood on parenting.

Before we begin it is necessary to clarify what is meant by the term "mood." Moods are hypothetical constructs depicting an individual's emotional state. Researchers typically infer the existence of moods from a variety of behavioral referents (e.g., skeletal muscle activity, physiological measurements, speech patterns, and verbal reports). The term "mood" is sometimes distinguished from the terms "affect" and "emotion" (e.g., Lewis & Michalson, 1983), with moods referring to emotional or affective states of relatively long duration. In the present discussion we will not make this distinction, and the term mood will refer to both transient and long-term emotional states. Also, mood is frequently characterized along two dimensions: (a) hedonic tone (positive-negative), and (b) arousability. The present discussion focuses on the positive-negative dimension of mood. With these clarifications made, we now turn to our major focus: The influence of parental mood on parent behavior.

## THEORETICAL HYPOTHESES ON THE EFFECTS
## OF MOOD ON PARENT BEHAVIOR

### Mood as a Setting Event

Most of our thinking about the way that mood impacts parent behavior has centered around mood operating as a setting event (see Wahler, 1980; Panaccione & Wahler, 1986). Using terminology from the behavioral perspective, setting events represent circumstances that influence "stimulus-response relationships already built up through past organism–environmental interactions" (Wahler & Fox, 1981, p. 329). That is, a specific child behavior (the stimulus) has the potential of eliciting a wide variety of parental responses. Setting events determine, in part, the specific parental response elicited. The notion that parental moods operate as setting events suggests that parents respond to child behavior differently when experiencing positive, relative to negative, moods. Several hypotheses on the mechanisms by which positive and negative parental moods might differentially influence parents' responses toward their children are presented in the next paragraphs.

One hypothesis that has been advanced by a number of psychologists is that mood enhances the perception and/or processing of mood-congruent material (Beck, 1967; Ingram, Smith, & Brehm, 1983; Rehm, 1977). Specifically, individuals in positive moods may selectively attend to and think about positive environmental events or selectively ignore negative environmental events. Individuals in negative moods, on the other hand, may operate in an opposite manner. Applying this reasoning to parenting suggests that parents in positive moods spend greater amounts of time watching and thinking about their children's positive behavior. Conversely, parents in negative moods presumably devote more time toward their children's negative behavior.

Social interaction theory and research (Burgess & Huston, 1979; Patterson, 1982) suggest that what parents perceive in terms of their children's behavior systematically elicits different parental responses. In other words, parents who are noticing and thinking about positive child behaviors may be more likely to respond toward their children in a positive manner (e.g., compliments, praise statements). On the other hand, when a parent is noticing and thinking about negative child behaviors, positive parental behaviors might decrease and parental attempts at correcting and punishing child behavior may increase.

A second potential mechanism pertaining to the effects of mood on parenting emanates from data on the impact of mood on memory.

Numerous experimental studies indicate that mood influences the accessibility of positive and negative cognitions (see Blaney, 1986, for a review). Specifically, positive moods tend to increase the probability that individuals retrieve positive information from memory, and they tend to decrease the probability that individuals retrieve negative information from memory. Negative moods, on the other hand, typically have the opposite effect. The impact of mood on memory is often used to suggest a reciprocal relationship between mood and cognition (Isen, Shalker, Clark, & Karp, 1978; Rehm & Naus, 1988; Teasdale, 1983). That is, individuals in negative moods tend to access negative thoughts from memory, and these negative thoughts function to maintain negative moods.

The first hypothesis suggested that mood might differentially influence the amount of time parents attend to their children's positive versus negative behavior. The effects of mood on memory suggest that mood might also bias *how* parents view or interpret their children's behavior when they are attending to it. Specifically, when parents are in positive moods they may be more likely to access positive memories about their children's behavior. Thus, when parents have to make inferences about their children and their children's behavior (e.g., when interpreting ambiguous child activities or when ascribing motives to their children), parents in positive moods may be more likely to access positive thoughts and make positive inferences. Parents in negative moods, on the other hand, might be expected to do just the opposite. For example, a father in a negative mood may hear his 4-year-old son crying in another room and interpret this crying in a negative manner (e.g., "That kid is trying to irritate me." or "He's fighting with his brother again."). This negative interpretation, in turn, may facilitate the occurrence of a negative response (e.g., "Shut up!"). The same father, however, in a positive mood may be more likely to think of other reasons why his child may be crying (e.g., "He's hurt or needs help.") and respond in a more positive manner (e.g., check to see why his son is crying).

A third way in which mood might influence how parents act toward their children is by lowering parental thresholds for tolerating child behavior (Lahey, Conger, Atkeson, & Treiber, 1984; Schaughency & Lahey, 1985). The threshold might be conceptualized to represent a variety of emotional and/or physiological factors (e.g., emotional capacity or patience to deal with general life events; arousal level, etc.), and the reduction of this threshold is hypothesized to make certain child behaviors more aversive to parents. That is, child behaviors that are not normally considered to be problems may be experienced as such when parents are in negative moods. As a result, parents may be more likely to act in a controlling or punitive manner (i.e., issue more commands and reprimands to correct and punish child behavior) when in negative, relative to positive, moods. Alternatively, lowered thresholds for dealing with child behavior may be associated with parents minimizing interaction with their children. That is, parents may recognize that they have less tolerance for child behavior when they are in negative moods and simply avoid interacting with their children during these times.

We have presented three hypotheses on how mood might operate as a setting event and facilitate the occurrence of certain parent behaviors. This discussion has referred to mood as a dichotomous variable (positive vs. negative). It is also important to recognize that the intensity of moods within the positive and negative ranges of the continuum (e.g., extremely positive affective states as opposed to mildly positive affective states) may also play an important role in determining parent behavior.

Several theorists have hypothesized that intense and/or depressed moods decrease the amount of thought and attention parents are able to devote toward their parenting behavior. For example, Kahneman (1973) posited that individuals possess a finite capacity for attending to events, and the experience of intense emotion is thought to draw from this limited supply. According to Kahneman, the experience of intense emotion presumably competes with cognitive activities and environmental factors for an individual's attention. That is, intense affective states may distract parents from attending to or thinking about their children's behavior. A similar conceptualization of the effects of intense emotional states has been presented by Isen, Means, Patrick, and Nowicki (1982). This conceptualization suggests that intense moods increase "cognitive load," and the increase in cognitive load is compensated for by a reduction in mental activity elsewhere. Also, Ellis and Ashbrook (1987) proposed that depressed moods, relative to nondepressed moods, reduce attentional capacity and "cognitive effort" available for processing other environmental events. In other words, depressed moods limit the cognitive resources that can be directed toward other environmental stimuli (e.g., child behavior).

A study conducted by Zussman (1980) illustrates how a cognitive activity that competes for a parent's attentional supply may influence parent behavior toward children. In an experimental design, Zussman examined parent–child interaction (parent with one preschool-aged child and one toddler-aged child) when parents were performing a mental anagram. The task was conceptualized as a cognitive activity that competed with child-care responsibilities for the parent's attention. Zussman found that the presence of the competing cognitive task had substantial effects on parenting. Specifically, when parents were performing the mental anagram, positive parental behaviors (e.g., frequency of interaction, responsiveness, and support) directed toward the preschool-aged children decreased and negative parental behaviors (e.g., criticisms, punishments) directed toward the toddler-aged children increased. Zussman interpreted these data to suggest that competing cognitive activities may cause parents to engage in "minimal parenting." In other words, competing cognitive activities decreased the amount of parent–child interaction and the delivery of positive parent behaviors, and simultaneously increased the amount of negative parent behaviors directed toward children.

To the extent that intense or depressed moods operate in a manner similar to Zussman's cognitive task, one might infer that parents who are experiencing these moods may interact less with their children and attend to fewer of their children's activities. Similarly, these parents may exert less effort when interacting with their children and bypass opportunities to deliver appropriate positive and negative feedback. Also, under these circumstances parents may make more "mistakes" in their parenting. For example, parents experiencing intense moods may tend to "give in" to demands or tantrums (e.g., giving a crying child a candy bar in order to quiet the child down) because it is an "easy" way to quiet their children. Also, since parents tend to believe that power-assertive methods yield immediate child compliance with little parental effort (Baldwin, 1955; Patterson, 1976), parents may tend to use such methods when experiencing strong or depressed emotional states.

Another way in which mood, and the intensity of the mood state, might influence parent behavior is by operating as an energy source that increases the intensity of parents' behavior (see Lewis & Michalson, 1983; Zillman, 1979, for reviews). In other words, specific moods and the intensities of these moods may act to energize behavior and, consequently, increase or decrease the intensity of parental actions toward a child. This notion suggests that a parent who is spanking his or her child and who is simultaneously experiencing intense feelings of anger would be more likely to deliver a harsher spanking (i.e., hit the child harder and more frequently) than when the same parent is experiencing less intense feelings of anger. Similarly, when a parent is playing with his or her child and is simultaneously experiencing intense feelings of elation, the parent may be more talkative and playful with his or her child than when the parent is experiencing mild feelings of elation.

## Mood as a Consequence

The preceding discussion has focused on the role of mood as a setting event in influencing parent behavior toward children. Mood might also be conceptualized to act as an operant. This conceptualization of mood is related to the issue of hedonism (i.e., individuals act with a motive of increasing pleasure and reducing pain), with the emotional consequences of an act regarded as an important cause of that act. This viewpoint suggests that positive moods represent a form of reinforcement and negative moods represent a form of punishment. As such, parent behaviors that result in positive moods should increase, and those that dispel positive moods should decrease. Similarly, parent behaviors that cause negative moods should decrease and the behaviors that alleviate negative moods should increase.

According to this viewpoint, knowledge of how a parent's behavior affects the parent's mood is important in predicting future parent behaviors. For example, consider a situation in which a child is misbehaving and the parent is experiencing a negative mood. If the parent strikes the child and this alleviates the parent's negative mood, an operant conceptualization suggests that the parent should be more likely to strike his or her child under similar circumstances (i.e., other situations when the child is misbehaving and the parent is in a negative mood). Similarly, the frequency of parent-initiated interactions should be predicted by parental moods resulting from parent–child interaction. Specifically, parent-initiated interactions should be more frequent in families where parents experience positive moods as a result of interacting with their children, and less frequent in families where parents experience negative moods when interacting with their children.

The results from several studies suggest that this reasoning may have merit. For example, as we indicated at the beginning of the chapter, numerous studies have linked parental depression with child problems (Beardslee et al., 1983; Forehand et al., 1987; Orvaschel, 1983). This relationship is often discussed in a unidirectional manner, with parental depression influencing child behavior. However, theories on the etiology of depression (e.g., Lewinsohn, Weinstein, & Shaw, 1969) and parent–child interaction (Patterson, 1982, p. 280–283) as well as anecdotal reports from parents indicate that the relationship is bidirectional. Assuming that parental interaction with problematic children can cause depressed parental moods, it would be predicted that parent–child interaction should decrease in families with problematic children. This hypothesis is consistent with the findings of numerous studies indicating lower levels of parental involvement in families with behavior problem children and adolescents (see Maccoby & Martin, 1983; Snyder & Patterson, 1987 for reviews). Further, the results from a short-term longitudinal study (Maccoby, Snow, & Jacklin, 1984) suggest that "difficultness" ratings for sons at 12 months of age predict decreases in maternal involvement with their sons during a teaching task at 18 months of age. Again, although low parental involvement is typically conceptualized as a cause of child problems, it can easily be argued that parents do not enjoy interacting with problematic children and, therefore, avoid it at times.

In sum, a number of hypotheses have been presented to explain how parental mood may influence parent behavior toward children. These hypotheses included: (a) increasing the likelihood that parents will attend to and/or process the occurrence of positive or negative child behaviors; (b) influencing the way parents access memories to interpret their children's behavior; (c) altering parents' thresholds for dealing with child behavior; (d) competing with other environmental factors for parents' attention (i.e., increasing cognitive load); (e) energizing the parent; and (f) operating as a reinforcer or punisher for the performance of particular parent behaviors. Figure 10.1 depicts the major constructs and pathways of influence described in this chap-

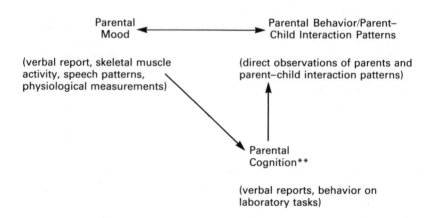

**Cognition refers to the mental processes of perceiving, judging, remembering, and reasoning.

It should be noted that parental behavior may also influence parental cognition and that parental cognition may influence parental mood. These pathways of influence, however, were not emphasized in this chapter and, consequently, are not depicted in the model above.

FIG. 10.1. Parental mood and parent behavior toward children: constructs, measures of constructs, and major pathways of influence.

ter. Although there are some contradictions between theories of how mood might affect particular parent behaviors, most of the theories suggest that positive parental moods should facilitate the performance of positive parental behaviors (e.g., compliments, praise) and increase the frequency of parent–child interaction. Negative parental moods, on the other hand, should increase the likelihood of negative parental behaviors (e.g., criticisms, reprimands), and decrease the frequency of parent–child interaction.

## EMPIRICAL WORK ON THE RELATIONSHIP BETWEEN MOOD AND PARENTING

Data examining the relationship between parental mood and parent behavior is primarily correlational and focuses on parental depression. These studies, however, are pertinent to the present discussion because they suggest specific behaviors that may be influenced by parental mood. It is important to emphasize at the outset that the correlational findings cannot be interpreted as evidence indicating that parental mood affects parent behavior. First, the syndrome of depression includes symptoms other than negative moods (e.g., fatigue, diminished ability to concentrate), and depression is often accompanied by family factors that have been correlated with dysfunctional parenting (e.g., marital discord, social isolation). Thus, variables other than parental mood may be responsible for an association between parental depression and dysfunctional forms of parent–child interaction. Second, due to the correlational nature of these studies, it is unclear whether parent behavior represents a cause or effect of depressed parental mood. Because of these problems, our review of the correlational data is brief. It includes only a few studies incorporating observational measures of parent–child interaction patterns. In addition, the review focuses primarily on parenting with children in the 3- to 6-year-old age range.

### Correlational Data

Panaccione and Wahler (1986) examined the relationships between maternal depression and mother–child interaction. The sample consisted of 33 mother–preschooler dyads (mean child age = 4.4 years). Mother–child dyads were observed for 30-minute periods on at least 3 separate days, and mother and child aversive and affectionate behaviors were coded. Maternal depression was assessed with the Beck

Depression Inventory (BDI). Results from the study indicated a moderate positive correlation between maternal depression and maternal aversive behavior ($r = .43$). Depression, however, was not significantly correlated with any of the other observational codes.

Radke-Yarrow, Cummings, Kuczynski, and Chapman (1985) examined patterns of mother–child attachment in families with depressed and nondepressed mothers. The literature on attachment suggests that emotional availability, responsiveness toward children's needs, and warm and involved parenting are all associated with the development of secure attachments in children. The sample consisted of 99 mother–child dyads: 42 of the mothers were diagnosed with unipolar depression, 12 of the mothers were diagnosed with minor depression, 14 of the mothers were diagnosed with manic depression, and 31 of the mothers comprised the normal control group. Children ranged from 16 to 44 months in age. Patterns of attachment were assessed with a modified version of Ainsworth and Wittig's (1969) Strange Situation. Results from the study indicated that secure attachments were more common among children of control mothers and mothers with minor depression relative to children of mothers with unipolar depression and manic depression. Further, secure attachments were more frequent in children of mothers with unipolar depression relative to manic depression.

In addition to examining the quality of attachment in children of depressed and nondepressed mothers, Radke-Yarrow and colleagues (1985) assessed mothers' mood and expressed affect during the course of their investigation (3 days) and examined how these measures related to mother–child attachment. Self-reports of maternal mood were obtained on each of the three days on which the study was conducted, and approximately 6 hours of observational data were collected on expressed affect. Mothers of securely attached children expressed positive affect more often and negative affect less often than mothers of insecurely attached children. Interestingly, there were no significant differences between diagnostic groups in expression of affect, and there were no significant findings involving mothers' self-reports of mood.

Mills, Puckering, Pound, and Cox (1985) contrasted the parental interaction patterns of 39 depressed mothers and 21 normal controls. Children in this sample were 2 to 3 years of age. Mother–child interaction was assessed during two home observation sessions (at least 3 hours of observational data had been collected on each dyad). Behaviors coded were maternal "links" (maternal behaviors expanding upon the child's ongoing behavior or introducing new material relevant to the child's ongoing behavior) and child responses to these links.

Maternal depression was determined via interview. Results from the study indicated that depressed and nondepressed mothers emitted a similar number of links, however, a greater proportion of the links emitted by nondepressed mothers were responded to by the toddlers. These data were interpreted to suggest that depressed mothers failed to "mesh" in their interactions with their children. Reasons offered by the authors for this failure to mesh included poor maternal timing in the delivery of links and a failure to deliver links appropriate for their particular child.

Forehand, Lautenschlager, Faust, and Graziano (1986) examined the association between maternal BDI scores and the frequency of beta commands in a sample of 37 clinic-referred children. Children in this sample ranged from 2 to 9 years of age. Beta commands were defined as "vague or interrupted commands to which the child cannot comply" (p. 74). Mother–child dyads were observed during four 40-minute home observation periods. Results from the study indicated a small, but significant, positive correlation between maternal depression and frequency of beta commands ($r = .25$).

Observational studies examining the association between parental depression and parent behavior in samples of children at other age levels report similar findings. For example, studies conducted with infants and toddler-aged children indicate attachment disturbances in families with depressed parents (Gaensbauer, Harmon, Cytryn, & McKnew, 1984; Lyons-Ruth, Zoll, Connell, Grunebaum, 1986; Zahn-Waxler, Cummings, McKnew, & Radke-Yarrow, 1984). Sameroff, Seifer, and Zax (1982) found depressed mothers to be less spontaneous, happy, vocal, and proximal toward their 4-month-old children than nondepressed mothers. In a sample involving children ranging from 3 to 16 years of age, Hops and colleagues (Hops et al., 1987) found that depressed mothers emitted higher rates of dysphoric affect and lower rates of happy affect than normal control mothers. It should also be noted that several studies incorporating observational assessments have failed to find significant associations between parental depression and parent behavior (Forehand, Wells, & Griest, 1980; Johnson & Lobitz, 1974; Rogers & Forehand, 1983).

In sum, the majority of studies attempting to link depression with parent behavior suggest that depressed parents behave more negatively toward their children and less positively toward their children than nondepressed parents. Also, the results from a couple of studies (Forehand et al., 1986; Mills et al., 1985) suggest that mothers in depressed moods may communicate less clearly with their children than mothers who are not in depressed moods. That is, depressed parents tend to deliver a greater number of statements that fail to elicit responses from their children (links) and a greater number of vague commands that make it difficult for their children to comply (beta commands).

## Experimental Data

Few researchers have attempted to examine the influence of mood on parent behavior or isolate the effects of mood, independent of the syndrome of depression, on parent–child interaction patterns. Zekoski, O'Hara, and Wills (1987) assessed the impact of depressed and elated maternal moods on mother–infant interaction. Their sample consisted of 30 mother–infant dyads who were randomly assigned to one of three mood induction conditions (a neutral, depressed, or elated mood induction). In this experiment, all mothers participated in a mood induction procedure, which involved reading statements from cards and attempting to feel the mood suggested by the statements (e.g., Neutral: "Utah is the Beehive State." Depressed: "I have had too many bad things happen in my life." Elated: "God, I feel great."). Following the mood induction, mothers played with their infants for a 10-minute period. Mothers and independent observers reported their perceptions of the mother–infant interaction that followed the mood induction on a 5-item questionnaire. Two of the questionnaire items assessed mothers' behavior toward the infant: (a) the contingent responsiveness of the infant to the mothers' positive behavior, which was rated on a scale ranging from −100 (mother's efforts prevent baby from responding positively) to +100 (mother's efforts cause baby to respond positively); and (b) the sufficiency of the mother's behavior in eliciting positive infant behavior, which was rated on a scale ranging from 0 to 100. According to observers' reports, infants of mothers in the depressed mood induction condition were lower on contingent responsiveness than infants of mothers in the neutral or elation mood induction conditions. Observer reports on contingent responsiveness failed to discriminate between the neutral and elation mood induction conditions, and mothers' reports on this measure failed to discriminate between any of the three groups. In addition, observers and mothers reported that mothers in the depressed mood condition were "less sufficient" in eliciting positive infant responses than mothers in the other two conditions. There were no significant differences on this measure between the neutral and elation conditions.

In our own research, we attempted to determine whether maternal mood influenced parent behavior with preschool-aged children. Our sample consisted of 40 mother–son dyads, with children ranging from 46 to 72 months in age. The experimental procedure involved two separate visits to our laboratory. During one of the visits mothers participated in a positive mood induction and during the other visit mothers participated in a negative mood induction. The order of the mood inductions was counterbalanced across subjects. Each mood induction consisted of listening to music while using imagery to relive a past negative or positive experience (depending on the condition the parent was in during that visit). The mood inductions each lasted for 8 minutes.

Observations of mother–son interaction followed the mood inductions. Observations were conducted in a playroom setting and consisted of a variety of interaction situations including: free play, two separate sorting tasks, and cleanup. Only the data collected during the free play situation are discussed in the present chapter. During free play interaction, mothers were instructed to allow their sons to play with the toys in the room. The free play lasted for 5 minutes and was always the first situation observed following the mood induction. Table 10.1 describes the observational codes for parent behavior during the free play.

Our assessment of the mood manipulation involved three measures. First, mothers completed the depression and hostility scales of the Multiple Affect Adjective Checklist (MAACL; Zuckerman & Lubin, 1965). The MAACL is a widely used self-report scale containing adjectives reflecting positive and negative moods (e.g., happy, glad, blue, irritated, sad). Second, mothers participated in a counting time test, which involved counting from one to ten into a tape recorder. Speech rate was later coded (in seconds) by observers blind to the experimental

TABLE 10.1
Observation Codes During the Free Play Interaction

| Parent Behavior Coded | Definition |
| --- | --- |
| Positive Statements | Any verbalization that expressed a favorable judgement of an activity, product, or attribute of the child. In addition, parental attempts at eliciting child activity in a positive manner (e.g., "I have a real fun thing for you to do") were coded in this category. |
| Negative Statements | Any verbalization that found fault with an activity, product, or attribute of the child. |
| General Verbal Interaction | This category included: teaching interactions, phrases that reflected or repeated child verbalizations, phrases that described objects or activities, and questions that did not request the child to do something. |

condition. On the basis of previous research (Clark, 1983), we predicted that mothers in the negative mood condition would count more slowly than mothers in the positive mood condition. Finally, mothers completed an 8-item "incentive" measure, which assessed mothers' desire to engage in a variety of activities (e.g., go to a party, engage in physical exercise). Similar measures have indicated that individuals in negative moods report less incentive to engage in activities than individuals in positive moods (Clark, 1983). Mood assessments were conducted immediately prior to the mother–son interaction period. The results of the mood induction on these four dependent variables are presented in Table 10.2. All manipulation checks demonstrated the predicted pattern of results.

Mood effects on parent behaviors during the free play interaction are presented in Table 10.3. Matched-pairs t-tests indicated that mothers issued fewer positive statements and engaged in less general verbal interaction with their children during the negative mood condition relative to the positive mood condition. These findings are consistent with the correlational data linking maternal depression with low levels of positive parent behaviors (Hops et al., 1987; Sameroff et al., 1982) and low levels of parent–child interaction (Sameroff et al., 1982). It is interesting to note, however, that we failed to find an influence of maternal mood on negative statements directed toward children. This result is inconsistent with the findings of several studies linking maternal depression with negative maternal behaviors directed toward children (Panaccione & Wahler, 1986; Hops et al., 1987).

In order to better understand *why* our mood manipulation failed

TABLE 10.2
Means for Mood Assessments Conducted After the Positive
and Negative Mood Conditions[a]

|  | Positive Mood Condition | Negative Mood Condition | T Value |
|---|---|---|---|
| MAACL Depression Subscale | 8.6 | 21.7 | 9.58** |
| MAACL Hostility Subscale | 6.5 | 13.2 | 6.49** |
| Incentive Measure | 47.9 | 33.7 | 6.46** |
| Counting Time Test | 7.0 | 8.2 | 4.14* |

[a] The higher the scores on the MAACL depression and hostility subscales, the more depressed and hostile, respectively, subjects reported that they felt. The higher the score on the Incentive Measure, the more incentive subjects reported to engage in positive activities. Means for the Counting Time Test represent the number of seconds it took subjects to count from one to ten.

*$p < .01$
**$p < .001$

to influence maternal negative statements, additional analyses were conducted. First, we examined whether maternal reports of depressive symptoms, assessed with the Beck Depression Inventory (BDI) prior to the beginning of the experimental procedure, were associated with the present study's assessment of maternal negative statements. In order to do this, a two-level variable of maternal depression was created by performing a median split on mothers' reports of depressive symptoms (median = 7.5). Mothers in the high depression group ($n$ = 20) had a mean BDI of 12.4, and mothers in the low depression group ($n$ = 20) had a mean BDI of 3.6. Then, negative statements from the positive and negative mood conditions were collapsed, and a between group t-test was computed. Results from this analysis indicated that mothers in the high depression group delivered significantly more negative statements ($M$ = 2.6) than mothers in the low depression group ($M$ = 1.4, $t(38)$ = 1.96, $p$ = .05). This result is consistent with findings from previous correlational studies (Panaccione & Wahler, 1986; Hops et al., 1987) and suggests that the failure to find a significant effect of mood on negative statements was not due solely to method differences between studies. Specifically, the lack of an experimental effect of mood on maternal negative statements does not appear to be the result of our observational situation or negative statements code.

In light of this finding, we assessed whether the mood manipulation influenced depressed mothers (i.e., mothers with BDI scores above the median) differently than nondepressed mothers. In order to test this hypothesis we conducted a series of mixed design analyses of variance (ANOVAs). In all analyses, maternal depression served as the between-group factor (group status was determined by the median split on the BDI, as stated above) and maternal mood (positive vs. negative) was the manipulated within-subject factor. A separate mixed

TABLE 10.3
Means for Observations of Parent Behavior During the Positive
and Negative Mood Conditions[a]

|  | Positive Mood Condition | Negative Mood Condition | T Value |
|---|---|---|---|
| Positive Statements | 1.0 | 0.5 | 2.09* |
| Negative Statements | 1.1 | 0.9 | 1.00 |
| General Verbal Interaction | 35.9 | 29.9 | 4.09** |

[a] Means represent the number of 6-second intervals in which the bahavior occurred.
* $p < .05$
** $p < .001$

design ANOVA was computed for each measure of mood (MAACL depression subscale, MAACL hostility subscale, incentive to engage in positive activities, and the counting time test). None of these analyses yielded a significant between group effect nor a significant interaction between maternal group status and the mood manipulation. Thus, mothers in the depressed and nondepressed groups did not appear to be differentially affected by the mood induction procedures.

Finally, we assessed whether maternal depression interacted with the mood inductions in predicting maternal negative statements. Again, a mixed design ANOVA was conducted with depression group status as the between-group factor and positive and negative maternal mood as the manipulated within-subject variable. This analysis failed to yield a significant interaction in predicting maternal negative statements.

In sum, the present results indicated that the mood inductions influenced the frequency of general verbal interaction and positive statements emitted by mothers. These findings are consistent with correlational studies linking parental depression with these two parenting variables and suggests that mood, independent of other factors in the syndrome of depression, plays an important role in influencing these behaviors. The mood inductions, however, failed to influence maternal negative statements. Interestingly, an assessment of symptoms of maternal depression prior to the experimental procedure predicted maternal negative statements, collapsed across the two mood induction conditions. Analyses attempting to detect whether maternal depression interacted with the mood induction procedure failed to yield significant results. The pattern of findings regarding negative statements can be interpreted a number of ways. For example, earlier in the review we mentioned that the syndrome of depression is associated with a variety of other symptoms and stressors (e.g., lack of energy, marital discord). These other factors, or a combination of these factors, may be more responsible for the association between parental depression and negative maternal statements than parental mood. Alternatively, the present findings may simply reflect differences between experimentally induced moods and moods experienced during major depressive episodes. Further research is necessary for a more comprehensive understanding of the association between depression and maternal negative statements.

## CONCLUSION

In conclusion, the theory and research presented in this chapter suggests that a better understanding of mood effects on parent behavior may be necessary for advancements in theory and clinical practice. From a theoretical standpoint, research in this area may help contribute to our understanding of the causes of parent behavior. Clinically, knowledge concerning the effects of parental mood on parent behavior may be useful in efforts at enhancing the quality of parent–child interaction patterns. If parental moods are found to be important determinants of parenting, clinical efforts directed at improving parenting skills may need to address factors that adversely affect parental moods.

## ACKNOWLEDGMENTS

The authors wish to acknowledge the assistance of Annette Farris, Stephanie Lecompte, and Renee McDonald in the preparation of this chapter.

## REFERENCES

Ainsworth, M., & Wittig, B. (1969). Attachment and exploratory behavior of one-year-olds in a strange situation. In B. Foss (Ed.), *Determinants of infant behavior* (Vol. 4, pp. 111–136). London: Methuen.

Baldwin, A. L. (1955). *Behavior and development in childhood.* New York: Dryden.

Bandura, A. (1986). *Social foundations of thought and action: A social and cognitive theory.* Englewood Cliffs, NJ: Prentice-Hall.

Beardslee, W. R., Bemporad, J., Keller, M. B., & Klerman, G. L. (1983). Children of parents with major affective disorder: A review. *American Journal of Psychiatry, 140,* 825–832.

Beck, A. T. (1967). *Depression: Clinical, experimental, and theoretical aspects.* New York: Harper and Row.

Belsky, J. (1984). The determinants of parenting: A process model. *Child Development, 55,* 83–96.

Blaney, P. H. (1986). Affect and memory: A review. *Psychological Bulletin, 99,* 229–246.

Burgess, R. L., & Huston, T. L. (1979). *Social exchange in developing relationships.* New York: Academic Press.

Clark, D. M. (1983). On the induction of depressed mood in the laboratory: Evaluation and comparison of the Velten and musical procedures. *Advances in Behavioral Research and Therapy, 5,* 27–49.

Ellis, H. C., & Ashbrook, P. W. (1987). Resource allocation model of depressed mood states on memory. In K. Fielder & J. Forgas (Eds.), *Affect, cognition, and social behavior.* Toronto: Hagrefe.

Forehand, R., Lautenschlager, G. J., Faust, J., & Graziano, W. G. (1986). Parent perceptions and parent–child interactions in clinic-referred children: A preliminary investigation of the effects of maternal depressive moods. *Behavioral Research and Therapy, 24,* 73–75.

Forehand, R., McCombs, A., & Brody, G. H. (1987). The relationship between parental depressive mood states and child functioning. *Advances in Behavioral Research and Therapy, 9,* 1–20.

Forehand, R., Wells, K., & Griest, D. (1980). An examination of the social validity of a parent training program. *Behavior Therapy, 11,* 488–502.

Gaensbauer, T. J., Harmon, R. J., Cytryn, L., & McKnew, D. H. (1984). Social and affective development in infants with a manic depressive parent. *American Journal of Psychiatry, 141,* 223–229.

Hops, H., Biglan, A., Sherman, L., Arthur, J., Friedman, L., & Osteen, V. (1987). Home observations of family interactions of depressed women. *Journal of Consulting and Clinical Psychology, 55,* 341–346.

Ingram, R. E., Smith, T. W., & Brehm, S. S. (1983). Depression and information processing: Self-schemata and the encoding of self-referent information. *Journal of Personality and Social Psychology, 45,* 412–420.

Isen, A. M., Means, B., Patrick, R., & Nowicki, G. (1982). Some factors influencing decision-making strategy and risk taking. In M. S. Clark & S. T. Fiske (Eds.), *Affect and cognition: The 17th Annual Carnegie Symposium on cognition* (pp. 243–261). Hillsdale, NJ: Lawrence Erlbaum Associates.

Isen, A. M., Shalker, T. E., Clark, M., & Karp, L. (1978). Affect, accessibility of material in memory, and behavior: A cognitive loop? *Journal of Personality and Social Psychology, 36,* 1–12.

Johnson, S. M., & Lobitz, G. K. (1974). The personal and marital adjustment of parents as related to observed child deviance and parenting behaviors. *Journal of Abnormal Child Psychology, 2,* 193–207.

Jouriles, E. N., Pfiffner, L. J., & O'Leary, S. G. (1988). Marital conflict, parenting, and toddler conduct problems. *Journal of Abnormal Child Psychology, 16,* 197–206.

Kahneman, D. (1973). *Attention and effort.* Englewood Cliffs, NJ: Prentice-Hall.

Lahey, B. B., Conger, R., Atkeson, B. M., & Treiber, F. A. (1984). Parenting behavior and emotional status of physically abusive mothers. *Journal of Consulting and Clinical Psychology, 52,* 1062–1071.

Lewis, M., & Michalson, L. (1983). *Children's emotions and moods: Developmental theory and measurement.* New York: Plenum Press.

Lewinsohn, P. M., Weinstein, M., & Shaw, D. (1969). Depression: A clinical-research approach. In R. D. Rubin & C. M. Frank (Eds.), *Advances in behavior therapy* (pp. 231–240). New York: Academic Press.

Lyons-Ruth, K., Zoll, D., Connell, D., & Grunebaum, H. U. (1986). The depressed mother and her one-year-old infant: Environment, interaction, attachment, and infant development. In E. Z. Tronick & T. Field (Eds.), *Maternal depression and infant disturbance: Vol. 34. New Directions for Child Development* (pp. 61–82). San Francisco: Jossey-Bass Inc.

Maccoby, E. E., & Martin, J. A. (1983). Socialization in the context of the family: Parent–child interaction. In P. H. Mussen (Ed.), *Handbook of Child Psychology: Socialization, personality, and social development,* (pp. 1–101). New York: Wiley.

Maccoby, E. E., Snow, M. E., & Jacklin, C. N. (1984). Children's dispositions and mother–child interaction at 12 and 18 months: A short-term longitudinal study. *Developmental Psychology, 20,* 459–472.

Mills, M., Puckering, C., Pound, A., & Cox, A. (1985). What is it about depressed mothers that influences their children's functioning? In J. E. Stevenson (Ed.), *Recent research in developmental psychopathology* (pp. 11–17). Oxford: Pergamon Press.

Orvaschel, H. (1983). Maternal depression and child dysfunction: Children at risk. In B. Lahey & A. Kazdin (Eds.), *Advances in clinical child psychology, Vol. 6* (pp. 169–197). New York: Plenum.

Panaccione, V. F., & Wahler, R. G. (1986). Child behavior, maternal depression, and social coercion as factors in the quality of child care. *Journal of Abnormal Child Psychology, 14,* 263–278.

Patterson, G. R. (1976). The aggressive child: Victim and architect of a coercive system. In L. A. Hamerlynck, L. C. Handy, and E. J. Mash (Eds.), *Behavior modification and families: Theories and research. Vol. 1;* pp. 267–316. New York: Brunner/Mazel.

Patterson, G. R. (1982). *Coercive family process.* Eugene, OR: Castalia Publishing Company.

Pfiffner, L. J., & O'Leary, S. G. (1987). *Effects of maternal discipline and nurturance on toddler behavior and affect.* Unpublished manuscript, State University of New York at Stonybrook.

Radke-Yarrow, M., Cummings, E. M., Kuczynski, L., & Chapman, M. (1985). Patterns of attachment in two-and three-year-olds in normal families and families with parental depression. *Child Development, 56,* 884–893.

Rehm, L. P. (1977). A self-control model of depression. *Behavior Therapy, 8,* 787–803.

Rehm, L. P., & Naus, M. J. (1988). A memory model of emotion. Paper presented at *Contemporary psychological approaches to depression: Treatment, research and theory,* R. E. Ingram (Chair), Conference at San Diego State University, San Diego, CA.

Rogers, T. R., & Forehand, R. (1983). The role of parent depression in interactions between mothers and their clinic-referred children. *Cognitive Therapy and Research, 7,* 315–324.

Sameroff, A. J., Seifer, R., & Zax, M. (1982). Early development of children at risk for emotional disorder. *Monographs of the Society for Research in Child Development, 47,* (Serial No. 199).

Schaughency, E. A., & Lahey, B. B. (1985). Mothers' and fathers' perceptions of child deviance: Roles of child behavior, parental depression, and marital satisfaction. *Journal of Consulting and Clinical Psychology, 53,* 718–723.

Skinner, B. F. (1953). *Science and human behavior.* New York: MacMillan.

Skinner, B. F. (1974). *About behaviorism.* New York: Alfred A. Knopf.

Snyder, J., & Patterson, G. R. (1987). Family interaction and delinquent behavior. In H. C. Quay (Ed.), *Handbook of juvenile delinquency* (pp. 216–243). New York: John Wiley & Sons.

Teasdale, J. D. (1983). Negative thinking in depression: Cause, effect or reciprocal relationship? *Advances in Behavioral Research and Therapy, 5,* 3–25.

Wahler, R. G. (1980). The insular mother: Her problems in parent–child treatment. *Journal of Applied Behavior Analysis, 13,* 207–219.

Wahler, R. G., & Fox, J. J. (1981). Setting events in applied behavior analysis: Toward a conceptual and methodological expansion. *Journal of Applied Behavior Analysis, 14,* 327–338.

Zahn-Waxler, C., Cummings, M., McKnew, D. H., & Radke-Yarrow, M. (1984). Altruism, aggression, and social interactions in young children with a manic depressive parent. *Child Development, 55,* 112–122.

Zekoski, E. M., O'Hara, M. W., & Wills, K. E. (1987). The effects of maternal mood on mother–infant interaction. *Journal of Abnormal Child Psychology, 15,* 361–378.

Zillman, D. (1979). *Hostility and aggression.* Hillsdale, NJ: Lawrence Erlbaum Associates.

Zuckerman, M., & Lubin, B. (1965). *Manual for the Multiple Affect Adjective Checklist.* San Diego, CA: Educational and Industrial Testing Service.

Zussman, J. U. (1980). Situational determinants of parental behavior: Effects of competing cognitive activity. *Child Development, 51,* 792–800.

# CHAPTER 11

# A New Look at Emotions and the Family: A Model of Effective Family Communication

**Elaine A. Blechman**
University of Colorado at Boulder

How does the family's emotional climate, in interaction with innate individual factors, promote either competence or psychopathology in family members?

Skinner, in his opening chapter to *Emotions and the Family: For Better or for Worse,* answers this question with reference to the behavior analytic principles that have revolutionized the science of psychology in this century. He concludes that although feelings are a kind of behavior that can be subsumed under these principles, "as a source of data for science . . . [they are] . . . largely of historical interest only" (Skinner, p. 9, this volume).

In response to Skinner's chapter, and mindful of how their own work has been shaped by his ideas, the other contributors to this volume argue for an expanded behavioral perspective on emotions in the family. Feelings must be subjected to rigorous scientific study because they provide unique information about the environment's impact on individual well-being. Happy family members are primed for competence with family and friends, at work and at school; unhappy family members are primed for incompetence and psychopathology.

Are the family's emotional climate and family members' moods epiphenomena or do they signal the operation of a mechanism that influences learning and performance of skills required for achievement and social competence? Addressing this question, I developed an empirical model of effective family communication consistent with the findings of contributors to this volume and with my own work (Blechman, 1990).

In this chapter, I summarize and integrate contributions to this book with reference to the family communication model. The model is meant to encourage debate and research about the nature of effective family communication and about its mechanism of influence.

The model of effective family communication presented addresses the confluence of nature and nurture with three propositions:

1. A good mood signals prolonged contact with pleasurable consequences and optimal preparedness for learning and performance.
2. Effective communication promotes good moods in all family members.
3. Family members who are often in good moods are primed for competence and shielded from psychopathology, despite cultural, biological, and socioeconomic handicaps.

## A Clinical Example

The following clinical example will be used to illustrate the perspectives of contributors and the proposed model. A family recently called for help with their 13-year-old, school-phobic son, David. David never liked leaving his mother; in the last 2 years he has persistently called on various aches and pains to justify not going to school. David's two older brothers are married and avoid coming home. Mrs. Smith is a depressed, middle-aged woman who has never worked outside the home and looks about twice her husband's age. Mr. Smith (who is a year older than his wife) is a successful, handsome attorney who has had a number of affairs during his marriage. He drinks frequently and excessively. Violent arguments between the couple, which sometimes end with physical assault on Mrs. Smith, have increased in the last few years. According to Mrs. Smith, her love for her children and her pride keep her in the marriage. According to Mr. Smith, feelings of contempt tempered with pity and loyalty for his wife and love for his children keep him in the marriage.

## Skinner's Perspective on Feelings

Skinner (chapter 1) focuses on environmental forces that influence the individual's expression of specific feelings, particularly love, anxiety, and fear. He provides an evolutionary, radical-behaviorist position on the private experience of feelings and their public expression.

He suggests that physiology, individual learning history, and cultural evolution combine to determine what bodily sensations are felt, and how these feelings are expressed to others.

Skinner's analysis might be applied to Mrs. Smith's feelings in the following way. Arguments between the Smiths often begin when Mrs. Smith sees her husband drinking and begins to cry. He asks his wife, "What's wrong?" She says: "I'm afraid you are drinking too much. I'm worried that you will get drunk again and hit me." Her public expression of fear derives from: (a) her current, private bodily condition (i.e., churning gut); (b) public antecedents to this bodily condition (i.e., seeing her husband finish a bottle of brandy); (c) her history of reinforcement (i.e., she usually feels her gut churning when she sees her husband getting drunk. When drunk, her husband often hits her. When she cries, he often backs away and stops hitting her.); and (d) how she communicates her history of reinforcement (e.g., "I am afraid you will hit me again.")

Presenting the radical behaviorist perspective, Skinner might emphasize that Mrs. Smith's feeling of fear is caused not by an unobservable, hypothetical trait of fearfulness or masochism, or solely by a churning gut. Her expression of fear is a product of private and public, past and present circumstances that have taught her to label a churning gut in a situation of impending physical harm as "fear," to expect physical harm when her husband is drunk, and to expect the cessation of harm when she cries.

Skinner acknowledges the existence of feelings without granting them motivational status as a cause of behavior. Fear does not cause Mrs. Smith's churning gut or her reports of fear. A hysterical personality trait evidenced by perpetual provocation of violence does not cause her fear. The cause of her fear (including her bodily condition and her emotional expression at the sight of her husband getting drunk) resides in Mr. Smith's past violence when drunk. Although Skinner does not place all the causes of feelings in the external environment, he argues that physiologists are best trained to study the private bodily conditions that contribute to feelings, whereas behavior analysts are best equipped to study the public conditions that contribute to feelings.

Presenting a cultural evolutionary perspective, Skinner conceives of three reinforcement mechanisms that contribute to the survival of the species, the individual, and the culture, via three types of love. In eros, the physical pleasure of sexual activity has a genetic, biochemical basis and contributes to the survival of the species. In philia, the behavioral tendency to seek out people who provide reinforcing consequences is based in the individual's learning history and contributes to the individual's survival. In agape, group members' preference for people whose actions contribute to the greater good is based in cultural values and contributes to the culture's survival.

Expression of positive and negative feelings shape human relationships; friendship, love, marriage, family, and culture. In turn, these feelings are shaped by biological, individual historical, and cultural conditions. Therefore, when things go wrong at the level of individual, family, or culture, Skinner's advice is to alter the controlling history of reinforcement. Following this advice is no easy matter. Control over significant aspects of the individual's reinforcement history lies in the hands of the family. Families often resist yielding power to their members and changing the status quo.

For better or for worse, families exercise substantial control over their members' feelings, thoughts, and actions. In the case of Mrs. Smith, her feelings of fear (rather than anger) are surely maladaptive for every family member in the long run. However, in the short run, her fearful behavior is often reinforced by the termination of her husband's violence. Thus, to follow Skinner's advice about altering the individual's history of reinforcement, this woman's emotional behavior must be observed and altered in the context of her own family.

## A NEW BEHAVIORAL LOOK AT EMOTIONS IN THE FAMILY

Skinner's acknowledgment of the origins of feelings in physiology, reinforcement history, and culture is elaborated upon by several contributors to this volume (e.g., Hatfield & Rapson; Plutchik & Plutchik; Greenberg & Johnson). In fact, R. Plutchik is widely cited for his psychoevolutionary theory of emotions. Skinner's emphasis upon environmental reengineering as a means of improving individual adjustment and generating social change is concretized and amplified by other contributors to this book. Some contributors focus on describing and altering the individual's skills, including the ability to communicate and cope (Plutchik & Plutchik), regulate emotions (Saarni & Crowley), recruit and provide social support (Wills). Other contributors focus on describing and altering the family's skills, including the ability to communicate and regulate negative affect (Lindahl & Markman; Greenberg & Johnson; Dumas; Jouriles & O'Leary), and to establish a level of intimacy acceptable to husband and wife (Hatfield & Rapson; Fruzzetti & Jacobson).

Although Skinner questions the value of scientific inquiry into emotions, his work has contributed to a "dramatic change in how we think about emotions," particularly, "the shift from an intrapsychic to a relational view of emotions" (Campos, 1989, p. 633).

Without Skinner's revolution of psychology, few chapters in this volume could have been written. The field of behavioral family therapy, represented by a number of contributors to this volume, encompassing innovative treatments aimed at improving marital and parenting relationships, is a child of Skinner's imagination.

Yet, in response to Skinner, the other contributors make four cogent arguments that demand an expanded behavioral perspective on the family's emotional climate.

*1. Include Physiology.* Skinner suggests that if behavior analysts study emotions, they proceed by focusing on the external expression of emotions along with the external antecedents and consequences of emotions. In his opinion, physiologists should be left to study the bodily conditions that precede overt emotional expression.

Hatfield and Rapson begin their chapter with an example of the interdependence of social interaction and physiology. In accord with their example, other contributors argue that physiology must be included in the study of emotions given a continuous interplay between private experience and public emotional expression (e.g., Fruzzetti & Jacobson; Greenberg & Johnson; Hatfield & Rapson; Jouriles & O'Leary; Lindahl & Markman; Plutchik & Plutchik). Their perspective is consistent with an "emerging theme in the study of emotional development" that "autonomic responses are being reconceptualized as relational phenomena" (Campos, Campos, & Barrett, 1989, p. 398).

The model of family communication presented later, suggests that effective family communication helps family members attain the subjective experience of good moods. A good mood signals that physiological conditions (such as vagal tone and autonomic arousal) are at optimal levels for learning and performance.

*2. Include Social Context.* Dumas (chapter 9) argues most emphatically for a new operant perspective, taking into account molar interpersonal context. He contends that a four-part contingency (context-antecedent-behavior-consequence) must replace the usual three-part contingency (antecedent-behavior-consequence). In the expanded paradigm, context moderates the influence of history of reinforcement on current behavior.

Dumas describes lawful relationships between stress and behavior. Consistent with these relationships, a stressful family context disrupts parenting behavior and obstructs direct attempts to improve parenting behavior. The problem of Mrs. Smith can be used to illustrate this argument. Her unhappy marriage moderates her interaction with her infant, Denise. On days when her husband is drunk, she is impervious to specific antecedents (she may not notice when Denise smiles), she responds maladaptively to these antecedents (she may hit Denise when she cries), and she is impervious to the long-term consequences of her behavior (even though the pediatrician has expressed concern about Denise's fearfulness). On days when her husband is abstinent, Mrs. Smith is far more responsive and nurturant to Denise. Mrs. Smith has no deficiency in her parenting skills repertoire. Her performance of these skills is, however, suboptimal when her husband is drunk. Mrs. Smith will derive the most help from learning to adjust her parenting behavior to her family context.

Dumas' argument is consistent with a second "emerging theme in the study of emotional development," that "to understand emotion, one must understand that the human being lives in a web of interrelationships with social and physical objects" (Campos, Campos, & Barrett, 1989, p. 397).

The model of family communication presented later, suggests that a stressful global context creates prolonged contact with aversive consequences (evident in a bad mood). Desperate efforts to abolish the bad mood disrupt learning and performance.

**3. Account for the Apparent Causal Role of Emotions.** Skinner denies that emotions cause behavior; he places the cause of covert feelings and overt emotional expression in events in the external environment. In contrast, several contributors give emotions an intrapersonal, motivational role (e.g., Jouriles & O'Leary; Greenberg & Johnson). Jouriles and O'Leary describe a pathway from stress to maternal mood to disrupted cognitive processes to ineffective mothering. Thus they assign to mood the role that Dumas assigns to a stressful context.

Like intrapersonal psychological theories, most naive belief systems invest emotions with motivational power. Ask the Smiths' elder son, "Why don't you ever go home for the holidays?" He replies, "Because I get so angry at my father that I feel like I'll explode." Ask again, "Why so angry?" Now his answer refers to events in the social environment that have, in the past, reinforced emotional experience and expression. "Look at how he treats my mother. He hits her the way he used to hit me. Look at the problems my kid brother is having. Wouldn't you be angry?"

Radical behaviorist, intrapersonal, and naive views of emotions can be reconciled. In an attempt at such a reconciliation, the model of family communication presented later views mood as a signal (to self and others) of extended contact with hedonically relevant consequences and of the quality of current functioning. A good mood signals extended contact with pleasurable consequences and optimal capacity for learning and performance. A bad mood signals extended contact with aversive consequences and suboptimal capacity for learning and performance. Thus mood is a subjective assessment of the environment's impact on current functioning. Mood, in this model, is neither a cause of behavior nor an internal representation or mediator of the environment's impact. Mood is instead a global judgment by the individual (or onlookers) about the individual's intersection with the environment.

### 4. *Include Developmental, Temperamental, and Sex Differences.* In this volume, as elsewhere, Skinner adopts a universalistic stance that transcends differences between animal species, human cultures and subcultures, and individuals within cultures. His analysis of feelings, illustrating fundamental behavior-analytic principles, necessarily ignores individual differences rooted in development, temperament, or gender.

Individual differences in the experience and expression of emotion (in combination with the private nature of emotional experience) are the wellspring of family conflict, argue contributors to this volume, and cannot be ignored.

Saarni and Crowley describe predictable changes in children's understanding of the social impact of emotional expression. They propose that innate temperamental differences (e.g., in reactivity to stimulation) influence children's capacity to regulate emotional expression and to optimize favorable consequences.

Gender differences in tolerance of emotionally arousing discussions are described by Lindahl and Markman and by Fruzzetti and Jacobson. Compared to men, women seek more intimacy and emotional closeness and are less apt to avoid concomitant physiological arousal. The gender-linked communication gap makes it difficult for men and women to feel understood by each other and to trust one another. Both teams view the resolution of the communication gap as crucial to marital satisfaction and propose relevant clinical strategies for distressed couples.

Hatfield and Rapson view the communication gap as a universal problem for close relationships, rooted in all the past experiences (including those linked to ethnicity) that produce different individual styles of emotional experience and expression. The intimacy-building skills they propose are relevant to the establishment and maintenance of any close relationship.

The following model of effective family communication suggests that in all close relationships, information exchange about feelings is a prerequisite for behavior management and problem solving. Without information exchange, couples cannot get feedback about their impact on each other and cannot compromise. With information exchange, couples can compromise on a combination of individually preferred activities. This compromise paves the way for good moods, the experience of intimacy, and long-term marital satisfaction.

## A MODEL OF EFFECTIVE FAMILY COMMUNICATION

### Proposition 1: A Good Mood Signals Prolonged Contact with Pleasurable Consequences and Optimal Preparedness for Learning and Performance

According to this proposition, a good mood signals that biological, cognitive, and behavioral processes involved in learning and performance are optimal. A bad mood signals that functioning is suboptimal. Actions undertaken during a good mood have numerous positive consequences that reinforce successful functioning along with efforts to stay in a good mood and keep others in a good mood. Actions undertaken during a bad mood have numerous negative consequences that obstruct successful functioning, and perpetuate own and others' bad moods.

*Defining Moods.* Moods are summary statements about the individual's response to the environment. Moods, defined this way, are readily assessed through daily administration of a mood adjective checklist and of an inventory of daily hassles and major life events that take place at home, with friends, on the job, and at school (see Wills, chapter 5). A good mood is a statement that every aspect of individual interaction with the environment is successful and that the consequences of interaction are highly reinforcing. A bad mood is a statement that every aspect of individual interaction with the environment is unsuccessful and that the consequences of interaction are punishing. Cognitive processes underlying learning and performance such as attention, perception, and memory are suboptimal in a bad mood and optimal in a good mood (Dumas, Jouriles & O'Leary, Hatfield & Rapson, this volume; Leventhal & Tomarken, 1986).

*Defining Preparedness for Learning and Performance.* Preparedness for learning and performance can be assessed by observation of behavioral and physiological responses to stressful stimulation. Attentive, exploratory behavior that keeps the individual in maximal contact with important features of the current environment signals optimum opportunities for learning and performance; behavior that escapes or avoids the current environment signals minimal opportunities. Specific behavioral and physiological indicators of preparedness for learning are suggested by the infant temperament literature.

Children vary in their "reactivity" to different levels of stimulation along the dimensions of latency, threshold, and intensity of response (Rothbart & Derryberry, 1981). Some children are consistently high on reactivity or "irritability"; others are consistently low on reactivity and high on "inhibition" (Campos, Campos, & Barrett, 1989; Worobey & Lewis, 1989).

Children who are high on "reactivity" or "behavioral inhibition" have few chances for learning given their overt behavior (active protest or passive avoidance) and their covert physiology (low vagal tone) during challenges (Fox, 1989; Kagan, Reznick, & Snidman, 1988). Children who exhibit curious, sociable behavior and high vagal tone have many chances for learning during exposure to challenges (Kagan, Reznick, Clarke, Snidman, & Garcia-Coll, 1984).

Heart-rate variability or vagal tone (more precisely, the respiratory component of heart-rate variability, RSA) was chosen by Fox (1989) as a measure of reactivity based "on a well-documented association between it and reaction to sensory stimulation." According to Fox, individual differences in resting heart-rate variability influence the magnitude and direction of heart-rate response to sensory stimuli (Porges, 1974), reaction time (Porges, 1972, 1973), attention and distractibility (Richards, 1987), attention to novel stimuli (Linnemeyer & Porges, 1986), and developmental outcomes in normal and pre-term infants (DiPietro, Larson, & Porges, 1987; Fox & Porges, 1985). Fox (1989) collected longitudinal data from 88 healthy infants with high and low heart-rate variability or vagal tone. The sample appears to have included infants ranging from low on reactivity (behaviorally inhibited) to moderate on reactivity (called reactive by Fox). Infants with high vagal tone were more reactive to positive and negative events at 5 months and more sociable at 14 months.

In light of the literature just reviewed, vagal tone seems a fine physiological index of preparedness for learning and performance. High vagal tone (given its presumed reinforcing consequences) and good mood should go hand in hand. This hypothesis, supported by Fox's data about sociability and vagal tone, requires more study.

*Defining New-Information Questions.* A behavioral index of preparedness for learning and performance, useful after early childhood, can be based on the frequency with which the individual asks new-information questions during challenges. New-information questions are counted only if they elicit answers (and thereby put the individual in contact with important features of social and nonsocial tasks). The index excludes unanswered questions, questions that were asked and answered earlier in the same conversation (showing inattentiveness), and "why" questions about motives ("Why do you always act so miserable?"). Motivational "why" questions are usually answered with irritation or anger, whereas scientific "why" questions elicit new information (Plutchik & Plutchik, chapter 3).

Popular children use new-information questions as a method of peer-group entry ("How do you play this game?"). Good students use new-information questions as a method of understanding task requirements ("Will you take points off for spelling errors?"). Families effective at diverse laboratory tasks (e.g., tower building, 20 questions) ask numerous new-information questions before they begin; ineffective families respond without question to experimenter instructions (Blechman, Tryon, et al., 1989). In general, new-information questions show genuine interest in other people.

Any individual can be confronted with a variety of challenges; social ("Get acquainted with this person.") and nonsocial ("Find the errors in this picture."). The frequency with which new-information questions are asked during these challenges should predict success and a good mood. Empirical confirmation of the reinforcing consequences of new-information questions is needed.

*Mood Transfer.*    An individual in a mood, good or bad, is still in contact with the consequences that created that mood. The individual may have left the setting that gave rise to hedonically relevant consequences and entered a neutral setting, but sustained contact with old consequences prevents discrimination of the setting change (Dumas, chapter 9). In this way the individual transfers mood across settings.

Sustained contact with consequences across settings may occur at a biochemical or physiological level. Thus, Zillmann's (1971) excitation-transfer theory attributes the transfer of moods across situations to the slow dissipation of sympathetic nervous system activity. Sustained contact with consequences may occur at a cognitive level; this happens when a bad mood is perpetuated by irrational and pessimistic thoughts (Hatfield & Rapson; Saarni & Crowley; Greenberg & Johnson).

Sustained contact with consequences across settings may also occur at an interpersonal level (Lindahl & Markman; Jouriles & O'Leary; Dumas; Fruzzetti & Jacobson). Arriving home early from work in a bad mood, Mr. Smith finds David and his mother playing cards. Mr. Smith comments sarcastically that truancy looks like fun. David runs to his room and slams the door. Mrs. Smith begins to cry. Mr. Smith's mood blackens.

In this example, Mr. Smith's bad mood is transferred from one situation to another (work to home) by physiological, cognitive, and interpersonal responses that continue his contact with mood-congruent consequences at home. Mr. Smith transfers his bad mood to his wife and son (emotional contagion), by interpersonal behavior that puts them in contact with consequences congruent with his mood.

*Mood Regulation.* Mood is regulated through actions that contact consequences congruent with the mood (leading to mood transfer and intensification) or incongruent with the mood (lead to mood shift). Individuals regulate their own moods and others' moods. Some individuals are particularly skilled at shifting themselves and others into good moods despite contrary circumstances.

Contributors agree that the emotion-regulation skills required to shift from a bad mood to a good one are gradually developed. The acquisition of these skills is influenced by the child's innate reactivity threshold (Saarni & Crowley). These skills are learned through interaction with parents, beginning with the mother's first attempts to soothe her crying newborn (Lindahl & Markman) and culminating in parents' responses to their adolescents' complaints (Wills). Contributors further agree that in maritally dissatisfied couples partners trap each other and their children into bad moods, and are inept at promoting good moods in themselves and other family members. Unarmed with emotion-regulation skills, children are at risk for social incompetence (Parke & Asher, 1983), and for drug use in adolescence as an artificial method of mood regulation (Wills, chapter 5).

*Mood and Learning.* Mood has been defined as a signal of contact with hedonically relevant consequences and of preparedness for learning; vagal tone, as a leading physiological indicator of such preparedness. In mood regulation, family members influence each other's moods, which are their contact with mood-relevant consequences and their preparedness for learning.

Familial mood regulation was studied by Gottman and Fainsilber-Katz (1989). They measured vagal tone in parents and 5-year-old children as an index of the child's ability to focus attentional processes and inhibit inappropriate action (Porges, 1984). They found that maritally distressed couples who used a negative parenting style were physiologically underaroused (low husband vagal tone, low skin conductance in husband and wife) during a parent–child teaching task. Children of maritally distressed couples evidenced a high vagal tone (along with anger, noncompliance, and high levels of stress hormones). They concluded that, in the short run, children's vagal tone might buffer them against the deleterious impact of negative parenting; in the long-run, children's hypervigilance might tax the child's physiology and reduce the child's vagal tone. In this study, maritally distressed couples with chronic bad moods seem to have put their children in contact with mood-congruent consequences through a negative parenting style involving ineffective communication.

## Proposition 2: Effective Family Communication Promotes Good Moods in All Family Members

According to this proposition, effective family communication hinges on the exchange of information about feelings. Information exchange allows family members to influence each other's behavior and to solve problems and resolve differences through compromise. As a result, in families characterized by effective communication, members have equal chances to engage in activities that for them, are reinforcing and mood-elevating. Via information exchange, married couples achieve a communication compromise crucial for marital satisfaction, blending male-preferred cool activities and female-preferred hot discussions. The emotional climate in families using effective communication is intimate, enjoyable, and relaxing.

In contrast, in families using ineffective communication, the honest exchange of information about feelings does not take place often enough to support behavior management, problem solving, or the compromises necessary for marital satisfaction. In these unhappy families, few members can avoid activities that promote bad moods or engage in activities that promote good moods. Instead, the family permits only emotionally cool activities (the disengaged family) or only emotionally hot discussions (the "overinvolved" family).

*Defining Effective Family Communication.* In any episode of effective communication, the impact of participants' verbal and nonverbal behavior matches their intentions regarding information exchange, behavior management, and problem solving (Blechman, in press). In information exchange, a listener gets a message a speaker intended to send. In behavior management, a speaker influences a listener's behavior in the intended direction. In problem solving, speaker and listener address a mutually defined problem in a mutually agreeable manner. Any discussion can be subjected to molecular coding; the resulting codes can be classified into the molar categories of information exchange, behavior management, and problem solving (Dumas & Blechman, 1990). During a discussion, the fit between impact and intent can be quickly assessed by participants by using Gottman's talk-table (1979).

The majority of human communication involves the exchange of spontaneous messages about feelings and symbolic messages about abstract ideas; messages about feelings predominate (Buck, 1984). Feelings are omnipresent, immediately sensed, and rapidly communicated. Ideas are more slowly formulated and translated into symbols for communication. Although feelings can be communicated without an accompanying abstract idea, abstract ideas are difficult to communicate without affect (Zajonc, 1980). When spontaneous information exchange succeeds, the speaker accurately describes private experience to an interested, attentive listener. Speakers know they have succeeded at information exchange when listeners indicate, "I accept and understand how you feel."

The capacity to exchange messages about feelings is the cornerstone of effective family communication. Information exchange is a prerequisite for behavior management, because it is impossible to influence a listener who is unresponsive to one's words and actions. A combination of information exchange and behavior management are prerequisites for problem solving, because it is impossible to reach a compromise about a mutual problem with a partner who is unwilling to make concessions. In sum, compromise (the most desirable end-product of effective communication) is impossible without information exchange.

In the Smith family, for example, information exchange is unsuccessful. When Mrs. Smith tries to tell her husband how worried she is by a call from David's teacher, Mr. Smith explodes at her and walks away. When Mr. Smith tries to tell his wife how much he wants her affection and how angry he is at her for giving all her affection to the children, Mrs. Smith accuses him of preoccupation with sex and dissolves in tears. Behavior management is also unsuccessful. Mr. Smith ignores David's problems at school. Mrs. Smith neglects her appearance and refuses to let her husband touch her. Finally, problem solving is unsuccessful. The couple has not achieved a compromise that allows them to discuss David's problems in a manner that makes each parent feel loved and appreciated by the other.

*Defining Intimacy, Social Support, and Stress.* If a good mood signals general contact with pleasurable consequences, then psychological intimacy signals such contact in a specific relationship. Mr. Smith explains his most recent extramarital affair in just these terms, "She listened to

all my problems. She always saw my point of view. She really understood me. Just seeing her made me feel good."

Given the multiple reinforcing consequences of a good mood, it is
understandable why involvement in an intimate relationship is inherently appealing (Fruzzetti & Jacobson, Greenberg & Johnson, Hatfield
& Rapson). According to Fruzzetti and Jacobson, unhappy married
couples crave intimacy above all else.

Intimacy usually refers to close adult relationships that keep partners in a good mood. Social support describes the mood-elevating
process that can prevail in any human relationship; stress describes
the process by which any relationship induces or maintains a bad mood
(Wills, chapter 5).

*Information Exchange, Mood, Intimacy, and Stress.*   In an intimate
relationship, participants exchange feelings honestly yet without injuring others' self-esteem (Hatfield & Rapson, Plutchik & Plutchik, this
volume; Rogers, 1954). The skill of gauging the impact of one's own
feelings on others is learned gradually by all children and with particular difficulty by children who are highly reactive (Saarni & Crowley,
this volume). The skill of recognizing and expressing one's own feelings despite others' disapproval is particularly difficult for those who
are behaviorally inhibited, unassertive, or shy (Plutchik & Plutchik,
this volume).

A balance between psychological freedom and psychological safety
(Rogers, 1954), between autonomy and connection (Baumrind, 1971),
is achieved when family members express genuine positive and negative feelings to each other, listen in an accepting manner to each other's
disclosures, and avoid statements that either escalate conflict or deny
genuine disagreement (Fruzzetti & Jacobson; Lindahl & Markman;
Saarni & Crowley, this volume).

Conducted in this way, an exchange of information about feelings
promotes the subjective experience of a good mood, intimacy, social
support, and marital satisfaction. Information exchange may also be
the critical ingredient in attachment of infants to their caretakers
and in romantic love (Greenberg & Johnson, Hatfield & Rapson,
this volume). Nurturant parents and infatuated lovers attend with
exquisite sensitivity to the external manifestations of internal feeling
states; each of their responses aims to promote feelings of comfort
and pleasure in the objects of their affection (Lindahl & Markman,
Saarni & Crowley, this volume).

In ineffective communication, information exchange may be absent
(as in denial, repression, and suppression), or the exchange of hostile,
critical feelings may be unregulated (as in aggression or coercion).

Either way, the result for all family members is the subjective experience of a bad mood, stress, and relationship dissatisfaction (Hatfield & Rapson, Fruzzetti & Jacobson, Greenberg & Johnson, Lindahl & Markman, this volume).

When family members are in foul moods, their ineffective communication puts others in contact with aversive consequences. Mothers and fathers, stressed by unsatisfactory marital relationships, communicate with children and adolescents in ways that engender perceived and real behavior problems and social incompetence (Dumas, Jouriles & O'Leary, Fruzzetti & Jacobson, Lindahl & Markman, this volume). Instead of asking new-information questions and listening to the answers, these parents criticize, lecture, and escalate conflict (Plutchik & Plutchik, Lindahl & Markman, Wills, this volume).

*Defining the Communication Gap.* Men and women, on average, are reinforced by and achieve a good mood and a sense of intimacy from different kinds of exchanges. Gottman pointed out the communication gap between the sexes in his observation of married couples. Particularly during conflict-laden discussions of emotionally hot topics, men attempt to escape from conflict through "stonewalling," whereas women confront conflict (Gottman, 1979).

Four explanations of the communication gap deserve consideration. First, the communication gap may be attributable to men's lower arousal thresholds and consequent aversion to discussion of emotionally hot topics (Gottman, 1979; Fruzzetti & Jacobson, this volume). Second, the communication gap may be attributable to women's superior communication skills and their delight in exchanging information about feelings (Buck, 1984; Gottman, 1979). Third, the communication gap may be attributable to different methods of same-sex relationship formation (Lindahl & Markman, this volume). Male friends maintain their relationships through participation in mutually enjoyable activities (e.g., watching or playing sports); female friends maintain their relationships through discussions about relationships (e.g., with men). Partners in close heterosexual relationships inevitably confront their differing activity preferences (e.g., he wants to watch football with her; she wants them to talk about the future of their relationship.) Fourth, the communication gap may reflect the social power differences that are inevitable in close relationships. The partner with less control over personal outcomes and fewer alternatives to the relationship is more concerned about relationship maintenance and seeks more discussion of the relationship's status (Thibaut & Kelley, 1959). Wives often occupy the low-power position in marriage.

All possible explanations of the communication gap are intertwined,

making confirmation of one and rejection of others unlikely. Taken
together, the foregoing explanations provide a thorough description
of the kinds of joint activities that promote a good mood (in the short
run) and a sense of intimacy (in the long run) in men and in women.
Men prefer "cool" activities, blends of distracting activity and talk
about neutral topics. Women prefer total absorption in "hot" activities
centered in intense discussions of personally relevant and conflict-
laden topics. In any close relationship, the person with less power is
likely to prefer "hot" discussions.

*The Communication Compromise and Marital Satisfaction.*   If hot discussions promote a good mood and a sense of intimacy in women, and
cool activities have the same effect on men, how do couples resolve
their differences and achieve good moods, intimacy, and marital satisfaction?

Studies reviewed later along with the clinical strategies recom-
mended by Lindahl and Markman, Fruzzetti and Jacobson (this volume) suggest that satisfied couples resolve the communication gap
through compromise. One compromise concerns the nature of hot
discussions and the frequency of cool activities; wives make sure that
hot discussions are palatable, husbands embed these discussions in a
stream of cool activities. A second compromise concerns the outcome
of hot discussions; solutions always recognize the validity of both partners' positions.

Wives in satisfied marriages often take responsibility for scheduling
and managing hot discussions. (In egalitarian marriages, psychologi-
cally minded husbands may well play the same role.) She raises an
important, emotionally hot topic only when she and her husband can
engage in a thorough and relaxed discussion. When her husband
indicates that he is ready and willing to discuss the topic, she questions
him about his feelings, listens attentively to his answers, asks pertinent
follow-up questions, and reciprocates with self-disclosures about her
own feelings. The wife's new-information questions apparently serve
several functions. They help her understand her husband's point of
view, encourage his self-disclosure, make him feel his position is valid,
encourage him to ask new-information questions of her, and move the
couple in the direction of a compromise solution.

Husbands in satisfied marriages (and nontraditional wives in egalitarian marriages) may take responsibility for scheduling and managing
cool activities and for embedding hot discussions in a stream of cool
activities. A man may tell a joke to end a hot discussion with his wife,
suggest that they discuss a family problem over dinner at a favorite
restaurant, or disclose a work problem while the couple is enjoying

the afterglow of good sex. He may teach his wife to enjoy watching or participating in his favorite sports and hobbies. Working together at cool activities may eventually satisfy the wife's concerns about her husband's affection and diminish her desire for hot discussions of relationship problems.

More is known about the way satisfied couples manage hot discussions than about the way they combine hot discussions and cool activities in their daily lives. In 30 married couples, Levenson and Gottman (1983) found a powerful relationship between current marital satisfaction and the couple's physiological "linkage" or interrelatedness during conversational interaction. Linkage indicates the degree to which each spouse's physiological arousal (across all measures) can be predicted from the partner's reactivity, while controlling for autocorrelation. High linkage was associated with low marital satisfaction. Linkage predicted over 60% of the variance in current marital satisfaction. Three years later, Levenson and Gottman (1985) reassessed 19 of these couples' marital satisfaction. Arousal during the initial study (rather than linkage) was the best predictor of a decline in marital satisfaction over 3 years; couples who were initially the most aroused showed the greatest decline in satisfaction. Arousal predicted over 80% of the variance in satisfaction change.

In two longitudinal studies of marital interaction, Gottman and Krokoff (1989) found that a different pattern of results predicted concurrent marital satisfaction as opposed to improved satisfaction over 3 years. Disagreement and anger exchanges were found to relate to unhappiness and negative interaction at home concurrently, but they predicted improved satisfaction longitudinally.

McEnroe, Blechman, and Sheiber (1988) examined the relationship between marital satisfaction and concurrent performance on hot and cool activities. The study engaged 16 couples varying in level of marital satisfaction in hot discussions of conflict-laden topics and in cool activities (building towers from blocks and playing 20 questions). During the hot discussions, measures of physiological arousal were collected from each partner. Videotapes of hot discussions were subsequently coded to determine participants' use of molecular communication codes in the categories of information exchange, behavior management, and problem solving (Dumas & Blechman, 1990). Satisfied couples differed on hot and cool activities from dissatisfied couples. During the hot discussion, they used significantly more information exchange and behavior management codes and evidenced less physiological arousal. In addition, their problem-solving outcomes on the cool activities were significantly better. A hierarchical multiple-regression analysis predicted 72% of the variance in marital satisfaction from a combination of physiological arousal, communication skill during hot discussions, and problem-solving outcomes at cool activities. Compared to distressed couples, satisfied couples were less aroused during hot discussions and more skilled at hot discussions and cool activities.

*Achieving a Communication Compromise.*   There is general agreement that marital satisfaction requires a compromise that limits husbands involvement in female-preferred hot discussions. There is disagreement about how this compromise takes place in spontaneously satisfied marriages and about how this compromise can be encouraged during behavioral marital therapy. Gottman and Krokoff (1989, p. 52) suggest that women take responsibility for engaging men in palatable hot discussions. In this volume, Lindahl and Markman and Fruzzetti and Jacobson suggest that men and women share this responsibility.

A thorough ecological analysis of days in the lives of long-term satisfied couples may reveal that one partner schedules and manages hot discussions and the other partner embeds hot discussions in a stream of cool activities. Although the ingredients in the normative communication compromise remain to be described, long-term happily married couples are proud that they have learned to resolve their differences (Krokoff, Gottman, & Roy, 1988; Notarius & Vanzetti, 1983).

When couples fail to compromise, unhappiness is inevitable. In disengaged "pseudo-mutual" relationships, couples favor cool activities and avoid clear exchanges of information about feelings (Gottman & Fainsilber-Katz, 1989; Krokoff, Gottman, & Roy, 1988; Minuchin, 1974). In emotionally overinvolved, intrusive relationships, couples favor hot discussions and obsessively exchange information about hostile and critical feelings (Leff, Kuipers, & Berkowitz, 1983; Valone, Norton, Goldstein, & Doane, 1983). The emotional climate in the latter families (high "expressed emotion") has been shown to be detrimental to schizophrenic, depressed, and recent-onset manic patients who relapse quickly when they return home from hospital (Hahlweg et al., 1989).

*The Causal Role of New-Information Questions.*   The central thesis of the family communication model is that effective communication promotes good moods, which signal contact with favorable consequences and openness to learning. New-information questions have been proposed as a behavioral index of openness to learning and vagal tone, as a physiological index. Although an interaction between new-information questions and vagal tone is presumed, new-information questions are viewed as the quintessential communication tool used by an individual to investigate the social environment. Thus, new-information questions (e.g., "What's new?", "How are you feeling?", "What's wrong?", "How can I help?", "What do you feel like doing?", "What should we make for dinner?") are given a causal role in this model, driving effective communication and all its favorable global consequences (including intimacy, perceived social support, relationship satisfaction, and compromise).

## Proposition 3: Family Members Who Are Often in Good Moods Are Optimally Prepared for Competence. Family Members Who Are Often in Bad Moods Are At Risk For Incompetence and Psychopathology

When family communication is effective, family members' frequent good moods signal that they are primed for competence despite cultural, biological, and socioeconomic handicaps. When family communication is ineffective, family members' frequent bad moods signal that they are disposed to incompetence and psychopathology despite cultural, biological, and socioeconomic advantages.

*Defining Competence.*    Measures of social and achievement competence represent the bottom-line success of an individual's response to challenges in interpersonal relationships, at school, and on the job (Blechman & Brownell, 1988; Blechman, McEnroe, & Carella, 1986; Blechman, Tinsley, Carella, & McEnroe, 1985). An individual who is socially competent is liked by others despite the differences of opinion and preference that characterize human relationships. An individual who is high on achievement competence does well at school and on the job, despite the inadequacies and hardships of these settings. Emotional competence (or resilience) describes the outcome of prolonged adaptive coping with the regulation of emotional arousal (Saarni & Crowley, Lindahl & Markman, this volume; Blechman & Tryon, in press-b). An individual who is emotionally competent overcomes depression and anxiety despite circumstances that put most other people in lingering bad moods.

*Defining Coping.*    Measures of coping (Wills, this volume) tap all the adaptive and maladaptive ways in which people respond to diverse challenges (Plutchik & Plutchik, this volume). Skills are adaptive methods of coping that are presumed to lead to competent ends. Social or communication skills are generally presumed to lead to social compe-

tence. Yet children's social competence cannot be completely accounted for by their social skills (Parke & Asher, 1983).

***From Communication to Competence.***   The central thesis of the family
communication model is that effective family communication optimizes family members' competence despite their cultural, biological,
and socioeconomic handicaps. The evidence supporting this thesis
includes correlational data, longitudinal data (e.g., Harrington, Block,
& Block, 1987) and concurrent data (e.g., Blechman & McEnroe,
1985).

My co-workers and I have demonstrated that children relatively
high on academic and social competence come from families in which
communication is relatively effective. We have demonstrated this relationship for children from suburban and urban families (Blechman &
McEnroe, 1985) and for minority children from inner-city families
(Blechman & Tryon, in press-a). In the latter study, we also demonstrated that mothers' competence is even more strongly tied to effective
family communication than their children's. We have shown that children relatively high on social and academic competence are the happi-
est and most free from behavior problems and symptoms of depression, and that children evidencing both social and academic
incompetence are most prone to depression and behavior problems
(Blechman, McEnroe, & Carella, 1986; Blechman, Tinsley, Carella, &
McEnroe, 1985). In a study now in progress, preliminary data indicate
that diabetic children with the best metabolic control come from families effective at communication (Blechman & Delamater, in press).

Lindahl and Markman (chapter 6) describe how marital communication influences children's capacity to cope with emotional challenges
and how those strategies, in turn, determine children's subsequent
emotional and social competence (see also Saarni & Crowley, chapter
4). Wills (chapter 5) describes how parent–adolescent communication
influences teens' strategies for coping with interpersonal challenges
(peer pressure to use drugs) and how these strategies, in turn, determine subsequent risk for addiction.

In sum, the central thesis of the family communication model (that
effective family communication optimizes mood and competence despite handicaps) is abundantly supported but largely by correlational
evidence. Skeptics are free to point out that families composed of
competent members are likely to be good at communication, or that
genetic endowment for intelligence influences both competence and
communication. The family communication model will remain suspect
awaiting convincing evidence of causality (from communication to

competence holding handicaps constant) and the defeat of alternative explanations.

## CONCLUSION

Does effective family communication optimize every family members' mood and competence despite cultural, biological, and socioeconomic stressors and handicaps? Answering "yes," this chapter presented a model of effective family communication. The model was proposed to integrate contributions to this book into an expanded behavioral perspective on emotions in the family. This new look encourages scientific inquiry into emotions in close relationships considering: physiology and social context, the apparent causal role of emotions, developmental, temperamental, and sex differences.

The model's three premises are consistent with evidence presented by contributors:

1. A good mood signals prolonged contact with pleasurable consequences and optimal preparedness for learning and performance.
2. Effective communication promotes good moods in all family members.
3. Family members who are often in good moods are primed for competence and shielded from psychopathology, despite cultural, biological, and socioeconomic handicaps.

Considerable research is required before the family communication model can be invested with validity.

*Describe Mood and Communication.* The first task for future research involves the collection of data thoroughly describing the distinctive features of good (as opposed to bad) moods and effective (as opposed to ineffective) family communication. Such descriptive data might address the following questions. Is a good mood a reliable signal of optimal individual preparedness for learning and performance as indexed by new-information questions and vagal tone? Under what circumstances is mood a misleading signal? What are the distinctive features of effective communication that transcend cultural and socioeconomic differences between families? What kinds of compromises about communication are typical among long-term satisfied married couples?

*Test the Causal Impact of New-Information Questions.* A second task for future research involves microanalytic studies of the relative impact of new-information questions (compared to other questions and statements). Do new-information questions promote information exchange, behavior management, and problem solving? Do new-information questions promote good mood (and high vagal tone) in self and others? Do they improve response to social and nonsocial challenges? Do they promote compromise?

*Test the Causal Impact of Effective Communication.* A third task for future research involves molar studies of the functional impact of family communication on mood, competence, and psychopathology. The causal role of communication must be assessed, taking into account family members' biological, cultural, and socioeconomic handicaps and advantages. The ultimate, critical test of the family communication model will compare alternative causal pathways: from communication to mood to competence, from competence to mood to communication, and from a third variable (such as parental intelligence) to mood, competence, and communication.

*Teach Information Exchange.* Assuming that the burden of empirical evidence eventually supports the family communication model, how can that benefit the Smith Family? The principle clinical implication of this model concerns the value of new-information questions. Clinicians will profit from using these questions as a means of engaging distressed families in information exchange. Families will profit from extended practice at asking each other such questions and listening to the answers they get. If the family communication model is correct, a two-stage approach to behavioral family therapy is in order. In the first stage, the family learns to exchange information until they feel good with each other. In the second stage, they learn to influence each other's behavior and solve the mutual problems that brought them into treatment.

## REFERENCES

Baumrind, D. (1971). Current patterns of parental authority. *Developmental Psychology Monographs, 75,* 43–88.
Blechman, E. A. (in press). Effective communication: Enabling the multi-problem family to change. In P. Cowan & M. Hetherington (Eds.), *Advances in Family Research, Vol. 2.* Hillsdale, NJ: Lawrence Erlbaum Associates.
Blechman, E. A., & Brownell, K. D. (1988). Competence and physical hardiness. In E. A. Blechman & K. D. Brownell (Eds.), *Handbook of behavioral medicine for women* (pp.

439–450). New York: Pergamon Press.

Blechman, E. A., & McEnroe, M. J. (1985). Effective family problem solving. *Child Development, 56,* 429–437.

Blechman, E. A., McEnroe, M. J., & Carella, E. T. (1986). Childhood competence and depression. *Journal of Abnormal Psychology, 95,* 223–227.

Blechman, E. A., Carr, R., Chanler, A., & Saenger, P. (1989). Family communication and metabolic control among Type 1 diabetic youth. Unpublished manuscript, Department of Psychiatry, Albert Einstein College of Medicine, Bronx, NY.

Blechman, E. A., & Delamater, A. M. (in press). Family communication and Type 1 Diabetes: A window on the social environment of chronically ill children . In D. Reiss & R. Cole (Eds.), *Advances in Family Research, III.* Hillsdale, NJ: Lawrence Erlbaum Associates.

Blechman, E. A., Tinsley, B., Carella, E. T., & McEnroe, M. J. (1985). Childhood competence and behavior problems. *Journal of Abnormal Psychology, 94,* 70–77.

Blechman, E. A., & Tryon, A. S. (in press-a). Inner-City Families: Competence, Depression, and Communication. *Journal of Clinical Child Psychology.*

Blechman, E. A., & Tryon, A. S. (in press-b). Familial origins of affective competence and depression. In K. Schlesinger & B. Bloom (Eds.), *Boulder Symposium on Clinical Psychology: Depression.* Hillsdale, NJ: Lawrence Erlbaum Associates.

Blechman, E. A., Tryon, A. S., McEnroe, M. J., &, Ruff, M. H. (1989). Behavioral approaches to psychological assessment: A comprehensive strategy for the measurement of family interaction. In M. M. Katz, & S. Wetzler (Eds.), *Contemporary approaches to psychological assessment.* New York: Brunner/Mazel.

Buck, R. (1984). *The communication of emotions.* New York: Guilford.

Campos, J. J. (1989). A reconceptualization of the nature of affect. [Review of *The emotions.* New York: Cambridge Press.] *Contemporary Psychology, 34,* 633–635.

Campos, J. J., Campos, R. G., & Barrett, K. C. (1989). Emergent themes in the study of emotional development and emotion regulation. *Developmental Psychology, 25,* 394–402.

DiPietro, J. A., Larson, S. K., & Porges, S. W. (1987). Behavioral and heart rate pattern differences between breast-fed and bottle-fed neonates. *Developmental Psychology, 23,* 467–474.

Dumas, J. E., & Blechman, E. A. (1990). INTERACT/BLISS: A computer coding system to assess small group communication. Unpublished ms., University of Montreal.

Fox, N. A. (1989). Psychophysiological correlates of emotional reactivity during the first year of life. *Developmental Psychology, 25,* 364–372.

Fox, N. A., & Porges, S. W. (1985). The relation between neonatal heart period patterns and developmental outcomes. *Child Development, 56,* 28–37.

Gottman, J. M. (1979). *Marital interaction: Experimental investigations.* New York: Academic Press.

Gottman, J. M., & Fainsilber-Katz, L. (1989). Effects of marital discord on young children's peer interaction and health. *Developmental Psychology, 25,* 373–381.

Gottman, J. M., & Krokoff, L. J. (1989). Marital interaction and satisfaction: A longitudinal view. *Journal of Consulting and Clinical Psychology, 57,* 47–53.

Hahlweg, K., Goldstein, M. J., Nuechterlein, K. H., Magana, A. B., Mintz, J., Doane, J. A., Miklowitz, D. J., & Snyder, K. S. (1989). Expressed emotion and patient–relative interaction in families of recent onset schizophrenics. *Journal of Consulting and Clinical Psychology, 57,* 11–18.

Harrington, D. M., Block, J. H., & Block, J. (1987). Testing aspects of Carl Rogers' theory of creative environments: childrearing antecedents of creative potential in young adolescents. *Journal of Personality and Social Psychology, 52,* 851–856.

Kagan, J., Reznick, J. S., Clarke, C., Snidman, N., & Garcia-Coll, C. (1984). Behavioral inhibition to the unfamiliar. *Child Development, 58,* 1459–1473.

Kagan, J., Reznick, J. S., & Snidman, N. (1988). Biological bases of childhood shyness. *Science, 240,* 167–171.

Krokoff, L. J., Gottman, J. M., & Roy, A. K. (1988). Blue-collar marital interaction and a companionate philosophy of marriage. *Journal of Personality and Social Relationships, 5,* 201–222.

Leff, J. P., Kuipers, L., & Berkowitz, R. (1983). Intervention in families of schizophrenics and its effect on relapse rate. In W. R. McFarlane (Ed.), *Family therapy in schizophrenia* (pp. 173–188). New York: Guilford.

Levenson, R. W., & Gottman, J. M. (1983). Marital interaction: Physiological linkage and affective exchange. *Journal of Personality and Social Psychology, 45,* 587–597.

Levenson, R. W., & Gottman, J. M. (1985). Physiological and affective predictors of change in relationship satisfaction. *Journal of Personality and Social Psychology, 49,* 85–94.

Leventhal, H., & Tomarken, A. J. (1986). Emotions: Today's problems. *Annual Review of Psychology, 37,* 565–610.

Linnemeyer, S. A., & Porges, S. W. (1986). Recognition memory and cardiac vagal tone in six-month-old infants. *Infant Behavior and Development, 9,* 43–56.

McEnroe, M. J., Blechman, E. A., & Sheiber, F. (1988). Communication and Marital Satisfaction. Poster presented at the 22d Annual Meeting of the Association for Advancement of Behavior Therapy, New York, NY.

Minuchin, S. (1974). *Families and family therapy.* Cambridge, MA: Harvard University Press.

Notarius, C. I., & Vanzetti, N. A. (1983). The marital agendas protocol. In Erik E. Filsinger (Ed.), *Marriage and Family Assessment* (pp. 209–227). Beverly Hills, CA: Sage.

Parke, R. D., & Asher, S. R. (1983). Social and personality development. *Annual Review of Psychology, 34,* 465–510.

Porges, S. W. (1972). Heart rate variability and deceleration as indexes of reaction time. *Journal of Experimental Psychology, 92,* 103–110.

Porges, S. W. (1973). Heart rate variability: An autonomic correlate of reaction time performance. *Bulletin of the Psychonomic Society, 1,* 270–272.

Porges, S. W. (1974). Heart rate indices of newborn attentional responsivity. *Merrill-Palmer Quarterly, 20,* 131–154.

Porges, S. W. (1984). Heart rate oscillation: An index of neural mediation. In M. G. H. Coles, J. R. Jennings, & J. A. Stern (Eds.), *Psychophysiological perspectives: Festschrift for Beatrice and John Lacey.* New York: Van Nostrand Reinhold.

Richards, J. E. (1987). Infant visual attention and respiratory sinus arrythmia. *Child Development, 58,* 488–496.

Rogers, C. R. (1954). Towards a theory of creativity. *ETC: A Review of General Semantics, 11,* 249–260.

Rothbart, M. K., & Derryberry, D. (1981). Development of individual differences in temperament. In M. E. Lamb & A. L. Brown (Eds.), *Advances in developmental psychology* (Vol. 1, pp. 37–86). Hillsdale, NJ: Lawrence Erlbaum Associates.

Thibaut, J. W., & Kelley, H. H. (1959). *The social psychology of groups.* New York: Wiley.

Valone, K., Norton, J. P., Goldstein, M. J., & Doane, J. A. (1983). Parental expressed emotion and affective style in an adolescent sample at risk for schizophrenia spectrum disorders. *Journal of Abnormal Psychology, 92,* 399–407.

Worobey, J., & Lewis, M. (1989). Individual differences in the reactivity of young infants. *Developmental Psychology, 25,* 668–523.

Zajonc, R. B. (1980). Feeling and thinking: Preferences need no inferences. *American Psychologist, 35,* 151–175.

Zillmann, D. (1971). Excitation transfer in communication-mediated aggressive behavior. *Journal of Experimental Social Psychology, 7,* 419–434.

# Author Index

## A

Ackerman, R., 63, *71*
Acredolo, C., 81, *97*
Adcock, S., 76, *96*
Ainsworth, M., 146, *151*, 190, *197*
Albert, J., 110, *113*
Alden, L., 150, *151*
Allgeier, A. R., 28, *31*
Altman, I., 28, *31*
Anderson, C. A., 138, *152*
Antonovsky, A., 76, 91, *94*
Argyle, M., 28, *31*, *151*
Arthur, J., 118, *134*, *198*
Asarnow, R. F., 169, *175*
Ash, M., 103, *115*
Ashbrook, P. W., 185, *197*
Asher, S. R., 211, 220, *224*
Atkeson, B. M., 184, *198*
Averill, J. R., 166, *174*
Azar, S. T., 168, 169, *174*

## B

Bacon, S. J., 167, *174*
Baddeley, A. D., 167, *174*
Baer, D. M., 158, 163, 166, *174, 175*
Baer, J. S., 82, *96*
Baker, E., 86, *98*
Baldwin, A. L., 186, *197*
Balsam, P. D., 158, *174*
Bandura, A., 133, *134, 197*
Baranowski, T., 93, *94*
Barker, C. B., 83, *95*
Baron, R. A., 20, *31*
Barrera, M., 78, *94*
Barrett, K. C., 55, *71*, 205, 206, 209, *223*
Barry, W. A., 37, *51*
Baucom, D. H., 118, *134*
Baum, A., 78, 80, 81, *95, 97*
Baum, C. G., 162, *174*
Baumrind, D., 214, *222*
Beach, S. R., 169, 170, *174*

## H

Hahlweg, K., 118, *134*, 218, *223*
Halberstadt, A. G., 14, *32*
Hall, A., 76, *95*
Hall, J. A., 14, *33*
Haring, M. J., 82, *97*
Harlow, M., 142, *152*
Harmon, R. J., 55, *71*, 191, *198*
Harper, L., 79, *96*
Harrington, D. M., 220, *223*
Harris, P. L., 56, 57, 62, *72*
Harris, T. O., *94*, 118, *134*, 169, *175*
Harter, S., 84, *95*
Hatfield, E., 11, 12, 16, 17, 20, 21, 22, 27, 28, 29, *31, 32*, 37, *51*, 204, 205, 207, 208, 210, 214, 215
Haviland, J. M., 14, *33*, 60, *72*
Hawkins, R. C., 87, *94*
Hawkins, R., 37, *50*
Hay, J., 22, *32*
Hayden, M., *176*
Haynes, S., 79, *95*
Hazan, C., 145, 146, *152*
Head, J., 103, *114*
Heisenberg, W., 173, *176*
Hekimian, E., 168, *174*
Heller, K., 82, *95*
Henderson, S., 76, 78, 79, 91, *96*
Herbert, E., 163, *176*
Hertel, R. K., 37, *51*
Hetherington, E. M., 102, 103, *113*, 59, *176*
Hill, J., 63, *71*
Hirsch, E., 156, *175*
Hoberman, H., 78, *94*
Hockey, G. R. J., 167, *176*
Hoelter, J., 79, *96*
Hoffman, E. H., 161, *178*
Hoffman, J. A., 118, *134*

Holahan, C. J., 79, 92, *96*
Holtzworth-Munroe, A., 118, 130, *135*
Hops, H., 118, *134*, 191, 194, 195, *198*
Hornyak, L. M., 104, *114*
Horowitz, L. M., 138, *152*
House, J. S., 77, 78, 82, *96*
Howes, P., 108, 109, 111, *113, 114*
Huesmann, L. R., 28, *32*
Hughes, C. F., 81, *97*
Hull, J. G., 82, *96*
Husaini, B. A., 78, *96*
Huston, T. L., 183, *197*

## I

Ilfeld, F. W., 89, 169, *176*
Ingham, J. G., 78, *96*
Ingram, R. E., 169, *176*, 183, *198*
Isen, A. M., 184,185, *198*
Izard, C. E., 12, 13, 14, 19, *32*, 138, 142, *152*

## J

Jacklin, C. N., 188, *198*
Jackson, C., *176*
Jackson, D. D., 37, *51*, 143, *153*
Jackson, J. L. 164, *176*
Jacobson, D. S., 103, *113*
Jacobson, N. S., 117, 118, 126, 128, 129, 130, *134, 135*, 143, 147, 150, *152*, 170, *176*j, 204, 205, 207, 210, 214, 215, 216, 218
Jamieson, K. J., 37, *51*
Jandorf, L., 82, *97*
Janis, I. L., 167, *176*
Jemmott, J. B., 80, *96*

# Subject Index

## A

adolescents, social support of
  affect, 80—81, 82
  community integration, 85
  coping skills development, 84
  health, 76—79, 81—82
  peer influences, 85—86, 88—92
  prevention and, 93
  problem solving skills, 83—84
  substance abuse, 88—89
affect regulation, negative
  as developmental task, 110—111
  defined, 99
  escalation, 101, 130—132
  gender differences, 106—107
  marital distress and, 102—110
agape, 4
anxiety, 5—6
attachment theory, 146
attraction, law of, 21
attribution theory, 58
autonomic nervous system, 16—17

## B

behavior
  analysis of, 9, 158—159, 171—172
  changing, 164
  contextual variables and, 171—173
  in families, 100—101, 164—166, 201—222
  motivation, 141
  operant conditioning, 4—5 156—158, 170—171
  regulation of, 61—64
  reinforcement, 3—5, 20—23, 203—204
  response classes, 163—166
behavioral marital therapy (BMT), 117—134
brain chemistry, 16